D1030849

Approaches to Nature in the Middle Ages

medieval & renaissance
texts & studies

Volume 16

Approaches to Nature in the Middle Ages

Papers of the Tenth Annual Conference of the Center for Medieval & Early Renaissance Studies

Edited by
Lawrence D. Roberts

medieval & renaissance texts & studies
Center for Medieval & Early Renaissance Studies
Binghamton, New York
1982

Center for Medieval & Early Renaissance Studies
State University of New York at Binghamton
Binghamton, New York

Library of Congress Cataloging in Publication Data

State University of New York at Binghamton. Center for Medieval and Early Renaissance Studies. Conference (10th : 1976)
Approaches to nature in the Middle Ages.

(Medieval & Renaissance texts & studies; 16.)
1. Philosophy of nature—History—Congresses. 2. Nature in literature—Congresses. 3. Nature (Aesthetics)—History—Congresses. I. Roberts, Lawrence D., 1937- II. Title. III. Series. Medieval & Renaissance texts & studies; 16.
BD581.S714 1976 113'.09'02 82-8264
ISBN 0-86698-051-2

Printed in the United States of America

Contents

Preface

The present volume contains the papers and commentaries from the Tenth Annual Conference of the Center for Medieval and Early Renaissance Studies at the State University of New York at Binghamton in October, 1976. The purpose of the Conference was to set forth medieval views of nature from the perspective of several disciplines, including literature, art, philosophy, and science.

Medieval conceptions of nature were influenced by several traditions, particularly the Biblical accounts (especially Genesis), Greek philosophy, and classical Roman literature. These traditions combined with developments in theology, philosophy, medicine, science, literature, and art, to produce a wide diversity not only of views of nature, but also of methods for approaching nature. But this wide diversity in medieval discussions of nature does not detract from the importance of the topic. Though the views of a culture on the topic of nature are of interest in themselves, they also can provide insights about the way people view themselves in relation to the universe: medieval views of nature, by manifesting beliefs about the relation of nature to God and man, illuminate the entire medieval *Weltanschauung*.

The topic of nature in the Middle Ages is preeminently a literary one in that the most explicit statements about nature and its various manifestations are found in literary works. But the uses to which representations of natural objects are put in medieval visual arts also reveal the artists' ideas and attitudes towards nature. Similarly, although the natural philosophers of the period attempt to present an objective view of how certain natural phenomena operate, their writings also reveal their attitudes toward nature in relation to God and man. For the most part, the essays in the present volume are engaged in the analytical task of clarifying the approach to nature exhibited in a particular field. The papers scrutinize specific works and argue hypotheses about the status of nature in these works. Such analytical studies are the foundation for a larger synthesis.

Although most of the papers in this collection are predominantly within one discipline, Bernard Huppé's paper brings together poetry and the visual art of the early Middle Ages. In "Nature in *Beowulf* and *Roland*," Professor Huppé is searching for a common perception of nature underlying the two literary works and the visual representations in the *Book of Kells* and the Bayeux tapestry. Pointing out that the illuminations of the *Book of Kells* give the impression that nature is hostile and dangerous, Huppé argues that a similar view of nature is present in a number of passages in *Beowulf*. He also holds that the hostility of nature in the *Book of Kells* finds a counterpoint in the protective power of the Gospels, and he finds a parallel counterpoint in God's providence in *Beowulf*. Responding to this argument, George Economou objects that he cannot find either the coherence or the Christianity in the picture of nature presented in *Beowulf*.

Winthrop Wetherbee, in "Some Implications of Nature's Femininity in Medieval Poetry," presents a study of the "goddess" *Nature*, in Bernard Silvestris' *Cosmographia* and Alain de Lille's *De planctu naturae*. Wetherbee finds that the relationship of man to *Natura* in these works has similarities to the relationship of man to woman in poetry of the same period. He relates *Natura* both to God and to man in his fallen state. Wetherbee attempts to show that in the poetry man's inability to have a fully satisfactory relationship with nature is both connected with and parallel to man's inability to have a satisfactory relationship with a woman. Enlarging the context, Francis X. Newman suggests that Wetherbee's emphasis on the medieval literature in which women are associated with Nature should be balanced by an investigation of the literature in which women are associated with *Sapientia*.

Dorothy Glass's paper, "*In Principio*: The Creation in the Middle Ages," focuses on the work of visual artists who treated the Genesis account of creation. The view of nature that Glass finds in the works of art shows little concern with nature as an entity in its own right; rather, the artists found nature important primarily in its relations to God and to man. Whether this view reflects the general outlook of the Middle Ages or arises from the particular subject, the Genesis account of creation, is not pursued here. But David Simon argues that creation is closely associated with salvation in medieval art, so that many depictions of Genesis refer not only to creation, but also to the fall and redemption. Simon's comments underscore Glass's view that nature as such is not of primary importance in the representations of Genesis.

In his paper, "The Origin of the Fleur-de-lis and the *Lilium candidum* in Art," Robert Koch is concerned with the origin of the fleur-de-lis as a heraldic emblem. His thesis is that the *lilium candidum* is the model for the fleur-de-lis, and in support of that thesis he points both to the medicinal value commonly attributed to the *lilium* and to its general religious symbolism. These arguments again reflect a concern not with nature in itself, but rather as useful to man (medicinally) or as symbolically representing a higher being. Discussing Koch's paper, François Bucher first offers a catalogue of types of medieval representations of nature; then he asks to what extent the subjugation of nature to a higher order hindered the anlysis of visible phenomena. The implication is clear: one would expect that a concern with nature as symbol would lead to second-rate analyses of nature. This question is an empirical one which needs investigation.

James Weisheipl in "Aristotle's Concept of Nature: Avicenna and Aquinas" traces the notion of nature as it appears in Aquinas and Avicenna back through Aristotle and Plato, and he contrasts the medieval and Greek view of nature as a dynamic source anterior to things with the mechanistic view of nature prevalent in our century. Weisheipl's discussion directly concerns individual natures rather than nature as a whole: nature operates through the natures of the individual things. Highlighting some points of difference between Aquinas and Avicenna in regard to the operation of individual natures, Weisheipl concludes that Aquinas attributes more intrinsic powers to natures and that Aquinas's view of nature results in a greater continuity between man and nature and, within man, between body and mind.

Taking up one point raised by Weisheipl—the different types of causality of motion—William Wallace proceeds to settle a problem in the interpretation of Galileo's writings. Historians of science have focused on one text of Galileo, in which he appears to treat the causality of motion as uninteresting in comparison to the description of the motion. While this apparent rejection of causal explanation has often been cited as marking an important step from medieval to modern science, Wallace calls attention to another passage in which Galileo discusses the cause of motion in a falling body and suggests that, in the latter passage, Galileo meant to affirm some sort of *intrinsic* cause of motion in falling bodies, while in the former he wanted simply to deny the importance of the much discussed question of the *extrinsic* cause of motion in a falling body.

John Murdoch's paper, "The Analytic Character of Late Medieval Learning: Natural Philosophy without Nature," discusses medieval treatments of certain questions about nature: Do indivisibles such as points exist in nature? How do points relate to a continuum and to its beginning and end? How are the beginning and ceasing of motions or any change to be understood? Murdoch's emphasis is not on the problems or their solutions, but rather on the manner in which the late medieval philosophers treated these problems. He shows how linguistic analysis and procedures according to imagination, rather than empirical study, were brought to bear on the study of nature. These methods were common in much fourteenth-century philosophical discourse, especially in the literature of the *Sophismata*. Murdoch concludes that in both method and results, the philosophy of nature appears to have little connection with nature itself.

In his response to Murdoch, Norman Kretzmann points out that the *Sophismata* always proceeded according to imagination, and disputes the connection made by Murdoch between proceeding according to imagination and using analytic methods. Kretzmann also emphasizes the point that the natural philosophers of the late Middle Ages did not use imagination merely to extrapolate from observed cases as contemporary scientists do; rather, the very cases which they discussed were derived from their imagination. To explain this neglect of nature in itself, Kretzmann advances the hypothesis that many (but not all) of the authors of so-called "physical" *Sophismata* view themselves as logicians rather than as natural philosophers. Whether this hypothesis is correct or not, the likely conclusion of the discussion of Murdoch and Kretzmann is that creative medieval thinkers in yet another area show a lack of interest in nature in itself. It is not clear that theological reasons concerning the relationship of God and man lie behind this neglect of nature; rather, a preoccupation with logic appears to be the explanation. Such preoccupation might be traceable to a desire to perfect the tool of logic for use in theology, or it might be traced to a faith that the formal methods of logic are the best means for finding the truth about the world, or it might have some other explanation.

One interesting recurring feature in this set of studies is the indirect approach to nature taken by many medieval thinkers. This indirectness takes several forms. The *Sophismata* literature discussed by John Murdoch, and the writings of Avicenna and Aquinas discussed by James Weisheipl, all are preoccupied with abstract theories rather than empirical confrontation with nature. Dorothy Glass's observations on nature in pictorial representations of creation bring out the links to God as Creator and man as user of nature. Robert Koch, Bernard Huppé, and Winthrop Wetherbee all emphasize various symbolic functions of nature.

As presented in these papers, nature in the Middle Ages emerges as a collection of entities whose value is subordinated to that of man and God and whose importance lies mainly in its symbolic functions. In the philosophical and artistic works discussed here, man is seen either as the culmination of nature or as a being so far transcending nature that he is not part of it. Even in the task of understanding nature, man's intellect and imagination are the main means to such understanding, with actual experience of nature playing either a subordinate role or no role at all. Nature has its importance, but this importance is mainly heuristic.

Lawrence D. Roberts

State University of New York
Binghamton, New York

Approaches to Nature in the Middle Ages

Nature in *Beowulf* and *Roland*

Bernard F. Huppé

The affinities between the Old English poetic art and the Hiberno-Saxon art of manuscript illumination are obvious.[1] For example, John C. Leyerle has made instructive use of the analogy between the Hiberno-Saxon interlace pattern and what may be called the backward-forward design of the Old English poetic art.[2] In a more general way I have observed that "The Old English poem . . . at its most complex is like one of the great signature pages of the *Book of Kells*, where the eye first sees only a maze of serpentine lines until suddenly the initial stands out in sharp relief."[3] The page is a web of lines as the Old English poem is a web of words.

Another affinity may be adduced from a non-initial page of the *Book of Kells*, folio 19v, the Argument to the Gospel of St. John (fig. 1), where we find three examples of deliberate disjunction in the text, analogous to rhetorical disjunction (*tmesis*). These visual disjunctions are marked by the "head under wing" symbol which indicates that the syllable or syllables immediately following are to be attached to the syllable at the next line:

toribus ------┐ pas↓   bat --------┐ doce↓   tismus ------┐ bap↓

Such visual disjunction has affinities with the structural disjunction characteristic of Old English verse.

Thus at the beginning of *Beowulf*, lines 4–67, the story of Scyld is developed in a series of disjointures of the temporal sequence of events. The narrative begins with his rise to power, returns to his mysterious beginnings, then back to his rise to power and dominion. Before describing his death and burial the narrative looks forward to his successor, Beowulf. At the same time, the descrip-

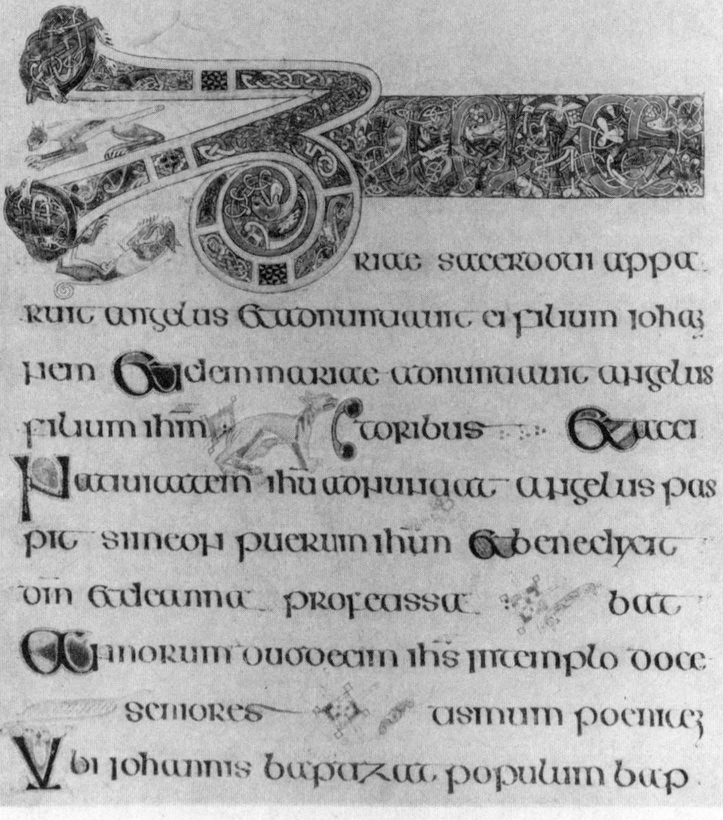

Figure 1

tion of the son's growing fame looks backward to the time of Danish suffering prior to the coming of Scyld. The paragraph describing Scyld's burial includes backward looks at his beginnings. The accession and reign of Beowulf is then introduced, but between this and the accession of his son, Healfdane, the narrative turns back briefly to the death of Scyld. Then are introduced Healfdane's sons and daughter. The expected sequence is now curiously broken, for no mention is made of the reign of the oldest son, Heorogar; instead the regal triumphs of Hrothgar are introduced. The missing link in the chain receives no mention until lines 467–69 and 2158–62. This kind of narrative disjunction is as basic to the total effect of the poem as the visual disjunction is to the total impression of the page from the *Book of Kells*.

We should expect to find similar affinities between the role Nature plays in *Beowulf* and in the manuscript illumination of the *Book of Kells*.

Clearly Nature was not to the miniaturist of the *Book of Kells* what it was for the miniaturist of the later Middle Ages who delighted in pleasant gardens, in manicured forests, and in the hunt. The feeling that emerges from the *Book of Kells* is of the hostility of Nature, its terrifying dangers, as in the page just under discussion, with its initial monsters, intertwining serpents, and the menacing animal who introduces the eye to the first symbol of verbal disjunction. These ominous figures are overpoweringly omnipresent in the *Book of Kells*. But these dangerous presences are external, in effect, to the sacred Word. They are in the exterior darkness, exorcised, as it were, by the Word, and thereby made symbols of what the Gospel saves us from. Indeed, this process is completed in the several denatured, heraldic presentations of the traditional symbols of the gospel writers. The Word protects from the present dangers of an inimical world of cold and devils, storm and spiritual tribulation, pestilence and eternal damnation.

On the surface, the role of Nature in *Beowulf* does not appear analogous; our first impression of the poem is of an abundance of nature description. Yet much of this impression results from single epithets and phrases, which are left undeveloped. They are merely part of the narrative development, locating the action in space and time: *hronrade,* 10; *brimes faroð*, 28; *flodes æht,* 42; *ofer yðe*, 46; *fealwe stræte*, 916; *mid ærdæge*, 126; *morgenleoht / scofen ond scynded,* 918–19, etc.[4] The examples of sustained or special development of nature description are surprisingly few. The major ones appear in descriptions (1) of Grendel's mere; (2) of the sea; (3) of the dragon; (4) of sea journeys; and (5) in metaphors of light and dark.

These five examples of extended descriptions of, or metaphorical reference to, Nature in *Beowulf* provide the anticipated underlying affinities with the *Book of Kells* (and with other Hiberno-Saxon and Frankish art). There appear in these passages from *Beowulf* the same sense of the hostility of Nature, its lurking monsters and dangerous dark, its gripping cold and violent storm.[5] There appears also the same counterpoint between the exorcizing power of God's providence and the hostility of man's natural surroundings. This counterpoint, I believe, is basic to the thematic development of *Beowulf*, where pagan heroism is shown to exemplify both God's mercy (in Beowulf's early adventures) and his justice (in Beowulf's doom).[6] But to demonstrate this point about thematic development would take me away from my subject. Here it will be sufficient, through analysis of nature passages in *Beowulf*, to establish that there are affinities between it and the *Book of Kells*.

First, however, to illustrate the posited counterpointing, the poet's account of Scyld's burial, lines 47–52, may be noted, although it is not particularly marked by natural description:

> Then above his head they set on high
> the golden standard, gave him to the ocean,
> let the sea take him; their souls were saddened,
> their hearts mournful. Here under the heavens
> no warrior or counsellor had the wisdom to say
> into whose keeping that cargo would come.

The darkened minds of Scyld's followers who know only the fearful mystery of Scyld's final journey into the unknown are implicitly counterpointed against the enlightened Christian mind to which the narrator has appealed in saying, line 27, that Scyld had gone "into God's protection." The faith of his audience provides the evidence of things unseen by which to understand the meaning of the journey.

Such counterpoint is given explicit development in the first passage in the poem where sustained natural description appears, lines 87–114:

Glory's demon glowered in the darkness
where he waited wracked in torment
as he listened each day to the loud music
resounding in the hall, where the notes of the harp
joined the song of the scop. (He spoke who knew
the ancient account of the creation of man,
he declared that God created the earth
the shining shore surrounded by the sea,
in victory He set the sun and the moon
as lamps to light those living in the world,
and made beautiful with leaves and branches
the regions of land, and also gave life
to every kind of animate creature;
thus lordly men lived blessedly
in happiness until the fiend in hell
began to do his wicked deed).
Grendel was the name of the grim demon
famed as a wanderer of wasteland and fen,
the moor his stronghold; the miserable wretch
had inhabited for long the land of the giants
after Cain's race had the Creator's curse
laid upon it; the Lord avenged
the slaying of Abel, his savage murder;
Cain's feud was joyless as far from men
God sent him into exile because of his sin.
From him arose all monstrous races,
elves and ogres and evil spirits,
the giants too who contended with God
for enduring time —their toil He repaid.

It should be observed that my translation reflects a difference from the usual punctuation of the passage, where, as in Klaeber's edition, the Song of Creation is made to end at line 98, with *drihtguman,* "lordly men," taken to refer to the Danes, and *feond on helle* of line 101 to refer to Grendel, *se grimma gæst* of line 102. With either punctuation the problem of suspended reference exists, an inevitable result of the poet's method of narrative disjunction. But the linking sign, the "head under the wing," is most clearly the repetition of the *gæst* in *ellengæst,* line 87, and *se grimma gæst,* line 102. Further, Grendel is not literally the *feond on helle.* He is, of course, frequently designated as *feond,* even *feond moncynnes,* 164, 1276, but when he is called *helle gæst,* 1274, the phrase is used in the context of his defeat by Beowulf to designate the place to which he will go; and in line 852 it is said that "hell received him," *him hel onfeng.* The most obvious referent for *feond on helle* is the Devil himself, not Grendel. The referent for *drihtguman* is more ambiguous. Indeed, if the immediate context of the word were the feasters in the hall, there could be no question that it must refer to the Danes. In fact the immediate context is the creation of animate life, *cynna gehwylcum þara ðe cwice hwyrfaþ.* In such a context the reference of *drihtguman* to human creation in Eden is natural, indeed is an almost necessary sequence to the mention of animate creation. In such context, moreover, the stirring of Satan's revenge is equally natural and demanded. Creation and Fall are interlocked as primordial cause and model of man's beleaguered estate, of his finding himself in hostile environment. The poet's narrative ambiguity appears designed to awaken in his audience the recognition that the attack on Heorot was foreshadowed by the primordial attack. Certainly such awareness has been prepared by the poet's prophecy of the flaming doom of Heorot in concluding his picture of its glorious completion, 74–85, for Heorot appears intended to recall both the Tower of Babel and the Eden of the Fall.[7]

The passage thus interpreted has clear affinities with the menacing dragons of the *Book of Kells* exorcized by the Word. These are the monsters like Grendel who would inflict themselves with revenge against the holy truth and against the pagan Danes who live in their false Eden, Heorot. The anachronism of the biblical paraphrase of Genesis being sung in pagan Denmark is designed precisely to suggest in words what the *Book of Kells* suggests visually. God's creation, Nature, is everywhere beautiful, but the Fall has caused the monstrosity which makes human life at war with itself and with Nature. Cold and heat are not enemies in the temperate zone of God's love, and the darkness does not threaten the light in God's day; but the threatening monsters do overcome the worldly Eden, except as they are banished by redeeming grace or by providential design.

(1) *Grendel's Mere.* In picturing post-lapsarian Nature as hostile to man except through the intervention of providential design, the passage is a paradigm for all the remaining passages of nature description in *Beowulf* noted above—thus Grendel's tarn is the occasion for the most developed and expanded "nature" description in the poem.[8] The detailed descriptions are foreshadowed in the passage where the men following Grendel's tracks in the morning come to the mere, lines 847–52:

> There the water   bloodily welled
> with boiling surge   of battle gore
> flung up in clots;   the drear waves closed
> over the melancholy   death-doomed monster
> who surrendered   his body and soul,
> in his fen haven   —there hell received him.

Then in the narrative of the attack of Grendel's mother mention is made, 1260–65, "of her enforced dwelling in the dread waters / of frozen streams," as a descendant of Cain who had fled from men "to inhabit the wasteland." After her attack she returns "to the moor," 1295. But the first full elaboration appears when Hrothgar tells what he has heard of the monster's dwelling, lines 1345–76:

> I have heard tales   told by my people
> counsellors of my court   and country folk;
> they tell of seeing   two such enormous
> haunters of the moor,   monstrous creatures
> keeping the fenland;   so far as they
> could get at the truth   one of the two
> was womanlike,   the other wretched creature
> on the path of exile   appeared to be male,
> except he was more giant   than he was man;
> in days of old   those who dwell in the land
> named him Grendel,   they know of no father
> or of mysterious demons   that might have been
> begotten before him.   They inhabit a hidden
> land of wolf dens   windswept headlands
> a hideous fenland   where from the heights

a cataract falls and flows within
the headland mists; not far from here
measured in miles does the mere stand;
over it hang hoar-frosted trees,
the fast-rooted woods shadow the water;
on its surface each night fire can be seen
in menacing portent; no living person,
no son of man, may sound its depths;
if the antlered hart crossing the heath
harried for long by pursuing hounds
should seek the wood, at the water's edge
it would stand and die rather than dare
to plunge within; it is not a pleasant place;
in wild surges its waters blackly
strive toward the skies when the wind stirs
menacing weather and the heavens weep
from rain-dark clouds.

The unnatural nature of the tarn, terrifying in its alien hostility, is thus first described from the perspective of the tales told about it and the monsters who inhabit it. This leads to an elaborate description of the journey, lines 1402–41:

The traces she left
crossing the fields to the forest trails
were widely seen as straight she went
over the murky fen, fleeing with the soulless
body of a lord and best of those
whose duty under Hrothgar was to rule the Danes.
Then a noble youth by way unknown
through narrow passes and lonely paths
climbed the steep and stony cliffs,
the looming headlands where sea-monsters lived;
with a few experienced men he went before
to have a look at the lay of the land,
when he suddenly chanced on a cheerless wood
of mountain trees with trunks which bent
over gray rocks. A grisly pool
bloodily churned below; the Scylding lords
and Danish retainers with difficulty

tried to endure the dire grief
each of them felt after they found
the head of Asher on the high sea-cliff—
as the people gazed the steaming pool
bloodily surged. The battle-horn sounded
its song of death as the troop was seated;
they looked about them at the teeming lake
where the monstrous serpents, the sea dragons swam
or other times lay along the slope;
then that morning they watched the monsters,
seeing the serpents venture on the sea
in joyless voyage —in violent anger
they headed away when they heard the trumpet
loudly resound. The lord of the Geats
took aim at one and killed it with an arrow
as it swam in the water so that the war shaft
pierced its body —in coursing the pool
it was more sluggish when it was slain;
through speedy engagement and spirited attack
with the barbed hooks of the boar spears
it was grappled in the water and the strange wave-goer
was pulled to the shore; the people gazed
at the baleful visitor.

This is one of the great set pieces in *Beowulf,* evoking the *Aeneid* and the Apocrypha to describe a scene of menacing and hellish nature. It ends, however, with a startling reversal, as Beowulf and his men become hunters, he slaying one of the monsters with an arrow and they hauling it ashore with boarspears. Implicit in the image of the deadly hunting game is the reflection of the menacing monsters in mutually menacing man, and the very futility of the hunt of the one sea monster serves as ominous foreshadowing of Beowulf's subsequent invasion of the tarn when he becomes, in turn, helpless against the sea monsters.

In contrast Beowulf's descent and his encounter with Grendel's mother in the cave below are told with minimal descriptive detail. As against his earlier prowess as a hunter he is here powerless. Attacked by the *brimwylf,* 1506, and by *sædeor monig* with their *hilde tuxum*, 1510–11, he cannot retaliate, and only his armor saves him; finally he is carried helplessly into the *nisele*. Of this cave we are told only that the *færgripe flodes* cannot enter, 1515–16, and nothing else, except for images of sun, light, and fire, which are best left for later discussion as part of the pattern of metaphoric detail interwoven into the structure of the poem as a whole. With the slaying of the monsters the tarn is purified, lines 1621–31:

the surging waters
in their mighty expanse were purified . . .
—the waters of the tarn
lay quiet under the heavens encrusted with gore.

From the alien place the men return by known ways carrying the monstrous head, lines 1632–39:

Filled with joy they crossed the fields
treading their way and retracing the footpaths
they remembered; four of the men
each of them hardy and high of spirits
with difficulty by prodigious effort
barely managed on a bloody spear
to carry away from the sea cliff
the head of Grendel to the golden hall.

The triumphant cleansing is counterpointed by the sheer monstrosity of what has been overcome.

Finally, in Hrothgar's ensuing reflections on the hilt of the purifying sword, the waters which the monsters inhabit are given their place in God's just design, lines 1687–93:

King Hrothgar spoke, gazing upon the hilt
the ancient relic on which was written
how strife began and how later the giants
were drowned in the rush of the raging flood,
the engulfing waters sent by the Lord God,
the eternal Ruler, to punish this race
of lawless exiles who lived by terror.

The water is itself both a purifying force and the habitation of forces that must be purified.

(2) *The Sea.* Perhaps elaborate description of watery menace and sea monsters in Beowulf's descent was preempted not only by the preceding elaboration in the description of the tarn, but also by the even earlier description of battling with sea monsters in the Breca episode. Hunferð's account makes mention only of the folly involved in facing the perils of the deep, lines 506–15:

> "Are you the Beowulf   who contended with Breca
> in a swimming match   on the open sea,
> where the two of you   tempted the waves,
> ventured your lives   through vanity
> and foolish pride? . . .
> There both of you measured   the might of the deep,
> with pressure of arms   and pull of hands
> and rode the currents;   the ocean was rough
> with winter storms,   together in the water's grip
> you labored for seven nights. . . ."

Beowulf's own account emphasizes the theme of menace; he speaks of cold, of storm, of night, and in addition tells of his conquest of sea-monsters, the providential outcome of his youthful folly, lines 539–67:

> We held hardened swords   bare in our hands
> when we swam the waves,   wishing protection
> against the whales. . . .
> For five long nights   we were never parted
> until surging sea   drove us asunder
> when the waves were stirred   by savage storm
> of northern wind   in the darkening night
> and rasping cold;   the waves were rough.
> The sea monsters   were aroused to madness.
> . . . A foully encrusted
> fiendish monster   forced me to the bottom
> fast in its grasp;   yet it was granted me
> that I should pierce   with point of sword
> my adversary of the sea;   savage battle destroyed
> the mighty beast   by means of my hand.
> So without respite   the loathly ravagers

pressed me sorely; with my dear sword
I waited upon them as was their due;
seated at the board at the bottom of the sea
looking forward to their fill of me
the evil fiends had no joy in the feast
for in the dawn cut down by my sword
in the sleep of death they lay on the surface
beside the shore. . . .

What again is described is Nature's fierce hostility, climaxed by the grimly ironic image of the foiled feast. The monsters are given the human role of being seated at a feast, but horribly upon a human; he, however, through his strength and God's grace, provides them with the sleep of death, not of repletion. Because of the prominence given to the feast in the poem, this image, even more than that of the hunt of the sea beast, juxtaposes and intertwines man and the monstrosity of nature; the monstrous intention of feasting is a reflection of fallen man, and the foiling of it is a sign of how, through God, man may overcome the horror of evil. The scene ends with a related counterpoint between the dark and the light of day, a counterpoint developed in the lines immediately following those quoted here. This imagery, however, like that in the battle with Grendel's mother, is best treated in a later discussion of a pattern of such imagery that runs through the poem.

(3) *The Dragon*. The dragon, like the other monsters, is a creature of the night, introduced as ruling "in the dark night," line 2211. His barrow, like the tarn and the sea, is the subject of an elaborate nature description. Like the tarn, it is in a place remote from man's knowing, but the monster of the barrow attacks only when its refuge is penetrated. The description of the barrow and its dragon, unlike the description of the mere and its monsters, is developed in brief and scattered passages which only cumulatively give a sense of alien antiquity, of the heart of darkness which man penetrates only in deadly peril. Indeed, even before the first mention of the dragon, there is a brief premonitory picture of a dragon and its barrow in the song of Sigemund, 884–97. There the dragon was "keeper of the treasure"; it lived "under the gray stone"; in death it "melted in its heat"; Sigemund takes the treasure. The first brief passage actually dealing with the dragon that Beowulf must face, and with its dwelling, appears when the awakening of the dragon is suddenly introduced, lines 2210–14:

But at the last began
in the dark nights   the rule of the dragon
who guarded the hoard   on the high heath
in a lofty stone barrow;   a path lay below
unknown to the people.

The next descriptive details do not appear until the narrative has turned back to the story of the ancient burial of the treasure, lines 2241–43:

A barrow on a headland
near the seashore   had been newly prepared
and made secure   through skillful concealment.

The dragon itself is not described until the account is given of its finding the treasure barrow that was its nature to seek, lines 2270–77:

The happy treasure
was found unguarded   by the ancient foe
the scaly dragon   who burningly scours
the land for barrows   and bound in flames
flies in the night;   he is greatly feared
by dwellers in the land;   he lives to search
for the buried hoard,   where hoary in age
he guards heathen gold   though he gains nothing.
Thus the threatening foe   for three hundred winters
held the treasure   in an earthen house
of rugged strength   until aroused. . . .

There follows a grimly humorous description of the dragon's angry circling of the barrow in search of the intruder, of his returning to the barrow to make sure of his loss, and finally of his waiting for the dark, lines 2287–311. In the passage the only descriptive detail is of the dragon's discovering no one *on þære westenne,* 2298. Emphasis, however, is given to the passing of day, the coming of night, and to the dragon's fiery menace. These images of fire, of burning, of the coming of day, dominate, in turn, the brief description of the dragon's attack, lines 2312–23:

Vomiting flames   the firedrake began
to burn the bright houses   —the blaze arose
to men's horror;   the monster in its flight
intended to leave   no one alive;
the Geatish folk   both far and near
were widely aware   of the violent war
the dragon waged   in deadly hate
with broad devastation;   at break of day
he hurried to the hoard   in the hidden hall
—he had wrapped in flame   and blazing fire
the people of the country   — —   trusting in his courage
and the barrow fastness;   his faith proved false.

The barrow and the dragon are next described when Beowulf goes to do battle with the thief as guide, lines 2410–16

Because only he   had come to the cave
and its sunken hoard   near to the surge
and fall of the sea.   Within it was full
of gold and gems;   the ungoodly guardian
and ancient warrior   held watch over the treasure
buried in the earth   —by no easy bargain
could any man   make it his own. . . .

The next description does not occur until Beowulf, seated on the headland, reflects at length on the past, then looks at the barrow, which is described in much evocative and mysterious detail, lines 2542–59:

The gallant man   who had managed to survive
many battles,   mighty clashes
of warriors in combat   saw by the wall
the stone arch rising,   from thence a stream
broke from the rock,   a rushing burn
of murderous fire;   not for a moment
could a man come   close to the hoard
without being burned   by the dragon's fiery blast.
Relentless in purpose   the lord of the Geats
swollen with rage   roared his challenge
from out his breast,   the sound of battle

resounding clearly   within the gray cliff;
hate was aroused,   the hoard keeper knowing
a human spoke;   little time was spent
in bid for amity;   first came a blast
from out the stone   —the sound shook the earth—
The adversary's breath   inflamed for battle
burned in the cave.

Of note here is the poet's interweaving of images. The stream issuing from the rock becomes one with the fiery stream issuing from the dragon, and Beowulf's battle cry penetrating within the barrow becomes interwoven with the emerging, answering breath of the dragon. The metaphoric effect of this interweaving of images is striking, and may have relation to the darkening tone of the final adventure. The monstrosity of Nature in the figure of Grendel fills Heorot because the hall is made by fallen man whose pride creates monstrosity; but Beowulf who, like Scyld, appears to have been sent by God, is juxtaposed against the monsters in providential triumph. Thus in his adventures in Denmark the interweaving of human and unnatural images serves largely to underscore the hero's triumph over evil begotten by humanity. Now, however, Beowulf feels estranged from God, whom he has a mysterious sense of having offended; he looks backward not forward and appears (from what Wiglaf and the narrator say) to be driven to attack the dragon by desire for gold, though in the mistaken hope that it will be for the good of his people. The interweaving of images in the passage under discussion would then suggest that man, estranged from God, is profoundly involved in the hostility of nature.

Except for the minimal requirements of the narrative, the battle itself is not marked by any developed description of either the dragon or the locale, but after the battle is over the barrow is briefly described again through the eyes of the dying Beowulf, lines 2715–19:

                The lord then went
beside the wall   and seating himself,
gazed in wisdom   on the work of giants,
the imperishable grave   supported within
by stone arches   set upon pillars.

Next the barrow is seen through the eyes of Wiglaf after he has entered. We are told of the treasure at which Wiglaf wonders and at the same time are reminded of the dragon through his absence. He looks at the treasure within *þæs wyrmes denn / ealdes uhtflogan*, 2759–60, but there is no sign of the dragon, *wyrmes*, 2771, who had *ligegesan wæg / hatne for horde,* 2780–81, *hioroweallande / middelnihtum, oþ þæt he morðre swealt*, 2781–82. Again the effect of the description is to interweave ancient human treasure with the alien, ancient terror of the dragon. The dragon's death does not lift the curse from the treasure; instead, it releases the power of its cursedness, as the messenger in his tale of coming disasters is aware. There is left only the hope that burying it again will help, and that the barrow Beowulf orders built on the headland, 2892, will preserve his glory. The mystery of the dragon is complex. The natural function of his monstrous terror is to find and avariciously keep earthly treasure, yet his covetous attempt to gain the treasure produces death and disaster. Earthly treasure gives function to the dragon, the greatest of nature's monstrosities, as it gives death to the humans who desire it.

Because the alien horror of the dragon is intertwined with the human—the barrow made by men to hold their treasure—the final description of the dragon fittingly juxtaposes him in death against the dead Beowulf. Thus Wiglaf looks at them both at the moment of Beowulf's death, lines 2821–35:

Then it remained   for the young man
in sorrow to look   upon his beloved
lying on the earth   his life at an end
pitiable in death.   The earth dragon,
his dread slayer,   also lay dead
crushed and lifeless;   the coiled serpent
no longer would rule   over the ring hoard,
for near the treasure   he had toppled to earth
finished by the stab   of the sharp sword
beaten on the forge   to battle hardness;
stilled by his wounds   the wide flyer
glorying in possessions   would never again
make an appearance   at midnight coursing
the clouds in flight,   for it had fallen,
struck at the hands   of the heroic king.
(As I was told   no man in truth

however mighty   ever met success
who undaunted   by the danger
braved the venomous   breath of the ravager
to rifle the hoard   in the treasure house
if he found the dragon   who dwelled within
awake in the barrow.)   For Beowulf's death
the treasure in part   was repayment;
the two together   had traveled to the end
of their transitory life.

This same linking in death of hero and monster occurs in the last view of the dragon when Beowulf's troop, upon returning, sees the dead Beowulf, lines 3033–37, and next to him the dragon, lines 3038–57:

First they had seen   the strange creature,
the loathsome dragon,   lying opposite
upon the field;   where he was felled
the firedrake lay   scorched by the flames
monstrously horrible   and measuring the length
of fifty feet;   once he flew joyously
in the dark sky,   and in the day returned
to his den below;   now fast in death
he had come to the end   of his use of caves.
Beside him were placed   goblets and pitchers
and plates were heaped   with precious swords
eaten through with rust   as they had rested
buried a thousand years   in the bosom of the earth;
for the heritage left   by legendary men
was made secure   enclosed by a spell
so that no man   might violate
the treasure house   unless the True God
the Victorious King   who protects mankind
gave permission   to such a man
as He saw fit   to open the hoard.

In the ensuing lines, which begin the next fitt, the significance of the curse upon the treasure is related to the mystery of God's design, the mystery emblemized in the intertwining in death of the dragon who hoarded the treasure and Beowulf who sought it.

The narrative of the battle with the dragon, then, is not marked by any set piece of natural description, but by scattered detail evoking the alien, ancient strangeness of the treasure barrow, guarded from mankind by its location in the wilderness, secured by the latent fury of the dragon and by the curse. It is the desire to keep and the desire to gain the treasure in which man and monster become intertwined. Unnatural Nature, hostile and inimical, is part of the estate of fallen man.

(4)*Sea Journeys.* When we turn to the accounts of Beowulf's journeys to and from Denmark, we appear to find a different kind of natural description, where Nature seems to be, as it were, smiling. In both passages, however, this effect does not result from any expressed pleasure in the sea, or in the journey upon it; rather it results from the sense of relief that the journey has passed with safety. The Geats put off from the shore, and with joy they come to the end of the voyage, "hurried by the winds." Happily the sea has not shown its accustomed enmity of storm and cold. The journey of the Geats has been made under God's protection, within the safety of the Sacred Word, as it were, where the hostility of Nature is held at bay. Nature is not smiling; rather its menace has been for the moment exorcised because Beowulf is an agent of God's mercy. It is not the sea that is beautiful, but the sturdy ship that carries the men safely across its dangers. The journey to Denmark is described in lines 210–28:

> The time had come,   on the sea under the cliff
> the ship waited;   vigilant warriors
> climbed the prow,   the sea currents
> merged with the shore;   the men carried
> onto the bosom of the ship   the bright treasure
> of polished wargear;   men with a will
> launched on the journey   the well-locked wood.
> Over the seaways   the wind-driven ship
> floated swanlike   with foamy neck;
> on the due hour   of the second day
> the curve-prowed craft   had come so far
> that the seafarers   could see the land
> its shining cliffs   and steep mountains,

the wide headlands,   the water was crossed
and harbor come;   then hastily the Geats
beached their ship   up on the shore,
moored the seawood;   their coats of mail
their gear clattered;   they gave thanks to God
that they had sailed   the sea in comfort.

The return journey is described in lines 1903–13:

He boarded his ship
and left Denmark   to cross the deep.
The robe of sail   with sheetings of rope
was tied to the mast;   the timbers creaked;
the wind did not hinder   the hastening ship
upon its course,   and the curved prow
foaming whitely   breasted the flood
upon its way   across the waters
until the cliffs of home,   the Geatish headlands
came into sight;   sped by the winds
the ship was beached   and rested on the shore.

In both passages what is emphasized is the beautiful sturdiness of the ship, the swiftness of the passage unhindered by storm, and most particularly, the providential safe arrival. Nature is not menacing because Beowulf and his men are safe within the page of God's merciful design.

(5) *Metaphors.* Finally there remain to be discussed the brief metaphorical passages of nature description. These center on the opposition between sunlight and dark, warmth and cold or fierce flame; there are, in addition, two intertwined examples of animal imagery. The sun and night imagery is pervasive, but exhaustive discussion is not necessary. The monsters are creatures of the dark and of the cold; they all wait for the sun to leave before they attack; they are associated with flame. All these descriptive details have already appeared in the passages dealing with Grendel's mother, including the strange fire burning in her den, and in those dealing with the dragon.

Grendel is introduced, lines 87–89, as a creature of darkness, inimical to day, and is so developed in the narrative of his attack on the Danes by selective, though scattered, descriptive detail. The attack begins with line 115, "After night had fallen"; the coming of day serves simply to reveal the horror, 126–29:

> At break of day   with the coming of dawn
> Grendel's power   was made apparent;
> after merriment   the morning brought
> loud lamentation.

The sun here brings no comfort and Grendel attacks "the very next night," line 135. Such comfort awaits the coming of Beowulf, the agent of providential design. In line 159 Grendel is called "the dark adversary and deadly shadow," who "in darkness held / the misty moors," 161–62; who "occupied Heorot . . . in the dark night," 166–67. Finally, the tale of "the cruel tyranny of terror in the night," 193, comes to Beowulf's ears.

In Beowulf's battle with him, Grendel is described in similar, scattered images of dark, lines 702–64:

> He came in the dark night
> stalking the shadows. . . .
> The sinful oppressor 705
> as was known to men   could draw no one
> into the night   if God wished it not. . . .
> Then Grendel bearing   the anger of God 710
> came from moor   under cover of darkness . . .
> from his eyes flared 726
> a fearful light   most like to fire . . .
> the grisly adversary 730
> was gleeful in mind;   before morning
> he intended   to tear apart
> each life and body,   to sate his lust
> with his fill of feast   —he was fated
> after this night   not to partake 735
> again of mankind. . . .
> His soul yearned for flight   and sought darkness 755
> in the company of devils. . . .
> The famed one wanted to get away 762
> as far as he could,   to flee from there
> to his fen haven.

In the Breca episode, as we have seen, the descriptive details emphasize the cold, the night and the water as the milieu of the monsters. In counterpoint, the sun appears after the monsters have been disappointed in their prey, lines 565–70:

> For in the dawn   cut down by my sword
> in the sleep of death   they lay on the surface
> beside the shore;   thereafter sailors
> held their courses   upon the high seas
> without any let;   the light came in the East
> God's bright beacon,   the storm abated. . . .

Clearly the appearance of the sun is not intended merely as an index of time, but in its designation as "God's bright beacon," 570, it takes on symbolic force, pointing to providential design as granting security to Beowulf against the monstrous dark. Additional emphasis is given to this symbolism by Beowulf's ensuing use of the motif in speaking to Hrothgar, lines 603–6:

> he who will may go
> proudly to the mead   when tomorrow comes
> and the radiant sun   shining in the South
> brings morning light   to the sons of men.

In the Finnsburh lay, which sheds its ominous light the length of the poem, nature description is employed with striking symbolic effect. After "the funeral flames," 1119, there comes a winter's peace, 1127–41:

> Then Hengest still   though he remembered home
> during the murderous winter   of his own will
> stayed in a house   in Finn's stronghold
> though free to sail   across the sea
> in ring-prowed boat;   in battle with the wind
> the stormy waters surged;   winter locked the waves
> in bonds of ice   until the better time
> made its stay on earth   —as it still does—
> when sunbright weather   observes its season
> in perpetual renewal.   Now with the passing of winter
> earth's bosom was fair;   the exile was bent

upon leaving the guesthall,   but his mind lingered
less on voyage   than upon revenge,
and upon the hope   he held in his mind
of hostile meeting   with the enemy men.[9]

The splendor of the poet's rhetoric is brilliantly illustrated in this image of the winter of peace made "murderous" by discontent. He inverts the customary associations: peace is maintained in the stormy winter; war will break out in the peace of spring. It is, of course, man with his warring mind who causes the inversion. The icy bonds of winter are the fetters of revenge unfulfilled; the ice of human hatred is melted only to release its fury.

In the battle with Grendel's mother, as has been noted, appears another striking set of images of fire and sun. Within the cave before he has grappled with the monster, Beowulf "saw a pallid light / a flame shining from a bright fire," 1516–17. He discovers that his sword, "the battle flame, had no power to bite," 1523, and in grappling with the monster hand to hand he fails. The light, however, enables him to see the sword with which God's grace permits him to triumph. After he has slain her, a light guides him, lines 1570–72:

The light glowed within   brightly gleaming
even as heaven's candle   in clear radiance
shines from on high.

As in the Breca episode the simile of 'heaven's candle" again suggests the providential design by which, "the Ruler of heaven / in wisdom determined the triumph of truth," 1555–56. Finally, Beowulf, guided by the light, finds Grendel and uses the sword to complete his task of purification by cutting off his head; the sword melts, lines 1605–11:

Then wondrously below
the blade of the sword   began in the blood
to melt away   in murderous icicles
until nothing was left,   most like to ice
when the deadly fetters   of the the binding frost
are freed by the Lord,   the true Father
who holds in His sway   time and season.

This simile stands in counterpoint to the inverted imagery of the winter of Hengest's discontent. The sword melts to signify the completion within God's design of the act of purification, the cruciform hilt alone remaining, and the ice of hatred, for this time, is melted. Finally, Beowulf's own account of his adventures is marked by contrapuntal images of light and dark. When he arrived home, lines 1964–66, he:

crossed the beaches
of the wide shore — the world candle shone
hastening from the south.

He begins his tale with reference to the sun and to night, lines 2072–74:

After heaven's jewel
had coursed the earth the demon came
terrible in the night. . . .

The battle is followed by a day of rejoicing until the dark and the next day's horror, lines 2103–28:

After morning came
and we took our places to partake of the feast
there was song and story. . . .
Thus in that place we took our pleasure
the entire day until the darkness of night
came again to man. . . .
After morning came the Danes could not
do as they wished for him who lay dead,
give him to consuming fire, set the beloved
upon the funeral pyre; in her fiendish clutch
she had taken his body into the water of the tarn.

Thus, in Beowulf's recapitulation the symbolism of day and night is given additional stress.

Two passages of bird imagery remain to be discussed. The first is a curious one that appears at the end of the feast celebrating Beowulf's victory over Grendel's dam, when, after "The shadow of night / darkened over the courtiers," 1789–90, Beowulf took his rest, lines 1799–1804:

> The hero rested —the roof towered high
> curved and gold-encrusted— the guest slept within
> until the black raven blithe-hearted announced
> the bliss of heaven. Then the bright sun
> advanced on its way. . . .

Why the raven, so commonly of ill-omen, should joyously announce the day is as puzzling as it is striking. My best guess is that its function is related to the thematic design of the poem in suggesting that in the city of the world, moments of happiness, of glory, carry within them the seeds of future disaster.

Be this as it may, the raven does reappear under much more usual circumstances to conclude the messenger's announcement of Beowulf's death and his prophecy of dire consequences, lines 3021–27:

> Therefore many a spear
> cold in the morning fingers must clasp
> and hands must raise; the song of the harp
> will never rouse the warrior, but the black raven
> settling on the doomed will have much to say
> in relating to the eagle his luck at the feast
> while he and the wolf worry the corpses.

In this final piece of nature description the raven unnaturally speaks in human terms of its relish in feasting on the feasters. This interweaving of human and animal serves to recapitulate the poet's treatment of Nature, as well as to show its resemblance to that found in the *Book of Kells*. It would appear that the analogies between the role of Nature in both books reaches some kind of metalinguistic, metavisual level of experience; the social consciousness of a people too close to Nature to see it as garden-like, and sustained by a missionary Christian faith. That much-quoted passage from Bede's *Historia* which tells of a pagan noble's reaction to the promise of Christianity most aptly expresses the sensibility suggested in *Beowulf* and in the *Book of Kells*. The passage is particularly serviceable; its straightforward narrative style differs from the style of the poem, while the burden of its message is the same. Thus by means of similarity in difference we come close to the metalinguistic level of contemporary understanding of Nature; the ultimate climate of belief expressed both in straightforward and convoluted styles:

> "Your majesty, when we compare the present life of man with that time of which we have no knowledge, it seems to me like the swift flight of a lone sparrow through the banqueting-hall where you sit in the winter months to dine with your thanes and counsellors. Inside there is a comforting fire to warm the room; outside, the wintry storms of snow and rain are raging. The sparrow flies swiftly through one door of the hall, and out through another. While he is inside, he is safe from the winter storms; but after a few moments of comfort, he vanishes from sight into the darkness whence he came. Similarly, man appears on earth for a little while, but we know nothing of what went before this life, and what follows. Therefore, if this new teaching can reveal any more certain knowledge, it seems only right that we should follow it."

If the varied analogues drawn from what is, in effect, a missionary stage of Christian civilization do in fact point toward underlying experience, then at another period in Christian civilization, other such analogies should appear, and they should be of a different order. A brief analysis of the role of Nature in the Bayeux Tapestry and in the *Song of Roland* may provide, in conclusion, just such a test of the validity of the analogies between the *Book of Kells* and *Beowulf*. The embroidery and *Roland* are roughly contemporaneous, and they come from a later period when the missionary spirit has given way to what may be called an incipient crusading spirit.[10] When we turn to the Bayeux embroidery we are struck at once by the role of Nature. It has become merely part of a framing design, enclosing the central concern with the actions of man himself.[11] Nature consists chiefly of the fauna of fable, contained in the upper and lower margins; of the sea as a place of crossing where the centrality of human action forces the story to flow into the margins; and of the flora of trees which serve simply to frame narrative episodes.

These features are illustrated in the panels which depict Harold's first crossing to meet with William (fig. 2). The fauna consists of

3. BOSHAM. THE CHURCH.

4. HERE HAROLD HAS CROSSED THE SEA AND

5. WITH HIS SAILS FULL OF WIND HAS COME TO THE TERRITORY OF COUNT GUY.

6. HAROLD.

7. HERE GUY HAS CAPTURED HAROLD AND

8. LED HIM OFF TO BEAURAIN AND THERE

Figure 2

fables and frames the actions horizontally; the flora consists of two trees which frame the episode laterally; in the sea crossing, the sails flow into the upper margin, as figures do elsewhere—for example in the crossing of the quicksands before Mont St. Michel (fig. 3). Here the abbey pushes into the upper margin, and the lower margin reveals the denizens of the sea. The trees as devices for framing episodes are everywhere; one very interesting example, however, will suffice: the panels depicting the news of Harold's coronation being brought to William, and his decision to attack England (fig. 4). A tree introduces the sea journey of the messenger, as trees frame his landing and William's response, which is, of course, to build a navy. The trees on the right mark both the conclusion to this decision and the beginning of its actualization. In all this Nature serves merely as a backdrop, or frame of reference, for human events. In the narrative of man's deeds Nature serves a rhetorical function. As we might expect in an age of expansion, of released energy, Nature may retain something of the ominous. Concern with Nature is subsumed, however, in the overwhelming concern with the dynamics of man's deeds.

There is an exact analogue between the function of Nature in the embroidery and in the *Roland*, where it also does not loom very large, and where it serves most prominently to provide by repetition of selected details a narrative pattern, a framework of reference for the central action of men living within a providential design. Except for entirely symbolic nature description in a few depictions of the diabolical, in the omens of Roland's death, and in Charles' two visions, Nature appears in the *Roland* only in a pattern of five repetitive, selected details. They are: 1) the shade of an orchard, or of trees, pine, olive, yew, laurel; 2) the fairness of evening, the shining sun, the passage of day, the coming of night; 3) passes, ravines, valleys; 4) the green grass and flowers; 5) animals, used chiefly in similes.[12]

1) *Orchard and Tree*: The events with which the poem begins, Charlemagne's weariness leading to Ganelon's betrayal, are in particular framed by the tree motif. In Laisse 2, which shifts from Charles to Marsiliun, the latter is introduced going "into the shade of an orchard," *un verger suz l'umbre;* his messenger, Blancandrin, comes to Charlemagne who is "in a broad orchard," *en un grant verger*, where his throne is set "under a pine tree near an eglantine," *desuz un pin; delez un eglenter,* 8; next morning Charles assembles his

19. AND HIS ARMY HAVE COME TO THE MONT SAINT-MICHEL

20. AND HERE THEY HAVE CROSSED THE RIVER COUESNON
HERE EARL HAROLD WAS DRAGGING THEM OUT OF THE QUICKSAND.

Figure 3

35. HERE AN ENGLISH SHIP

36. HAS COME TO DUKE WILLIAM'S TERRITORY. HERE DUKE WILLIAM

37. HAS ORDERED SHIPS TO BE BUILT.

Figure 4

council "under a pine tree," *desuz un pin,* 12; Ganelon on his treacherous mission meets the Saracens "under a tall olive tree," *suz une olive halte,* 28; in 29 he tells Blancandrin of Charles' sitting "in the shade," *suz l'umbre,* as Roland presents him with a symbolic apple; Ganelon and Blancandrin dismount in Saragossa "under a yew tree," *suz un if*, where Marsiliun is enthroned "in the shadow of a pine," *suz l'umbre d'un pin,* 31; when Ganelon is threatened "he sets his back against the trunk of a pine tree," *suz le pin a la tige,* 37; Marsiliun, 38, withdraws "into an orchard," *Enz el verger.* There follows the treacherous agreement.

This pattern is not again repeated in such detail, but the three remaining instances have significant echoic effect, suggesting the result of the initial act of treachery. Thus, the wounded Marsiliun retreating from Charlemagne comes to Saragossa and dismounts "in the shade of an olive tree," *suz un'olive*, 187. Then Baligant, the ultimate foe, arrives and enthrones himself "under a laurel tree," *Suz un lorer,* and his messengers to Marsiliun dismount "under an olive tree," *dedesuz un'olive*, 192, 195. Finally Charles viewing the carnage caused by his succumbing to treachery finds the dead Roland when he "reaches the shade of two trees," *desuz dous arbres,* 206.

2) *Light and Dark:* Repetition of detail again serves a function in punctuating the initial act of treachery. After Blancandrin has made his treacherous proposal to Charlemagne, Laisse 11 begins, "The evening was fair, the sun shone brightly," *Bels fut li vespers e li soleilz fut cler*, and Charles has the Saracens lodged "in the broad orchard," *grant verger*, where they stay "through the night until the coming of the bright day," *la noit demurent tresque vint al jur cler.* It should be noted that this is the first example of the frequent intertwining of two or more motifs, here of the orchard and of day-night.

The central events of Roland's battle against Marsiliun and Charles' against Baligant are similarly punctuated. The battle of Roncesvalles is presaged by Charlemagne's first vision, which is framed by the motif of light and dark; before he sleeps, "The day passes, the night grows dark," *Tresvait le jur, la noit est aserie,* 56; when he awakens, "The night passes and the bright dawn appears," *Tresvait la noit e apert la clere albe,* 58. The approach of the pagan host against Roland is echoically announced, "The day was clear and the sun was fair." *Clers fut li jurz e bels fut li soleilz,* 79. When Roland's horn has told Charles of the treachery, "the evening lengthens, the day draws out," *Eslargiz est li vespres e li jurs,* 187. Charles' second vision, preliminary to his battle against Baligant, is punctuated as is his first by the repetition of the light-dark motif to introduce and conclude it: "The night is clear and the moon is shining," *Clere est la noit e la lune luisant(e)*, 184, and "Charles sleeps on until morning and the bright day," *Carles se dort tresqu'al demain al cler jur,* 186. Before his vision when Charles in pursuit of Marsiliun's host "sees the dark descending he dismounts on the green grass," and prays to God "to make the sun stand still and the night wait and the day go on," *Quant veit li reis le vespers decliner, / Sur l'erbe verte descent . . . si priet Damnedeu / Que li soleilz facet pur lui arester / La nuit targer e le jur demurer.* Gabriel tells him "the light will not fail," and for Charlemagne's sake, "the sun is standing still where it was," *ne falt clartet . . . li soleilz est remés en estant*, 179, 180. In contrast to the miracle of the light, when Baligant arrives his fleet unnaturally turns the night into day; its "tall prows gleam with carbuncles and lanterns which flash so brightly into the sky that at night they adorn the sea." And as the vessels approach the land of Spain, this brilliance floods the whole coast, so that it shines, *en cez haltes vernes / Asez i ad carbuncles e lanternes; / La sus amunt pargetent tel luiserne / Par la noit la mer en est plus bele; / E cum il vienent en Espaigne la tere, / Tut li pais en reluist e esclairet,* 190. In the next laisse the motif is repeated, his fleet is "spangled with lanterns so that it gleams brightly all night," *Asez i ad lanternes e carbuncles, / Tute la noit mult grant clartét lur dunent.* When he lands, "The day is clear, with brilliant sunshine," *Clers est li jurz et li soleilz luisant,* 192. Before the battle Charles awakes "In the morning, at the first light of dawn," *Al matin quant primes pert l'albe,* to be blessed by Gabriel, 204, and as the two hosts approach, "The day was clear and the sun was bright," *Clers fut li jurz e li soleilz luisanz,* 246.

Finally, the motif frames the final episode where justice is done to Ganelon. When Charles prepares to leave Saragossa, "The day passes and the night has grown dark," *Passet li jurz, la noit est aserie,* 272, and then, 273, "The night passes and the bright day appears, *Passet la noit, si apert le cler jor.* In the final laisse when justice has been done and Charles seeks rest, "The day is over and the night has darkened," *Passet li jurz, la nuit est aserie,* 298.

3) *Pass and Ravine.* This motif, as with the first two, punctuates the first episode of treachery. Marsiliun vows to Ganelon that he will attack Roland if he finds him "in any pass or ravine," *a port*

ne a passage, 52; Charles asks who will guard "the passes and narrow gorges?" *les porz e les destreiz passages*, 58; and Roland vows that Charles may go safely "on your way through the pass," *Passez les porz*, 63, and commands Walter to "hold the defiles and heights," *les destreiz e les tertres*, 65; finally "The peaks are high and the valleys are dark, the gorges awesome under the dun rocks," when Charles departs in anguish at leaving Roland "in the gorges," *Halt sunt li pui, e li val tenebrus, / Les roches bises, les destreiz merveillus . . . As porz,* 66.

The motif, as would be expected, appears prominently in the battle at Roncesvalles. Marsiliun's troops come "down the valleys and across the mountains," *e les vals e les munz,* 68. Oliver climbs "a peak, and looking to his right along a grassy valley," sees the pagan host, *desur un pui halçur, / Guardet sur destre parmi un val herbus . . . est desur un pui muntét,* 80, 81; Roland promises the pagans will suffer "for coming to this passage through the mountains," *Felun paien mar i vindrent as porz*, 83; Marsiliun advances "along a valley," *par mi une valee,* 113. When Roland retracts and promises to sound his horn which Charles "will hear as he makes his way across the pass," *Si l'orrat Carles ki est as porz passant,* 129, its sound rings over "the high mountains," *Halt sunt li pui,* 133, and Charles "hears it as he makes his way through the pass," *Karles l'entent ki est as porz passant,* 134. "The peaks are high and dark and huge, and the torrents dash through them," *Halt sunt li pui e tenebrus e grant, / Li val parfunt e les ewes curent,* 138, as Charles turns back. Before his last stand Roland looks "at the mountains and hillsides," *Rollant reguardet es munz e es lariz,* 140; in response to Roland's last horn call, "sixty thousand trumpets blare, and the sound crashes through the mountains, and the valleys echo," *Seisante milie en i cornent si halt, sunent li munt e respondent li val,* 156. Roland surveying the dead looks "through the valleys, along the mountains," *Cercet les vals e si cercet li munz,* 162; he recovers from his faint and "looks around him, down along the valleys, up to the mountains," *Guardet aval e si guardet amunt,* 166; again he faints, "The mountains are high, and the trees are tall," *Halt sunt li pui e mult halt les arbres,* 169. When Charles arrives at the scene of slaughter he commands "the field, and the valleys, and the mountains," *le champ e les vals e les munz*, to be guarded, 178. Finally the pagans in retreat are "confronted by the deep awesome and swiftly flowing waters of the Ebro," *mult es parfunde, merveill[us]e e curant,* 180.

The episode of the battle with Baligant shows sparing use of the motif. When Charles has made his preparations to meet the hosts of Baligant, his troops "ride past the peaks and rocky heights, the deep valleys, the tortuous defiles" and emerge "from the pass and the wild country," *Passent cez puis e cez roches plus haltes, / E cez parfunz, ces destreiz, anguisables / Issent des porz e de la tere guaste,* 230; between the two hosts now "there is neither mountain nor valley nor hill nor forest nor wood," *Entr'els nen at ne pui ne val ne tertre, / Selve ne bois,* 243. Finally, Charles on his journey home again "rides through the valleys and over the mountains," *e les vals e les munz,* 273.

4a) *The Green Grass*. This is perhaps the most striking of the patterns of repetition and one with which other motifs are frequently interlaced. The first episode is marked only once by the motif; when Charles awaits Ganelon's message he "stands on the green grass before his tent," *Sur l'erbe verte estut devant sun tref,* 54. But in the battle at Roncesvalles the motif is employed with imposing echoic effect. After the battle is engaged, Turpin attacks a pagan and "hurls his corpse onto the green grass," *Que mort l'abat desur l'erbe verte,* 122; as the battle nears its close Roland embraces Turpin, "and gently lays him down on the green grass," *Sur l'erbe verte puis l'at suef calchet,* 161; again when all the peers are dead, Roland faints, recovers, and looks "down along the valleys, up to the mountains"; on "the green grass" beyond his companions he sees Turpin, *Guardet aval e si guardet amunt; / Sur l'erbe verte ultre ses cumpaignuns / La veit gesir le nobile barun / Turpin /,* 166. Roland's death is framed effectively by repetition of the motif: "under a beautiful tree. . . . On the green grass he has fallen backward," and he "faints on the green grass," *desuz un arbre bel. . . . Sur l'erbe verte si est caeit envers, . . . Sur l'erbe verte li quens Rollant se pasmet,* 168, 169; dying, Roland goes "under a pine tree and lies down with his face to the green grass," *Desuz un pin i est alét curant, / Sur l'erbe verte s'i est culchét adenz,* 174.

The ensuing action is marked by contrastive repetition of the motif: the defeated Marsiliun flees to Saragossa and "dismounts under the shade of an olive tree . . . and lies down in wretchedness on the green grass," *Suz un'olive est descendut en l'umbre. . . . Sur la verte herbe mult laidement se culcet,* 187; Charles, in pursuit of the Saracens, "sees the dusk descending, he dismounts on the green grass of the meadow," *Quant veit li reis le vespres decliner, / Sur l'erbe verte descent [lors] en un pred,* 179; after Baligant's arrival his throne is placed "under a laurel," where a white silk robe has been thrown "onto the green grass," *suz un lorer . . . Sur l'erbe verte,* 192. When Charles reaches the scene of the slaughter, "he sees his nephew lying on the green grass," *Sur l'erbe verte veit gesir sun nevuld,* 206. Before the battle, after he has ordered his troops, Charles, preparing to pray, "dismounts and lies down on the green grass," *Sur l'erbe verte s'e[n] est culchet adenz,* 228. In the battle, Naimes is wounded, and Charles sees "his bright blood falling on the green grass," *Sur l'erbe verte le sanc tut cler caeir,* 256.

Finally, the ordeal which will settle Ganelon's fate is fought on "a broad meadow," *pree mult large,* 288, and when justice is done to him, "His bright blood streams out over the green grass," *Sur l'erbe verte en espant li cler sanc,* 296.

4b) *Flowers.* Mention of flowers is rare, but striking and subtly linked with the motif of the green grass. When Roland sees the multitude of his slain men, he prays that God will admit them "to Paradise," *otreit il pareïs,* and lay them down "on the holy flowers," *En seintes flurs,* 140. Later when only Roland and Turpin are left the Archbishop prays over the peers, begging God "to lay them down on the holy flowers of Paradise," *En pareïs les metet en seintes flurs,* 162. These symbols of martyrdom are given visible form when Charles comes to the battlefield and, searching for his nephew, "all over the meadow he finds wild flowers which are crimson with the blood of our knights"; when he discovers his nephew "lying on the green grass," *De tantes herbes el pre truvat les flors / Ki sunt vermeilz del sanc de noz barons,* 206, he mourns him saying, "may God set your soul among the flowers in Paradise," *en flors / En pareïs,* 208.

The few other flower images serve an entirely different purpose, contrastively linking Baligant and Charlemagne. The latter is described, Laisse 8, "His beard is white and his hair is in full flower," *Blanche ad la barbe e tut flurit le chef.* Ganelon, later trying to convince Charles that no battle has taken place, says to him, "You are old and white and flowery," *Ja estes veilz e fluriz e blancs,* 134, where the reference is clearly to his hair and beard. Roland before his death speaks of Charles whose "beard is in flower," *ki la barbe ad flurie,* 173. The tenth battalion of Charles' troops, comprising the barons of France, have "flowery hair and white beards," *Les chefs fluriz e les barbes unt blanches,* 227. Baligant too is white of hair and beard, but his hair is described in simile as "flowery"; "white as a flower," *Barbe ensement cume flur,* 232; "as white as any thorn flower," *Altresi blanche cume flur en espine,* 261.

One final minor pattern of references to flowers occurs in the battle of Roncesvalles and appears also to serve a contrastive effect. Duke Sansun attacks a Saracen general and breaks "his shield which is gilded and painted with flowers," *L'escut li freinst ki est a flurs e ad or,* 98; and Oliver near to his end strikes a pagan and smashes "his helmet through its flowers," *E flurs e pierres en acraventet jus,* 146. In the battle against Baligant, Guinemans attacks"the King of Lycia and smashes his shield painted with flowers," *Tute li freint la targe ki est flurie,* 248.

5) *Animals and Birds.* Sparing reference to animals and birds is made chiefly by way of simile.

Devouring animals are used to provide one minor pattern. Turpin tells Roland to recall Charles by blowing the horn so that they "will not be eaten by wolves or pigs or dogs," *N'en mangerunt ne lu ne porc ne chen,* 132; in contrast Ganelon tells Charles that Roland is blowing his horn in sport, "A single rabbit has been known to set him blowing his horn," *Pur un sul levre vat tute jur cornant,* 134. Charles when he comes to the battlefield commands that the dead be left "where they are lying and let no beast nor lion touch them," *Lessez gesir les morz tut issi cun il sunt, / Que n'i adeist ne beste ne lion,* 178. In contrast, after Marsiliun has fled to Saragossa, the Saracens, in despair, "hurl the image of Mahomet into a ditch for pigs and dogs to devour and befoul," *E Mahumet enz en un fosset butent / E porc e chen le mordent e defulent,* 187.

A dragon appears twice, but only as an image: Abisme, a Saracen, at the front of Marsiliun's host, "Bears a dragon as his device," *Sun dragun portet,* 114, and Baligant has a dragon device carried before him, 241, 245.

Birds and animals appear as similes in the battle of Roncesvalles. At the outset, after Roland has refused to blow the horn, "Roland's pride surpasses that of any lion or leopard," *Plus se fait fiers que leon ne leupart,* 88. Just before the main engagement, Turpin's horse is described in unique detail: "His war horse is swift and spirited, with cupped hooves and flat legs, short in the thigh, broad in the rump, deep-chested and high-backed, with a white tail, a yellow forelock, small ears, and his head fawn-colored all over," *Li destrers est e curanz e aates, / Piez ad copiez e les gambes ad plates, / Curte la quisse e la crupe bien large, / Lungs les costez e l'eschine ad ben halte, / Blanche la cue e la crignete jalne, / Petites les oreilles, la teste tute falve,* 115. In sequence three of the Saracen's horses are described by means of bird similes: Climborin's horse "is swifter than any sparrow / hawk or swallow," *Plus est isnels que esprever ne arunde,* 119; Valdebrun's "is more swift and nimble than any falcon," *Plus est isnels que nen est uns falcuns,* 119; Grandonies' is swifter "than any bird that flies," *Plus est isnels que n'est oisel ki volet,* 123. The whole is framed by recurrence to Roland, after Marsiliun is routed, where these similes of swiftness are reversed, "As stags before the dogs the pagans run before Roland," *Si cum les cerfs s'en vait devant les chiens, / Devant Rollant si s'en fuient paiens,* 141.[13]

This selection of five details from Nature used in repetitive chains clearly serves a structural purpose, framing some episodes, linking and contrasting others. As with the Bayeux embroidery Nature provides only the background, the framework for man's actions; it has a rhetorical function. The other, less pervasive, role that Nature plays in the *Roland* is metaphorical, even allegorical. This role is found in descriptions (1) of the diabolical; (2) of the upheaval of nature betokening Roland's death; (3) of Charlemagne's visions. In all three instances Nature serves to point to another reality, and it takes on reality only in symbolic setting.

(1) *The Diabolical.* When Ganelon brings back his treacherous message to Charles, explaining away the absence of the Caliph as hostage, he asserts that he fled with his followers rather than accept Christianity. To support his apparent fiction by appeal to providential verisimilitude he describes vividly the consequences of their flight; "Before they were four leagues out on the water, storm and tempest swallowed them up. They were drowned," *Einz qu'il oussent iiii liues siglet, / Si.s auqillit e tempeste e ored: / La sunt neiez,* 54. The description may be fictional, but it responds to the obvious symbolism of the drowning in the Red Sea of the Egyptians, that is, to an analogical level of reality. The remaining few descriptions of the diabolical are clear and direct. The Saracen Chernuble comes from a country where "the sun does not shine, the wheat cannot grow, the rain does not fall, dew never forms, and all the stones are black . . . a land inhabited by devils: *Soleill n'i luist, ne blet n'i poet pas creistre, / Pluie n'i chet, rusee n'i adeiset, / Piere n'i ad que tute ne seit neire. / Dient alquanz que diables i meignent,* 78. The bounty of Nature serves by inversion to describe the analogical devil's country.

The diabolical nature of Baligant's host is described, as has been noted, 190–91, by its unnatural illumination of the night. It is also designated by the unnatural nature of the races of which it is constituted: one army consists of "the vassals from Micenes with big heads. Like hogs they have bristles along their spines," *Micenes as chefs gros, / Sur les eschines qu'il unt enmi les dos / Cil sunt seiét ensement cume porc,* 236; another consists of men whose "skins are as hard as iron," *Durs unt les quirs ensement cume fer,* 239; the Emir's army contains "giants from Malprose," *jaianz de Malpruse,* 240.

(2) *Roland's Death.* After the first attack, and before Roland faces the main body of Saracens, the narrative is interrupted by two prophetic laisses: 110 which describes the grief Charles will feel when he learns of the disaster; and 111 which prophesies the death of Roland. In the latter there appears the single example of sustained nature description in the poem:

> And in France a terrible uproar breaks loose: a storm of thunder and wind, with rain and hail falling in cloudbursts. There is scarcely a pause between the strokes of lightning, and indeed the earth quakes . . . there is not a house without a broken wall. At high noon there is a great darkness and no light at all except when the sky is split with lightning, and no man sees it without terrible dread. Some say: 'This is the last day, and the end of the world has come.' But they know nothing; there is no truth in their words. For it is the great lamentation of the elements for the death of Roland.

Clearly the symbolic function of this description of the upheaval of Nature is to suggest that Roland's death is a martyrdom which gloriously echoes the Crucifixion in the *imitatio Christi.* The upheaval of Nature so vividly and realistically described has anything but a "realistic" function. Nature is a veil through which we perceive dimly the eternal reality.

(3) *Charlemagne's Visions.* Finally, there is grim realism in the description of animals in Charles' dreams, but it serves an entirely symbolic function. As the setting implies, the animals speak of a providential drama which is the reality behind appearances. The reader is expected to sense the role of Charlemagne as the agent of God.

The first vision is in two parts; part one contains a clear foreboding of Roncesvalles in which Ganelon is seen shaking Charles's lance till the splinters fly to heaven, 56. The second part,

57, contains an ambiguous foretelling of the ordeal preliminary to the execution of Ganelon, which is dominated by animal imagery, boar, leopard, and boarhound, reflecting hazily the animal imagery employed in the narrative of Roland's battle. Its ambiguity is in part a reflection of Charles's own weariness of perception, the weariness which led to the disaster.

The second vision also has two parts. It comes after the rout of Marsiliun's fleeing host, and before the climactic battle with Baligant. The symbolism of the first part, 185, is clear; Gabriel foretells the battle to come, "by means of a vision, whose significance is made plain in terrible omens. . . . Charles looks up toward heaven and sees thunderbolts, hail, rushing winds, storms and awesome tempests, and fires and flames appear to him falling suddenly upon his whole army. . . . Then bears and leopards come to devour them, serpents and vipers, dragons and devils, and more than thirty thousand griffons . . . his way is blocked by a huge lion which comes out the woods toward him." The details of the vision reflect those omens foretelling the death of Roland, and also the animal imagery of the battle of Roncesvalles. Charles cannot aid his men because of his own weakness; this is the lion which blocked his path to Roncesvalles. But the first part of the vision at the same time looks forward in terms of the first battle to the great one Charlemagne must face, where the lion is Baligant, and the animals and storms signify the diabolical host which Charles must rout. It will be a dubious battle, but with Gabriel's help Charles will slay the lion. Storms and animals are part of a visionary symbolism. They mean much the same thing as they did in *Beowulf,* except that here their reality is within the vision, and they will be conquered by God's Christian agent, Charlemagne.

In the second part, 136, the punishment after a dubious single combat is foretold. Ganelon appears as a bear, reflecting the narrative of Charles's dealing with Ganelon after he learns of the treachery. There he commanded that Ganelon be seized and turned over to the cooks who "put a chain on his neck as though he were a bear," 137. Also in the vision, a greyhound (Thierry) attacks the largest bear (Pinabel) "on the green grass," again reflecting narrative nature detail.

Except for Marsiliun's gifts of animals to Charles, and an occasional mule, none of which is really a part of Nature, this is the substance of the role which Nature plays in the *Roland.* Either details of nature are subsumed into the rhetorical structure of the poem as background and frame for man's actions, or the reality of Nature is treated symbolically as a veil through which spiritual reality may be glimpsed. The affinities between the conception of Nature in the poem as structural background or as veil and that in the embroidery are manifest, and appear to support the thesis that such affinities do reveal a primary level of social experience as in the affinities between the *Book of Kells* and *Beowulf.*

Notes

1. The seed of this essay on the role of Nature in *Beowulf* and *Roland* was cultivated in a seminar on Nature in the Early Middle Ages which Professor François Bucher and I conducted. I do not hold him responsible for the fruit, but attest that the process of cultivation was, I hope, mutually stimulating. I wish to thank Mrs. Sylvia Horowitz and Mrs. Anne Kish for their help in editing the final draft of this paper.

2. John Leyerle, "The Interlace Structure of *Beowulf*," *University of Toronto Quarterly* 37 (1967), pp. 1–17; Richard Heinzel, *Über den Stil der altgermanischen Poesie, Quellen und Forschungen* 10 (1875).

3. Bernard F. Huppé, *The Web of Words* (Albany: SUNY Press, 1970), p. xvi.

4. The other isolated nature details, serving pure narrative function, are: *isig,* (?)33; *ofer yða ful*, 1208; *wigge under wætere,* 1656; *ofer sealt wæter,* 1989; *meregrund gefeoll,* 2100; *ic on holma geþring,* 2132; *þæs wælmes,* 2135; *grundhyrde fond,* 2136; *holm heolfre weoll,* 2138; *in þam eorðhuse,* 2232; *hildlatan holt ofgefan,* 2847. Perhaps the scene of the father grieving over his son who has been hanged should be added, with its descriptive detail, *winsele westne windge reste / reote berofene,* 2456–57. It is possible also that some details in the descriptions of the funeral pyres should be added as giving further force to the intertwining of human slaughter and nature. The designation of swords as "battle-flame" may have a similar effect.

5. See Derek Pearsall and Elizabeth Salter, *Landscapes and Seasons of the Medieval World* (Toronto: University of Toronto Press, 1973), pp. 33–43. For a sensible perceptive commentary on the passages with which I deal

and excellently selective citations see Howell D. Chickering, Jr., *Beowulf* (Garden City; Doubleday, 1977), pp. 278 ff.

6. See Bernard F. Huppé, "The Concept of the Hero in the Early Middle Ages," in *Concepts of the Hero in the Middle Ages and the Renaissance*, edited by N. T. Burns and C. Reagan (Albany: SUNY Press, 1975). The thesis is being developed in my forthcoming book, *Beowulf: The Hero in the Earthly City*. The translations are from the manuscript text of this work in progress; punctuation follows the principles set forth in *Web of Words*.

7. Alvin A. Lee, *The Guest-Hall of Eden* (New Haven: Yale University Press, 1972), pp. 197–99.

8. Emile Pons, *Le Thème et le sentiment de la nature dans la poésie Anglo-Saxonne,* Publications de la Faculté des lettres de l'Université de Strasbourg, 24, (1925), pp. 89–91.

9. The translation differs from that presented at the conference and reflects my indebtedness to Professor Donald Fry's persuasive reading of the lines, *Finnsburh, Fragment and Episode* (London: Methuen, 1974), pp. 20–23; 43. The effect of adopting Professor Fry's explanation of Hengest's motivation, although this was not my reason for adopting his reading, is to reinforce the symbolism of the use of nature. The winter does not cause Hengest to remain, rather it reflects symbolically the frozen moment of truce locking for a time the flame of hatred.

10. See Rita Lejeune and Jacques Stiennon, *The Legend of Roland in the Middle Ages,* trans. Christine Trollope (London: Phaidon, 1971), vol. 1, pp. 20–23.

11. Ibid., pp. 29–38; vol. 2, figs. 14–19. Study of these figures reveals that nature functions in the Angoulême lintel as it does in the embroidery and in the poem.

12. Citations are from F. Whitehead, ed., *La Chanson de Roland* (Oxford: Blackwell, 1946). Translations are from W. S. Merwin, trans., *The Song of Roland* (New York: Random House, 1970). It should be noted that Merwin's laisse numbering differs at times from Whitehead's.

13. Lejeune, *Legend of Roland*, vol. 1, p. 38; vol.2, fig. 19. The parallel use on the Angoulême lintel and in the poem of the "metaphor" of the hunt is striking.

Comment

BY

George D. Economou

I am going to confine my comments on Professor Huppé's paper to four basic areas: first, the role of Beowulf; second, the extension of the interlace theory to include questions of theme and religious sensibility; third, the difficulty of establishing or defining the character of *nature* in the two poems; and fourth, my understanding of the Roland poet's uses of *nature* in two important moments in the poem.

It seems to me that Beowulf's role as the poem's hero has been severely diminished this morning. He has been defined more by his being a member of fallen mankind—a fairly low common denominator—than by his heroic actions and reputation in the poem; credit for the banishment of the monsters is directly (almost exclusively) shifted to "redeeming grace" or "providential design." One fairly popular view among critics who offer a Christian interpretation of the poem (and this, of course, covers a pretty wide spectrum of positions) is that Beowulf acts as an agent of providence. If one accepts the first premise, this is a view, it seems to me, with some merit. I am not quite certain what Professor Huppé thinks of this, for several important parts of his analysis suggest that the hero is to be defined by an even lower common denominator than the Fall of Man, that is, by the monsters themselves. "Man and monster become intertwined." But is this intimacy between man and monster not so because the man, who may be redeemed, *chooses* to fight the monsters, who are beyond redemption? When Beowulf shoots and kills one of the creatures that is swimming in Grendel's tarn, he does it because he is committed to fighting monsters and not, I believe, to "sport" or "game-playing." The characterization of this attack as "startling and gratuitous" I do not understand; for it seems to me that the character of the hero, as developed up to this point in the poem, justifies the attack. And gratuitous acts, to my knowledge, while common and significant in Gide, do not have an important function in epic tradition.

In connection with this issue, I would like to comment briefly on a point of translation. In support of another hero-monster juxtaposition, "through which the dragon hoarding the treasure and Beowulf in seeking it become intertwined in death," lines 2824–26 have been rendered "The earth dragon / his dread slayer lay dead *beside* [my italics] him / crushed and lifeless." The second half of line 2824 reads, "Bona swylce læg." The modern English version's offering of "beside" as the equivalent of "swylce," is as difficult for me to agree with as the idea of Beowulf and the dragon being intertwined in death; the corpse of one, after all, is pushed into the sea, while Beowulf receives a king's burial from his people and praise from his poet.

A translator, of course, cannot help but express his personal view of a poem in some of the choices he makes. Professor Huppé, whose translations today and in the past have given me pleasure, has been quite candid about his change of the punctuation at the end of line 98 whereby he extends the creation theme through line 101. I would add that Dobbie, as well as Klaeber, punctuates the end of 98 with a period, but it is not my intention to discuss in detail the choices of "lordly men" in the sense of first humans for *drihtguman* and "fiend in hell" in the sense of the Devil himself for *feond on helle*. These choices reflect the interpretation of the poem, which, in turn, has been described as sharing with *The Book of Kells* "the same counterpoint between the exorcizing power of God's providence and the hostility of man's natural surroundings." This "underlying affinity" is pointed up by the suggestion that the repetition of *gæst* in *ellengæst* (86) and *se grimma gæst* (102) represents a technical analogy between "the poet's method of narrative disjunction" and "the linking sign, the head-under-the-wing" device in *The Book of Kells*. Though the words in question are 15 lines apart and seem to me, therefore, to work more effectively as echoes (a practice for which the poet is well known), I will mention only in passing that we would have to deal with another set of implications if we were also to consider the question of the oral heritage of the poem; and though there is some interesting semantic ambiguity between *gæst* and *gast* here and elsewhere in the poem, I am primarily concerned with the expansion of the interlace theory to accommodate the interpretation of religious symbolism and sensibility.

In a well-known article, Professor John Leyerle and, more recently, Professor Peter Schroeder have explored in considerable detail the similarities between the technique of the interlace in Hiberno-Saxon art and the narrative style in *Beowulf* and other Old English poems.[1] For the moment, suffice it to say of this complex comparative recast of art and literature, that the basic analogy lies in their respective treatments of space and time. The interlace style or structure in the visual arts deals with the disposition of iconographic or plastic elements in space, while the interlace style or structure in poetry, specifically in *Beowulf*, deals with the disposition of plot elements in time, with "the treatment of narrative chronology," in the words of Professor Schroeder (p. 188). Professor Huppé uses this technical and structural parallel as a spring-board of his argument for a thematic parallelism between *Beowulf* and *The Book of Kells*. To my knowledge, it is an unique and original parallelism, and, so far as I am aware, it is also unusual in its categorical explanation of the meaning of the animal figures in *The Book of Kells*. Recalling Northrop Frye's statement that "there is always a sense in which criticism is a form of autobiography,"[2] I cannot help but wonder how much of this shared sensibility between *The Book of Kells* and *Beowulf* is in fact Professor Huppé's. I would also respectfully submit that the famous sparrow passage from Bede's *History* is much too linear to convey the sense of a relationship between two works which has been originally predicated on the structural principle of interlace.

While I do not agree with the basic thesis of Professor Huppé's paper, I do greatly appreciate his effort to see the depiction of *nature* in the poem whole. I must confess that I find it difficult to understand *nature* in *Beowulf*, or in *The Song of Roland* for that matter, as a coherent and systematically worked-out representation of an idea of nature. It seems to me that the *Beowulf* poet uses natural imagery with great effectiveness in isolated instances and that this limited effectiveness has been neatly pointed out several times this morning, but when these instances are made to carry the weight of concepts like "postlapsarian nature" and "unnatural nature" I find them buckling under their burden. What, for example, is a "metalinguistic, metavisual level of experience" of *nature*? If the role of capital *N nature* in works of art cannot be concretely depicted or articulated, can we be certain it is there? In effect, I am asking when is a raven a raven, and when is it a symbol of a larger unit of meaning? When is the sea the sea, and when is it *nature*? When are initial serpents, a rat, a cat, a mouse, themselves? When are they traditional iconographic motifs? And when are they "menacing" and "dangerous . . . repellent presences"? The need to ask these questions betrays my sincere reluctance to admit the presence of the larger context of *nature* that would obviate the need to ask them in the first place.

Turning finally to *The Song of Roland*, Professor Huppé's characterization of *nature* as a backdrop or frame for human actions by analogy with the Bayeux Tapestry has definitely helped me confirm my own feelings about the limited yet concise role of *nature* in the poem. There are, however, two passages in the poem in which *nature* is treated in a way that suggests a meaning that transcends that of the usual frame or setting detail. In laisse 110, when it is clear that the French will not get out of Roncesvalles alive, we are told of turbulent storms, rain, hail, lightning, earthquakes, and darkness at noon in France. Frenchmen, unaware of what is happening to the Twelve Peers, interpret these prodigies as signs of Doomsday, but the poem says they are wrong—it is sorrow for the death of Roland that is the cause. It is a reaction of sympathy from nature in the homeland in which France expresses its grief, "Ço est li granz dulors por la mort de Rollant" (1437). Whether we view it as an instance of a kind of pathetic fallacy or a tendency towards personification, we recognize it as an extraordinary and moving moment. Naturally, we are reminded of the prodigies that attend the crucifixion in the accounts of Matthew, Mark, and Luke, and the suggested analogy between Christ and Roland does not necessarily strike us as untenable, especially when we consider that Charlemagne also bears a figural relationship to Christ. It is noteworthy that such prodigies also attend the birth of another hero whose history was circulating and developing at the same time as Roland's—I am referring to Alexander the Great. In the versions of Pseudo-Callisthenes, of the Archpriest Leo's *Historia de Preliis*, and in the vernacular romances, there are storms, quakes, and a darkening of the day when Alexander is born. Is it possible that a parallel can also be drawn between Alexander and Roland? Both are great warriors, and the similarity of the signs that accompany the birth of one and the death of the other is strongly reinforced by the clear suggestion that Roland's death is in fact a kind of birth.

The second passage comes in laisse 179, the famous moment when Charlemagne prays for the prolongation of the day, and an angel tells him God will make it happen. Of course, this is a repetition of the miracle performed for Joshua (X) and suggests a figural connection between Charlemagne and Christ through the establishment of a connection between the Emperor and an Old Testament type of Christ. Interestingly, by a sort of literary interlacing, the careers of Charlemagne-Roland are connected with those of Alexander and Joshua, forming a pattern of heroism in which all three classes of the Nine Worthies are represented. But finally, the miracle in laisse 179 consists of a suspension of a natural law: the primary creative power of the universe alters the operation of the secondary creative power to answer a prayer so that a Christian monarch and leader of men might do what is necessary to fulfill—if I may borrow a phrase— a providential design.

Notes

1. John Leyerle, "The Interlace Structure of *Beowulf*," *University of Toronto Quarterly* 37 (1967): 1-17; Peter R. Schroeder, "Old English Art and Poetry," *Viator* 5 (1974): 185-98.
2. Northrop Frye, "Expanding Eyes," *Critical Inquiry* 2 (1975): 203.

Some Implications of Nature's Femininity in Medieval Poetry

Winthrop Wetherbee

Inseparable from the important developments which took place in the philosophy of nature in the twelfth century was the development of a strong interest in psychology, and in particular the psychology of love.[1] In a universe ordered by an all-embracing *natura*, love is a link between man, the *minor mundus*, and his macrocosmic environment, for human physical and psychological life are actuated by the same *vitalis motus* which sustains the natural order. Hence the question of how man experiences and interprets his affinity with this order is critically important. The philosophical implications of the relationship were a matter of general agreement: as in the greater universe, and in emulation of its regularity, man's faculties and impulses, rightly ordered, act in hierarchical submission to a dominant *ratio*. Thus governed, man's participation in the natural order can be a means to self-recognition and spiritual advancement. But the appeal of *natura* is complex, and the penetration of her secrets is made difficult by the clouding of man's reason through sin. Where unfallen man saw the essence of natural reality with the eye of reason, we are forced to "feel our way" by experience;[2] and the same perceptions which make for understanding can, by the appeal of their richness and variety, seduce us into mere *curiositas*, a finally aimless fascination with *naturalia* for themselves, a fornication with idols.

In this paper I will consider a sequence of allegorical treatments of the relationship of man with the personified "goddess" *Natura*, and suggest their relation to other medieval poetry on the theme of love. Repeatedly in the allegories of *Natura* a feminine appeal for recognition, vindication or fulfillment is set in confrontation with a masculine *ratio*, a principle or faculty responsible for realizing the implications of this appeal through order. The role of the *Natura* who appeals to God in Bernardus Silvestris' *Cosmographia* and to man in the *De planctu naturae* of Alain de Lille is in effect an intensification of the role of woman in a range of poetry of their period; and man's response to the goddess becomes a prototypical illustration of his ability or inability to respond adequately to the implications of the experience of love.

Before taking up these larger matters it will be useful to say something about the place of woman in twelfth-century Latin poetry. Like the authors of the *romans d'antiquité*, the Latin poets were fascinated by the Ovidian romantic heroine: innocent victims of passion like Iphys or Philomela, and the abandoned wives and lovers of the *Heroides* were an important precedent for the concern of twelfth-century poets with the articulation of certain human emotions—love, desire, the longing for acknowledgment or fulfillment, frequently accompanied by an implicit questioning of the place of love in the scheme of things. The fascination of the Ovidian heroines was two-sided: on the one hand, as Jean-Charles Payen observes, they illustrate the perils of a world unconstrained by Christian morality, a world of "natural force, unbridled sensuality, Eros triumphant;"[3] but at the same time it was possible to make the inevitably destructive working-out of passion a foil to the depiction of aspirations which could be isolated and vindicated over against their tragic context. This may be seen in a lyric from the Codex Buranus which treats with both irony and sympathy the growth and consummation of Dido's love for Aeneas.[4] From its opening lines the poem emphasizes the promise which seems implicit in the fated arrival of so worthy an object for Dido's largesse, and we are likely to ignore the quiet hint that the wanderer is finally more *felix* than the queen who receives him:

sed errat feliciter
dum in regno taliter
Didonis excipitur:
si hospes felicior
hospita vix largior
aliqua percipitur.

But his wandering was favored, since he was so well received in Dido's kingdom. And if the guest was highly favored, a nobler hostess may hardly be imagined.

The erotic force which Cupid, disguised as Ascanius, had exerted in Vergil's narrative here emanates from Aeneas himself, who appears to Dido "amoris quasi facie." She is urged on by her sister Anna, who stresses the promise of the marriage:

si iste
iungetur tibi suisque
extollet te virtutibus,
Carthago crescet opibus.

> If he be joined to you and sustain you with his greatness, the substance of Carthage will be increased.

The hunt, the storm, and Dido's revelation of her passion quickly follow, and the poet ends with a curiously un-Vergilian comment:

Et sic amborum in coniugio
leta resplenduit etherea regio;
nam ad amoris gaudia
rident, clarescunt omnia.

> And so at the marriage of these two the heavens shone in joyful splendor; for all creation smiles and shines on the joys of love.

The contradiction of Vergil in these lines is surely intentional. It may be seen as simply an ironic exposure of Dido's self-delusion, as commenting on the intensity of will with which she seeks to alter the course of nature, and at the same time as commenting on her passion in another way, projecting an image of ideal fulfillment as a way of suggesting the fullness and generosity of her love in itself.

The Dido of this lyric is neither the articulate and passionate but faintly comic protagonist of Ovid's epistle, whose eloquence seems capable of postponing her suicide indefinitely, nor the intense Euripidean figure of the *Aeneid*, but a heroine whose primary characteristic seems to be an openness to the promise of love. The irony of her unfulfillment is stressed in a second lyric from the same grouping in the Codex Buranus,[5] a death speech in which Dido repeatedly links her fate with that of her desert kingdom, *arens Libya*, the "realm of thirst." Their common barrenness is pointed up by the departure of Aeneas, 'the flower of Carthage," whose coming had promised so much. In the final stanza, again anti-Vergilian, Dido's grand passion is reduced to a pathetic injunction to her soul to follow Aeneas, bearing her love and the memory of her sorrow:

Eneam sequere,
nec desere
suaves illecebras
amoris,
nec dulces nodos Veneris
perdideris,
sed nostri conscia
sis nuntia
doloris!

Pursue Aeneas, do not abandon the pleasant allurements of love; so may you not lose utterly the sweet bond of Venus, but survive as both sharer and witness of my grief.

This treatment of Dido can hardly reflect a desire to rewrite the *Aeneid*, or to overturn the well-established medieval view of her as a lesson in the self-destructiveness of lust. What is important is its revaluation of these views, the largely original way in which Dido's passion commended itself as a subject to the twelfth-century lyrist, enabling him to see her primarily as expressing a natural impulse to fulfillment.

Such a thematic use of feminine emotion may help to suggest a context for appreciating the impulse toward realization and vindication which is dramatized on a cosmic scale in the *Cosmographia* of Bernardus Silvestris. The theme of Bernardus' allegory is creation as process, as the realization of qualities and aspirations which exist *in potentia* as "seminal virtues" until brought to fruition through the union of matter with form. Nature herself opens the *Cosmographia* with an appeal to Noys, the agent of the divine Wisdom, to order the formless existence of primal matter, which yearns for *figura*, for 'the shaping influence of number and bonds of harmony."[6] Bernardus emphasizes the "human," feminine aspect of the goddess, endowing her with the impassioned eloquence of an Ovidian heroine, a sense of slighted majesty which emerges as a faintly accusatory tone in her address to Noys, and an intense maternal concern for the well-being of natural life. Her speech is modeled on a speech in Claudian's *De raptu Proserpinae*, in which Jupiter reports the accusations brought against him by Nature for having disrupted the order of the Golden Age and left man to forage like a beast;[7] like Claudian's goddess she claims a nobler destiny for her progeny and demands a transformation of their existence. But Bernardus' goddess is not simply seeking redress; amid the formless squalor of the pre-creation her appeal is the first impulse toward articulation of life itself.

The immediate effect of Nature's personality and of the urgency of her appeal is to dramatize the aspiration which in Bernardus' view pervades material existence, the sense in which "matter desires form as female desires male."[8] The "flowering" of created life in response to the ordering power of Noys is the result of Nature's appeal, and this result not only affirms the dignity of Nature herself, but has important implications for man, the lesser universe. For the process through which Nature comes to fulfillment, the adaptation of her vitality to the operation of the Divine Wisdom, is to culminate in the creation of man. Man in turn will find his fulfillment in recognition of the completeness with which his own being corresponds to the pattern and activity of the macrocosm: the comprehension of this great affinity will be simultaneously a recognition of his own lordship and destiny, for it involves an act of realization which mirrors the ordering activity of Noys, confirming that man's mind is created in the image of the Divine Wisdom, and at the same time represents his taking possession of Nature and the natural order as his proper domain.

Since the *Cosmographia* concludes with the creation of man, his destiny is only alluded to within the allegory. The foreshadowings Bernardus gives of human history offer clear evidence of human guilt, but they also celebrate the fruits of human *ingenium* in art, science and technology, and the final impression which the *Cosmographia* creates is of the stoical dignity with which man labors to resist his own instability, ordering and perpetuating his existence against the insuperable force of necessity. Bernardus makes us feel the anxiety of an age newly engaged with the study of nature at the tenuous linkage of cosmic order and physical law, and the doubtful moral implications of this linkage. Like *Natura* herself he seems at times to be protesting against a divine indifference which excludes man from the secure continuity of cosmic life, and to be urging a new valuation, one which will allow for the constraints of man's situation and assess his achievements on their own human terms, conceding them an intrinsic dignity such as *Natura* claims for material existence in general.

Thus it is surely by design that the *Cosmographia* opens with

Natura's passionate appeal for fulfillment, and ends with an account of the genitalia, the means whereby man seeks, endlessly and in vain, to emulate the continuity and plenitude of the natural order through procreation. This suggestion of sexual complementarity provides a framework for the action of the *Cosmographia*, and points to the sense in which both man and *Natura* can achieve fulfillment only through creative union with one another: the creation of man is the consummation of the natural order, and the capacity to comprehend that order is the hallmark of man's divinity.

That Bernardus scrupulously avoids locating human guilt historically, and seems to accept death as a necessary stage in the fulfillment of man's destiny,[9] is at least as much a matter of the decorum of his philosophical *fabula* as a reflection of his theology. This avoidance of a historical location for human guilt suggests a concern to forestall any precipitous moralization of his view of man, and a desire to do justice to human life at the level of intention and intrinsic feeling, such as appears in much twelfth-century poetry. Precise definition is impossible in such matters, but it seems clear that the initial appeal of *Natura* orchestrates the yearning of newly intuited elements in human desire for assimilation to human nature as conceived by religious and ethical orthodoxy. In Bernardus's allegory, where an overt optimism is everywhere balanced by a persistent and finally unresolved doubt, we can feel the complex pressure which a new kind of psychological insight exerted on the twelfth-century mind.

In the *De planctu naturae* Alain de Lille explores not only the psychological but the theological implications of man's dilemma. The effects of the Fall are explored through an elaborate metaphor of sexual perversion, in a dialogue between *Natura* and the poet-narrator, whose lament over the denaturing of man serves as a proem to the allegory.[10] Intense but somehow dislocated energy marks the poet who cries out to us in this proem. Though he regards the perversions of human behavior with horror, his muse seems unable to stop coining new formulae for characterizing them—metaphors from grammar, logic, rhetoric, and a parade of mythological exempla. He uses poetry itself as an image for the perversion he seeks to describe: the trope which yields no significance beyond itself, *figurae* which veil only their own corruption; and the compulsive energy with which his own verse issues in a stream of rapid-fire images of this corruption suggests that his own sensibility has been affected by the malaise, that affirmation is somehow beyond him. When he seeks to express positive feeling, and addresses the image of a virginal female beauty, whose lips his degenerate contemporaries disdain to kiss, he can only speak in the subjunctive: "my spirit would issue forth in response to her kisses," he tells us, and even if he should die he would enjoy a new existence in her. But there is a missing term in the expression of his yearning, an "if only . . ." which is left unexplained.

Suddenly the poet is aware of *Natura*, introduced by way of a long *descriptio* of the sort prescribed in the *artes poeticae*, beginning with the goddess's face and body and expanding, through a survey of her crown and robes, into a panorama of the life of the universe. She approaches the poet and at the moment of recognition he falls unconscious, unable to express himself in response to the vision, and suspended in a state of "alienation" between life and death.[11]

Alain's choice of the conventional *descriptio* as a vehicle is significant. The *descriptio* was probably the single most important aspect of poetic composition as treated in the schools, and the description of a beautiful woman, usually prefaced by a brief celebration of God's or Nature's creativity, and centered on the *idonea membrorum coaptatio*, the aesthetically perfect union of the physical components of her beauty, was virtually the symbol of high poetic art, as giving embodiment to ideal perceptions of harmony and purity, intuitions which constitute the imaginative nucleus of medieval poetry on the theme of love. Alain's *descriptio*, moreover, abounds in images of fulfillment and renewal, suggesting the normative and generative powers of the goddess as a standard of creativity which man may emulate. That the poet is unable to respond to this archetypal poetic image points up again the peculiar disorder of his consciousness dramatized in the proem, and suggests a fundamental lack of rapport with his poetic materials.

The loss here dramatized may be described as a loss of the capacity for a fully appreciative *realization* of the beautiful and desirable, the insight which makes possible a truly fruitful engagement with *Natura* and *naturalia*. And in Alain's depiction of fallen human sexuality as the extreme instance of the "divorce" of will and reason we can detect the implication of a comparable loss, the failure of a sexuality which we can only hypothesize, in which will and appetite would collaborate with reason, and sexual activity would express a perfect psychophysical integration. Desire would a response to the appeal of the beauty of human dignity itself, and would be grounded in a fully enlightened sense of participation in the natural order; the pleasure of its fulfillment would be intensified by a full appreciation of the sense in which every procreative act figures the archetypal "kiss" which is the impress of the divine Wisdom on created life.

Viewed in this way poet and lover are effectively one and the same, and responsiveness to the feminine beauty of Nature is the image of their common fulfillment. In Alain's beautiful hymn to Nature, the veneration of the universe for the goddess is characterized in the same words used in the proem to describe the reverence which sinful man has ceased to feel for the "semi-divine" beauty of a Helen.[12] And when in the denouement of the allegory we are introduced to Genius, the generative principle who is Nature's priest, he is engaged in inscribing a parchment with representations of human beauty and dignity, centered around a Helen so beautiful as to constitute beauty itself. Genius's relations with the goddess, moreover, in whose presence he seems to breathe again the air of Paradise, are made to resemble the devotion of a troubadour to his lady.[13]

The association of the poet's work with that of Genius is important, for Genius's office, in the universe and within the sphere of human sexuality, is to administer the union of form and matter, ensuring the perpetual creation of *similia de similibus*. It is in this capacity that he is Nature's priest, harbinger and solemnizer of the incarnation of form, the agent through whom the potentiality of natural life is realized. And the poet, too, becomes a sort of priest to the extent that his perception of the *iunctura* among the components of cosmic life realizes the quasi-sacramental implications of the union of form and matter.

Alain emphasizes the role of man's sensory engagement with the external world in developing his understanding of higher reality, and the responsiveness of his spirit and intellect to all levels of cosmic life. His very sensitivity to the rich implications of the analogy between the "marriage" which binds together the creatures who decorate Nature's robe and the *iunctura elegans* which is the consummation of the art of poetry is at the same time an acknowledgment of the sense in which that art, and by implication all human creativity, is potentially a means of engagement with Nature. In all of these ways he suggests the terms in which man might realize that union with Nature implied by the unresolved sexual allegory of the *Cosmographia*.

But it must be recognized at the same time that Alain considers Nature only as a fulfilled, constant presence, the spirit of a self-contained and orderly universe whose sole flaw is due to man's abrogation of his place in its order. Man once possessed the power to realize fully both his relationship with Nature and its implications, but he has lost this power, and while we are shown vividly what its recovery would mean, we are also shown that Nature does not have at her disposal the means to such a recovery. Genius concludes the allegory by pronouncing an anathema on all who deviate from Nature's sexual standard, but the anathema in itself does no more than reinforce with Genius's authority the denunciation already made by the poet himself in his proem and reiterated by Nature. Once a natural solution has been shown to be impossible and the need for supernatural intervention is clear, Alain has no more to say. Nature and Genius are suspended, communing across the barrier of the Fall.

As Bernardus's treatment of Nature focuses a host of aspirations which are implicitly those of an imperfectly realized human nature, Alain provides a definitive illustration of the psychological crisis which underlies the failure of these aspirations within the context of human life; he shows us the impossibility, for man, of assimilating the complex appeal of a Nature who is beautiful, forceful and intensely sexual and who is at the same time the means through which man's imaginative perception is to guide him to moral stability and enlightenment. The dilemma thus defined in terms of man's relations with the goddess herself inevitably affects the relations of man and woman, and is implicit in a range of lyrics which treat the imaginative experience of love. With varying degrees of irony these lyrics expose the inevitable failure of the aspiration implicit in the lover's response to that female beauty of which Nature is the source and model, and suggest the psychological barrier which prevents man from wholly realizing the implications of this idealism. The simplest illustration is a lyric found in both the Arundel manuscript and the Codex Buranus which devotes nine of its ten stanzas to an elaborate *descriptio puellae*, beginning *ab ovo* with the idea of the maiden, preexistent from the beginning of time in the creative *ingenium* of Nature:[14]

A globo veteri
cum rerum faciem
traxissent superi
mundique seriem
prudens explicuit
  et texuit
    Natura,
iam preconceperat
  quod fuerat
    factura.

Que causas machine
mundane suscitans
de nostra virgine
iam dudum cogitans
plus hanc excoluit
  plus prebuit
    honoris,
dans privilegium
  et pretium
    laboris.

When the gods had called forth the visible universe from ancient chaos, and wise Nature was unfolding and coordinating the order of things, she had already preconceived all that she would fashion.

Giving energy to the motive forces of the world order, and thinking long in advance about my girl, Nature endowed her with extra refinement and beauty, offering her as the seal and mark of value of her handiwork.

After the full-scale *descriptio* the poet ends by alluding to the effect of the girl's beauty, which "steals him from himself":

nam Natura, dulcioris
alimenta dans erroris,
dum in stuporem populis
    hanc omnibus
    ostendit,
  in risu blando retia
    Veneria
      tetendit.

For Nature, letting us feed ourselves on the sweets of folly, in showing forth this maiden to the astonishment of all, sets the traps of Venus through that fair smile.

A subtler and more fully dramatized version of essentially the same theme is offered in one of the most intricate of the *Carmina Burana*, which centers on the effect of the *largitas* of the beloved.[15]

Cui tanta claritas
ac mira caritas,
fecunda largitas
semper et undique
arrident utique,
hanc opto denique.

Ne miretur ducis tante
quis sublimitatem,
que me verbi vi prestante
doctum reddit plus quam ante,
stillans largitatem!

She from whom such radiance, and wondrous charity, and abounding largesse radiate in all directions unceasingly, she it is in whom my hope rests.

Let no one wonder at the nobility of such a governor, she who by [endowing me with] a surpassing power of speech renders me more wise and eloquent than ever before through the effect of her bounty.

Here it would seem that a realization of the richness of the love he feels elevates the lover to a state of inspired eloquence, a fulfillment of his vision like that which Nature offers to the poet of the *De planctu*; but here as so often in Latin lyric a certain wry, clerical skepticism is lurking, ready to expose the willful element in the poet's idealism. He is not yet in possession of his desire; his transport is still a wholly imaginary state, like Alain's evocation of virgin kisses in the proem of the *De planctu*. And as he lingers in suspense and the fear of rejection grows, he comes at last to question the possibility of fulfillment:

Sed si nos, Discordia,
tuo more disponis,
mutabo iam primordia
mee professionis.

But if you, Discord, dispose our lives according to your ways, I will alter my profession at this early stage.

The notion of "discordant disposition" and the mention of the poet's *professio* (suggesting an assertion of both his vocation as lover and his *métier* as poet) call attention to the literary character of the experience, and hint at a disillusionment about the attainability of such bliss as his imagination had projected. In the final stanza his appeal to the regenerative power of his beloved, though primarily an appeal for the solace of sexual union, suggests at the same time the need for a renewal of imaginative energy:

> Ergo, nitidior sidere,
> respice, si me vis vivere!
> nam flores constat emergere;
> tuo me solatum federe
> da ludere!

> Brighter than a star, look upon me, if you would have me live! Now, as the flowers may be seen opening forth, allow me to rejoice, solaced by the pledge of your love!

The irony which is inseparable from the dramatization of aspiration in such lyrics confirms the hints of pessimism in Bernardus and the moral rigor of Alain. The divorce of man's nature from its primal dignity is irresolvable by natural means. Man is basically incapable of realizing through apprehension or action the full significance of his relation to nature at large. Sexual love, the imaginative idealism which celebrates it and all the other assertions of the value of human feeling seem finally to be abortive gestures toward an unattainable continuity. All that we are left with is the persistence of the gesture itself, the ongoing concern of medieval poets to endow human desire with the resources of poetic form and language.

Even Bernardus's rigorously qualified affirmation of the dignity of sexual man seems to be undercut by the version of man's relations with Nature offered by Jean de Meun in the *Roman de la Rose*. Jean's image for the severing of human life from its paradisal origins is the castration of Saturn at the hands of Jupiter, an act which brought into the world death and the obligation of labor, including the labor of procreation. As Jean makes plain it also meant the divorce of natural man from rationality, and perhaps from aspiration toward anything beyond sexual fulfillment.

It is impossible here to do more than touch on the significance of Jean's Nature, whose long speech to Genius on man's violation of her law ends in a plea for procreation which inspires the sexual conquest that concludes the poem. Two striking features of his treatment of her may be mentioned. First, Jean keeps Nature and man wholly separate: the goddess expresses her will only by way of a chain of command which descends through Genius, Venus and Cupid before expressing itself in the lover's consciousness. Second, while doing justice to the traditional beauty and authority of Nature in her cosmic aspect, Jean has greatly elaborated her personality, which seems to grow progressively more human as her speech unfolds. Eloquent in her survey of the broader patterns of her domain, Nature becomes simply garrulous as she descends to consider the bearing of her order on earthly life. She is distracted into long digressions on natural philosophy, the potential effects of storms, floods, or insurrections in the animal kingdom, and discussions of fate, destiny and free will. As she considers man's abandonment of her she is consumed with anger, and thinks, in what amounts to a grotesque parody of the dramatic situation of the Ovidian heroine, only of exposing him as a sodomite.[16]

Even Nature's relations with her priest Genius are affected by these all-too-human indulgences. When she presents herself to him for confession, Genius greets her with a sermon on the perils of reposing confidence in an avaricious wife, whose curiosity, greed, and loquacity will inevitably reduce her husband to exposure and humiliation. Genius, who is himself a model of tact and reserve, disclaims any specific application, but his anecdotal homily is in fact a fair representation of the relationship of Nature with man. For the survey Nature gives of the sublunar world, compounded of half-understood science and philosophy, alchemical and medical lore, and punctuated with hints of rebellion and discord among the elements, is an image of the random and capricious manner in which she presents herself to man and demands his obedience to her law of procreation. It is through this law, as it expresses itself through his sensual nature, that man is "married" to Nature, and in submitting to her authority, like the husband whom Genius shows entrusting his innermost secrets to his wife, he exposes the debility of his fallen nature to her scorn and humiliation. Yet in Nature's eyes man is equally to be despised if he withholds submission: witness her fierce outcry against sodomites, forgers and traitors, and the relish with which she anticipates their torments in hell.

There are many questions to be asked about the conclusion of the *Roman*—what, for example, we should make of the fact that Jean's lover in spite of himself obeys the commandment of Nature and impregnates the Rose: or of the fact that the Rose remains irreducibly a rose on a rosebush throughout the process. But it is plain that the bonds by which man is joined to Nature are those of an unenlightened sensuality. His knowledge of her is at best a learned fantasy, an imaginative projection of his imperfect science and philosophy distorted by anxiety and groundless speculation, and his conscious participation in the natural order has been reduced to the day-to-day comedy of bourgeois marriage.

The long process which begins with Nature's initial appeal to God in the *Cosmographia* and issues in the *reductio ad absurdum* of her role as man's guide and stay in the *Roman de la Rose* may be said to be summarized in the poetry of Chaucer. Chaucer's early poetry is very close in its concerns to the work of the twelfth-century allegorists, and his *Parlement of Fowles* gives a vivid survey of natural life which embraces both the traditional goddess who balances the elements and the more inchoate force that priketh us in our corages. But Chaucer was also acutely sensitive to the challenge posed by Jean de Meun, the need to locate and affirm the presence of Nature in a world where Platonic verities are obscured by the accidents and neuroses of human experience. And the process inaugurated in Jean's poem, whereby Nature's presence is materialized in proportion to the materialization of man's vision, leads in the poetry of Chaucer to the figure of the Wyf of Bath.

The Wyf's most obvious antecedent in the *Roman* is La Vieille, but she is a far richer, deeper character. Several aspects of her role and character recall Jean's Nature, and I think she may be viewed very broadly as a sort of surrogate for this figure, a link between the natural order and the world of the *Canterbury Tales*. Like Nature in her long plea for procreation the Wyf displays a prodigious intellectual and imaginative energy in affirming her sexual role, but there is also, as in Nature's long speech, an element of uncertainty; for both figures sexual assertiveness is balanced by deep feelings of betrayal and resentment. The comparison has definite limits: Nature's energy endures undiminished and threatens to overpower her incautious betrayers, while the Wyf, behind her various postures, is aging, barren, and resigned; fulfillment is accessible to her only in the imaginative recreation of her sexual career. But it is largely in this very *ingenium*, the imaginative power which animates her autobiography, that her importance consists. It expresses not only her admirable power of sheer endurance, but also a capacity for moral idealism which, though it emerges only in her Tale and is never reconciled with her conscious sense of herself, reminds us that she is at some level capable of aspiring to a more truly fulfilling role than the perpetual combat which has marked her quest for the fruit of marriage. In the hint of reciprocity at the conclusion of the Tale we may see a manifestation of the Wyf's own deep desire to be "realized," possessed and appreciated by a male sensibility commensurate with her own capacity for response. To the extent that we see such hidden desires as vindicating this deaf and garrulous old woman—and certainly the Wyf does what she can to make such a view difficult—we may see her as Chaucer's representative woman, and the challenge she presents as a version of the primal challenge of Nature herself. This is what Nature comes down to in a world like that of the *Tales*, where little scope is given to youth or generation, and desire is the stuff of fiction.

Notes

1. See the stimulating survey of Peter Dronke, *Medieval Latin and the Rise of European Love-Lyric*, 2nd ed. (Oxford, 1968), 1:57–96.
2. Richard of St. Victor, *Benjamin major* 2.4 (*Patrologia latina* 196.82CD).
3. "Figures féminines dans le roman médiéval français," in Maurice de Gandillac and Edouard Jeauneau, eds., *Entretiens sur la renaissance du douzième sieècle* (Paris, 1968), p. 412.
4. Alphons Hilka and Otto Schumann, eds., *Carmina Burana* (Leipzig, 1930–), vol. 1.2, no. 98. All subsequent references to the *Carmina Burana* will be by number to poems in this volume.
5. *Carmina Burana* 100.
6. C. S. Barach and J. Wrobel, eds., *Cosmographia* (Innsbruck, 1876, under title *De mundi universitate*), p. 7, 22; trans. Winthrop Wetherbee (New York, 1973), p. 67.
7. *De raptu Proserpinae* 3.33–45.
8. Calcidius, *Commentarius in Timaeum Platonis* 286, ed. J. H. Waszink (London-Leiden, 1962, p. 290. Cp. Aristotle, *Physics* 1.9.192a.
9. Though the Fall is referred to obliquely at several points in the *Cosmographia*, no clear moral emphasis is given. Mortality is accepted as a basic condition of human life by the goddesses who foretell man's destiny in Cosmographia 2.8 and 2.10 (ed. Barach-Wrobel, pp. 51.52, 55; trans. Wetherbee pp. 109, 114).

10. *De planctu naturae*, ed. Thomas Wright, in *The Anglo-Latin Satirical Poets and Epigrammatists of the Twelfth Century*, 2 vols., Rolls Series [no. 59] (London, 1872), 2:429–31.

11. *De planctu naturae*, p. 449.

12. *De planctu naturae*, pp. 458, 430.

13. *De planctu naturae*, p. 520. See also my article, "The Theme of Imagination in Medieval Poetry and the Allegorical Figure Genius," *Medievalia et Humanistica*, n.s. 7 (1976):56–58.

14. *Carmina Burana* 67.

15. *Carmina Burana* 61.

16. Felix Lecoy, ed., *Le Roman de la Rose*, ll. 19188–207 (Paris, 1965–70), 2:76–77. On the character of Nature in the *Roman* see William Calin, "La Comédie humaine chez Jean de Meun" in *Mélanges Charles Rostaing* (Liége, 1974), pp. 110–12.

Comment

BY

Francis X. Newman

Professor Wetherbee's subtle and suggestive paper opens up many avenues of discussion, both about the separate works that he treats and about the theory by which he links them. I want to limit myself to two comments, the first a particular query about one of the poems discussed, and the second a question about the over-all argument of the paper. Neither of these comments is intended to dispute points made by Professor Wetherbee, but rather to raise issues that I would wish to see discussed in great detail.

My first comment concerns the *De planctu naturae.* In his analysis of what he describes as the "psychological crisis" of failed aspiration in the poem, Professor Wetherbee stresses the importance of that moment early in the poem when the poet falls into a stupor at the approach of the goddess *Natura*: "stupore vulneratus . . . in exstasis alienatione sepultus." He sees in this behavior evidence of the "peculiar disorder" of the poet's consciousness: his loss of the capacity to realize the beautiful and the desirable. Although *Natura's* characterization of the poet's stupor ("ignorantiae caecitas . . . alienatio mentis . . . debilitas sensuum . . . infirmitia rationis") might seem to support such a reading, another interpretation suggests itself when we compare the passage with some similar scenes in Alain's other allegory, the *Anticlaudianus.* In the opening of the sixth book of that poem, *Phronesis*, guided by Theology, comes to the heavenly realm, where the light is so intense that her mind grows numb and she sinks into a death-like stupor. Eventually Faith rouses *Phronesis* from this trance and leads her gradually to the apprehension of God. *Phronesis* earlier had had a similar experience when, led this time by Reason, she had her first encounter with Theology. Alain dramatizes each of these exchanges of guides—which mark significant points of transition in the narrative—by means of the same narrative device. The meaning of the device seems clear: as *Phronesis* journeys upward she is not simply progressing spatially, but is advancing through higher and different modes of knowledge. Alain signals the transition from one mode to another by the narrative image of sleep and waking; the stupor of *Phronesis* reflects the inability of lower noetic powers to comprehend the truths of a higher kind, and her subsequent waking reflects her transition to a superior mode of knowledge. This narrative device is a convention of visionary encounters: we need only recall Boethius's lethargy before Lady Philosophy or Dante's several swoons in the *Comedy*. The falling asleep of the dreamer in vision poetry is customarily an initiation into illumination: "Ego dormio et cor meum vigilat." While this perspective by no means invalidates Professor Wetherbee's interpretation of the encounter of the poet and *Natura*, it suggests that a fully persuasive reading of the scene would have to take into account Alain's use of the sleep-waking motif in the structure of the poem as a whole. Insofar as this scene is important to Professor Wetherbee's interpretation of the *De planctu naturae* and thereby to the argument of the paper, I would wish to see it more fully treated.

My second comment has to do with the paper's essential argument. In relating the treatment of love in the *romans d'antiquité*, the *Carmina Burana*, the *Roman de la Rose*, and the *Canterbury Tales* to the philosophical allegories of Bernardus and Alain, Professor Wetherbee pursues a course of speculation similar to that pursued by Peter Dronke in his *Medieval Latin and the Rise of the European Love-Lyric* (Oxford, 1968). But the paradigm of male-female love relationships that each discovers in the philosophers is strikingly different. Professor Wetherbee sees the feminine *Natura* as the counterpart of the women of the love poems, sharing in a common search for "recognition," "vindication," or "fulfillment." Professor Dronke, particularly in chapter 2 of his book, relates the courtly love relationship to mystical, noetic, and "Sapiential" languages that depict the female as the formative partner in the relationship, a divine *telos* who shapes and transforms the inchoate yearnings of her male lover. Wetherbee's analysis concludes with Alice of Bath; Dronke's recurs frequently to Beatrice. Which of the two is the paradigmatic female? Is it *Natura* or is it *Sapientia* that we should take as the reference point for the role of women in the love poetry of the Middle Ages? *Natura* and *Sapientia* are neither identical nor antithetical in their implications, and the effort to relate both to medieval love poetry would be a complex task. It is a task, however, to which Professor Wetherbee is well suited; I can think of no better way of having the question I have raised answered than to imagine a future paper from him entitled "Some Implications of the Femininity of *Natura* and *Sapientia* in Medieval Poetry."

In Principio: The Creation in the Middle Ages

Dorothy Glass

The creation stands at the beginning of all nature. In the Middle Ages, the *Hexaemeron*, or six days of creation, was both a topic of extensive debate and the subject of innumerable illustrations in all media.[1] Interpretations of creation both written and visual encompass theology, philosophy, mathematics and even architecture—in fact, virtually the entire intellectual life of the Middle Ages. There are many excellent studies of individual theologians, motifs, and monuments.[2] But, on the occasion of an interdisciplinary symposium, it seems more fruitful to attempt to place illustrations of the creation in the broader context of medieval thought. My comments will be neither new nor surprising to art historians, but may be relevant to those in other disciplines who seek relationships between the written word and the visual image. In trying to place rather complex matters in a broader context, I share St. Augustine's fear that "I am also in danger of appearing to take advantage of the opportunity to parade my scrap of knowledge with more vanity than profit."[3]

The creation, as recounted at the beginning of Genesis, is seemingly well-known, and one can easily visualize a series of illustrations depicting the days of creation. In actuality, chapters 1 and 2 of Genesis are drawn from different traditions.[4] Chapter 2 repeats some of the essentials of Chapter 1, but also offers conflicting information and interpretations. The text must be carefully analyzed in order to appreciate the problems faced by medieval artists in their attempts to envisage the story. It will soon be evident that medieval artists must not be viewed as mere illustrators.

For example, during the six days of creation recounted in Gen. 1, God actually performed eight separate acts. On the third day,

He created not only the dry land (or earth), but also grass, seeds, and fruits.[5] On the sixth day, He created the beasts of the earth and both man and woman who were given dominion over them.[6] The artist was thus faced with a choice of events to be depicted within the canonical six days. The solutions to this problem are myriad.

The creation of Eve raises a different issue because the text gives two different versions of the story. Perhaps through familiarity with such renowned works as Michelangelo's frescoes in the Sistine Chapel, we tend to visualize Eve as being formed from Adam's rib and then slowly emerging from his side, as he reclines on the ground. Yet, in Gen. 1, it is simply written that "God created man in his own image, in the image of God he created him; male and female he created them."[7] No further details are given. It is not until Gen. 2:21–22, where the story is told again, that the motif of Adam's rib is introduced.[8]

Gen. 2 offers still other details that are omitted in Gen. 1. In Gen. 1:27, it is noted that "God created man in his own image,"[9] while in Gen. 2:7, we are told that God formed man from dust, breathed into his nostrils, and man became a living being.[10] The latter version is certainly the more appealing visual image. Gen. 1:24–28 places the creation of animals before the creation of Adam and Eve, but Gen. 2:7–22 places that event between the creation of Adam and the creation of Eve, and also includes the naming of the animals, an episode quite often represented in the visual arts. Gen. 2:10–14 also tells of the Garden of Eden and the four rivers of paradise; both are omitted in the more cursory account given in Gen. 1. The story of the creation is thus not a simple linear tale. There are choices inherent in the text itself. The two versions offer different interpretations and each offers information not contained in the other. An examination of the monuments will illuminate this point.

Of the few extant illustrated Early Christian manuscripts, only the Cotton Genesis (British Museum, Cotton Otho. B.VI) has an extensive creation cycle.[11] Perhaps made in Alexandria in the sixth century, it was seriously damaged by a fire in 1731 and reduced to about 150 severely charred fragments. Kurt Weitzmann's meticulous reconstruction suggests that there were originally at least 330 miniatures.[12] Fortunately, we need not rely solely on the remaining fragments of the manuscript; many years ago, the Finnish scholar, J. J. Tikkanen, realized that the thirteenth-century mosaics in San Marco, Venice were based on the Cotton Genesis.[13] Tikkanen's general thesis is universally accepted and thus the San Marco mosaics may be used as an example of an elaborate Early Christian cycle of Genesis illustrations (fig. 1).[14]

At San Marco, in a dome that is itself a reflection of the cosmos, the first chapters of Genesis unfold. The cycle begins in the innermost ring of the cupola with the image of the nimbed dove, its wings spread over the waters. The dove, usually associated with the third person of the Trinity, appears here as the spirit of God. Gen. 1:2 reads: "And the earth was without form and void, and darkness was upon the face of the deep; and the Spirit of God was moving over the face of the waters."[15] The cycle continues counterclockwise around the cupola. The creator, accompanied by an angel, separates light from darkness. On the second day, the creator, accompanied by two angels, suggesting the number of days, makes the firmament called heaven, and separates the waters above it from the waters below it. The third day is interpreted literally in that both the creation of dry land and the creation of grass, seeds, and fruit are shown.

Turning now to the second band of the cupola, we see that on the fourth day, the sun, the moon, and the stars are created. On the fifth day, God creates fish and fowl, but unlike the fourth day, both the accompanying angels and the creator follow in a separate panel. This new compositional arrangement was doubtless necessitated by the difficulties incurred in trying to fit so many figures into a single, coherently organized panel. The creation of animals and man on the sixth day also occupies two panels. But, instead of continuing the sequential illustration of Gen. 1, the artist introduced the more vivid version of the story recounted in Gen. 2:7. The creator is actually molding the dusky figure of Adam. The seventh day, which actually begins the second chapter of Genesis, seemingly completes the cycle. The creator blesses the seventh day, personified by an angel. But, immediately after the depiction of the sabbath, the second chapter of Genesis continues as the creator is shown giving Adam his soul, here personified as a small winged man. Gen. 2:7 simply states ". . . Man became a living being."[16] Immediately after receiving his soul, Adam is introduced into the garden of Eden, where the four rivers of paradise also originate.[17] The outermost band of the cupola begins with the naming of the

Fig. 1. Venice, S. Marco, atrium, Creation Scenes (Alinari).

animals and the creation of Eve, as told in Gen. 2:21–23, [18] and continues onward through the expulsion from paradise.

The San Marco mosaics illustrate all the significant events recorded in the first two chapters of Genesis. But, as seen in the creation of Adam, the presentation of his soul, and the order in which the events of the sixth and seventh days are represented, the mosaicist's interpretation is not precisely literal. Other departures from the text, such as the angels and the depiction of the creator, are of even greater interest. They must be examined in some detail because they reflect the ways in which Christian theological interpretations were grafted onto the Old Testament text. It is precisely these variations that give each illustration of the creation its own particular significance.

Throughout the San Marco cycle, the creator is depicted as Christ, recognizable by his cross-nimbus, rather than as God the Father. But, it must be remembered that the creation took place through the Word of God; the phrase "and God said" is repeated consistently. In the New Testament, Christ is clearly identified as the Word of God. One need only recall the opening verses of the Book of John: "In the beginning was the Word and the Word was with God, and the Word was God. He was in the beginning with God; all things were made through him, and without him was not anything made that was made."[19] The identity of Christ and the Logos was crystallized in the Nicene Creed and the creator is represented as either God or His Son, Christ.[20] Both appear regularly and sometimes interchangeably in countless illustrations of the creation. At San Marco, the cycle is unified by the consistent and regular appearance of this dual creator figure.

Another significant instance in which the San Marco cycle interprets rather than simply illustrates can be seen in the inclusion of the angels, who go unmentioned in the Genesis text. One angel accompanies the creator on the first day, two on the second day, and so forth. The angels are thus numerically symbolic of the days of creation.[21] Indeed they are mentioned in conjunction with creation several times in both the Old and New Testaments.[22] Even more important is Augustine's discourse on angels. In the *City of God*, he writes:

> For when God said: "Let there be light" and light was created, if we are right in interpreting this light as the act

> of creating the angels, surely, then, they have been made partakers of the eternal light, which is nought but the unchangeable wisdom of God itself, by which all things were made, and by which we call the only begotten Son of God.[23]

Augustine thus identifies the angels with the light that God created on the first day; their presence throughout the succeeding days of creation becomes understandable. Having elicited a relationship between the visual arts and theological speculation, one is tempted to pursue this task and delve more deeply into St. Augustine with the hope that his extensive comments on the creation will explain many other aspects of creation illustration. While the process would seem to be methodologically sound, one cannot say *caveat emptor* often enough. For it is the very same Augustine who argues that all the works of creation were accomplished in only one day and must, therefore, be viewed as one act.[24] To my mind, such a comment suggests a single image in which the creator appears only once and all the acts of creation are represented within one frame or panel.[25] This is certainly not the case at San Marco, a monument emphasizing that extraordinary care must be taken when discussing the relationship between art and theology. Rarely does the object of art illustrate one single theological thesis.

I have written about San Marco at some length both because it is such an extensive cycle and in order to illuminate some of the problems involved in interpreting images. Although the evidence remaining from the Early Christian era is limited, there is another series of Genesis illustrations standing in direct contrast to those at San Marco. I refer to the no-longer-extant frescoes of San Paolo fuori le Mura in Rome, originally painted in 440 to 461, during the pontificate of Leo I, and now known to us only through seventeenth-century drawings (fig. 2).[26] At San Paolo, only three scenes illustrate the first two chapters of Genesis. In the first panel, four days of creation are represented. A half-figure of God the Father appears in the arc of heaven and the first day of creation is indicated by the personifications of light and darkness. God's position in the heavens suggests the activity of the second day, the separation of the firmament above the waters from that below the water. The third day is seen in the firmament on which the personifications of light and darkness stand, while the fourth day is witnessed by

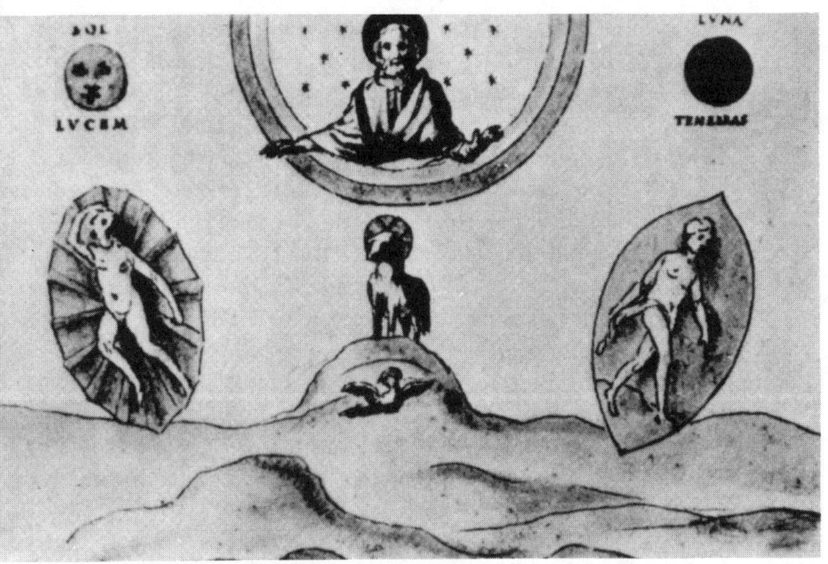

Fig. 2. Rome, Biblioteca Vaticana, Lat. 4406, 25.

the sun and the moon. The illustration is more symbolic and lacks the narrative quality seen at San Marco. The second fresco depicts the creation of Adam and the third fresco the creation of Eve. In both cases, God, rather than Christ-Logos, is the creator. There are no significant departures from the text, nor would there seem to have been room for theological speculation as at San Marco. The San Paolo frescoes do indicate, however, that, as early as the fifth century, several days of the creation were illustrated within the confines of one panel.

The evidence remaining from the Early Christian era is both sparse and subject to contention because so much of it is based on copies and reconstructions. It is not my intention to trace the subsequent influence of these two types of creation illustrations; that has been amply done by others.[28] Rather, I want to emphasize that, even at the very beginning of Christian art, a single series of events was subject to diverse depictions. Illustrations of the creation do not follow a linear pattern. Instead, the diversity, and the reasons for it, become increasingly complex.

Manuscript illumination was the primary art of the Carolingian era. For the first time, completely illustrated bibles were produced. These bibles will not concern us here, becuase, in treating the creation story, they usually begin with the creation of Adam and Eve, rather than with the first days of creation.[29] The Ottonian era is equally unfruitful because, although countless manuscripts survive, they are largely devoted to the New Testament; there was comparatively little interest in the illustration of the Old Testament. Indeed, it is not until the twelfth century that creation images again abound. Given the revival of intellectual life and the blossoming of the schools, it is not surprising to find a mass of literature relating to the *Hexaemeron,*[30] as well as a variety of solutions to the depiction of creation. Among the more interesting illustrations are those that relate the creation to the course of Christian history and thus place it in a more extensive context than we have seen previously. Equally significant is the fact that the creation appears in books other than bibles.

A manuscript of the *Antiquitates Judaicae* by Flavius Josephus (Paris, Bib. Nat. Lat. 5047, 2r) is of interest in this context (fig. 3).[31] Illuminated in northwest France toward the end of the twelfth century, it presents a seemingly unique solution to the depiction of the six days of creation. The folio illustrates the letters *IN*, so that the first word of the text serves as a physical support for the images. The letter *I* is represented by a standing figure of Christ-Logos. He stands on a green disk representing the earth while his head is in a blue disk symbolizing heaven. His posture indicates that He spans earth and heaven; His hand, raised in benediction, suggests that He is blessing the days of creation surrounding Him. His repose implies the rest of the seventh day, the Sabbath.

The six days of creation appear in medallions decorating the two vertical bars of the letter *N*. The first day of creation appears at the top left, and then one reads downward through the separation of the firmament and the creation of dry land. The fourth day, the creation of the sun, the moon, and the stars, appears at the top right and is followed by the creation of fish and fowl, and finally, the creation of Adam and Eve. The sequence of illustrations thus differs from the normative way of reading, because one must read from top to bottom, rather than from left to right. The innovative quality of these illustrations lies in the fact that in the depiction of the first five days of creation, an adolescent youth, rather than

Fig. 3. Flavius Josephus, Antiquitates Judaicae, *Paris, Bib. Nat. Lat. 5047, 2^r^.*

God the Father or Christ, holds the works of creation. There seem to be neither textual nor traditional reasons for this interpretation. Such personifications holding attributes are more normally associated with representations of the months or seasons. The number five does not yield such an interpretation. Moreover, the depiction of the youth is not consistent; there are obvious differences in both clothing and coiffure. The figure in the fifth day of creation has short, curly hair, while the personification in the third day has straight, longish hair descending to below the ears. Yet, the differences among the figures are not sufficiently great to permit an alternative interpretation such as the ages of man.

Another innovative aspect of this illumination is the medallion held by Christ and appearing on the diagonal bar of the letter *N*. A nimbed female figure, hands upraised in the orant position, sits on a bench and looks up at Christ. Heimann has sensibly identified this figure as the Virgin.[32] Compositionally and thematical ly, the appearance of the Virgin is significant. The diagonal on which she appears joins the first and last days of creation. The promise of the first day is compromised by the creation of Eve on the last day, for it is she who will introduce sin to mankind. The church fathers believed that Eve was the direct cause of man's fall from grace and that her sin could be redeemed only by another woman — the Virgin. In giving birth to Christ, the Virgin provided the possibility of redemption for mankind. This idea was aptly expressed by Tertullian as early as the third century:

> Into Eve, while still a Virgin, had crept the word constructive of death: into a virgin no less needed to be introduced the Word of God, constructive of life, so that, that which through the sex had gone astray into perdition should through the same sex be led back again into salvation. Eve had believed the serpent: Mary believed Gabriel. The sin which the former committed by believing, the latter by believing blotted out.[33]

In looking up at her Son and imploring Him in an orant postion, the Virgin appears to be interceding for mankind, much as she does in representations of the Last Judgment.[34]

Another manuscript of Flavius Josephus's *Antiquitates Judaicae* (Chantilly, Musée Condé 1632, 3r) has a unique and extraordinarily rich interpretation of the creation story (fig. 4).[35] The manuscript was made between 1170 and 1180 and comes from the Abbey of St. Trond. The interlocking letters *I* and *N*, the same letters that were illustrated in the previous manuscript, are decorated with seven medallions depicting the seven days of creation. The first day of creation, the separation of light and darkness, here personified by two bust-length figures, appears at the top of the *I*, while the second and third days flank it at the top of each vertical bar of the *N*. The tripartite division of the orb representing earth is interesting because it suggests the three continents known in the Middle Ages: Europe, Asia, and Africa. At the intersection of the two initials, Christ–Logos holds the sun and the moon. At the bottom, the fourth day, the creation of fish and fowl, and the sixth day, the creation of Eve, flank the seventh day, here illustrated by Christ–Logos seated on a faldstool and blessing.

Here, unlike the previous illustration, no single figure dominates.

Fig. 4. Flavius Josephus, Antiquitates Judaicae,
Chantilly, Musée Condé 1632, 3^r.

Yet, in a manner that is typical of the medieval mind, there is an underlying order within the apparent variety. The variety is evident in the depiction of the creator. Twice the Christ–Logos appears as a bust-length figure with one hand raised and the other resting on an unfurled scroll. Twice He is seated on a faldstool, and twice He is leaning forward while gesturing. The order is evident in the arrangement of the Christ-Logos figures. That is, the two medallions at each end of the *I* show Christ-Logos seated on a faldstool, the two medallions at the top of the *N* have Christ as a bust-length figure, while their opposite numbers at the bottom of the same letter show Him leaning forward. The conscious pattern is further emphasized by the fact that the first and last days of the cycle appear at either end of the *I*, while the other five images appear in normal chronological order.

The coherent organization of the two interlocking initials is but a prelude to the complexity of the entire illuminated page. The four rivers of paradise, all emptying urns, appear in the background and thus suggest the location of the events taking place within the medallions. Personifications of church and synagogue flank the fourth day at the center. Representing the old order and the new order, they suggest the course of biblical history and provide a thematic bridge to the three-quarter medallions attached to the frame of the initials.

At the top left, Aaron holds the golden urn filled with manna (Exod. 16:32–34),[36] an extraordinarily rare subject. The manna, or bread, eaten by the Jews during their forty years in the wilderness, can be typologically related to the bread appearing at the Last Supper. The same scene appears in this typological guise in the contemporaneous Klosterneuberg Altar by Nicholas of Verdun.[37] Aaron is also mentioned with Melchizedek in regard to the order of Old Testament priesthood. For example, Heb. 5:4–6 states:

> And one does not take the honor upon himself, but he is called by God, just as Aaron was. So Christ also did not exalt himself to be made a high priest, but was appointed by him who said to him:
>
> 'Thou art my Son
> Today I have begotten thee';
> as he says also in another place,
> 'Thou art a priest forever
> After the order of Melchizedek.'[38]

Thus, the Old Testament priesthood of Aaron and Melchizedek is linked to the New Testament priesthood of Christ.

The sacrifice of Isaac, at the top right, is a more common type of the sacrifice of Christ and appears throughout medieval art. The three-quarter medallions below Aaron and Isaac have tentatively been identified as a prophet at the left and an evangelist at the right,[39] thereby again suggesting the typology of the Old and New Testaments. Beneath the prophet is the Crucifixion, suggesting an obvious analogy with the sacrifice of Isaac. Its opposite number on the right depicts a personification of the Church holding a cross and a chalice. In a broad sense, the Church may be interpreted as both the bride and body of Christ,[40] while, more specifically, the chalice may refer to Christ's blood at the crucifixion and hence to the Last Supper. We have already related the manna in the golden urn held by Aaron to the Last Supper. The cross and chalice further suggest the priesthood typified by Aaron and Christ.

At the bottom left is a mummified figure reclining in a tomb. Possibly identifiable as Lazarus, he parallels Christ who also rose from the dead. Finally, at the bottom right, the Anastasis or Harrowing of Hell appears. Although more commonly represented in Byzantine art, this event, in which Christ descends into limbo, vanquishes the Leviathan, and frees the just, is appropriate here because it suggests the reward due a good Christian and the redemption made possible through the sacrifice of Christ. One manuscript page thus unfolds the entire course of Christian history from the creation through the redemption. It gives witness to the complexities of medieval typology and verifies the impression that one biblical event may be subject to a variety of interpretations which are largely dependent on the context of the episode. This extraordinarily compact image is both unique and far more complex than the previously discussed Flavius Josephus illumination. Yet, both illustrate the very same text. In this observation lies still another warning about the pitfalls involved in relating text and image.

The illustrations for Flavius Josephus's *Antiquitates Judaicae* place the creation within the context of church history. The creation also appears in other equally broad contexts as can be seen, for example, in the Gerona tapestry dating most likely from the early years of the twelfth century (fig. 5).[41] Although the reconstruction of the outer perimeter of the tapestry is problematic, the content of the scenes is easily identified. The center is occupied by a figure of

Christ blessing. The encircling inscription reads: "He said 'let there be light' and there was light."[42] Surrounding Christ are eight unequal wedge-shaped segments forming a circle. They illustrate the six days of creation, and the inscription around the circumference of the circle reads:

> IN PRINCIPIO CREAVIT D(EU)S CELU(M) ET TERRAM. MARE ET OM(N)IA QUA IN EIS SUNT. ET VIDIT D(EU)S CUNCTA QUE FECERAT ET ERANT VALDE BONA.[43]

Eight is obviously not the standard number of illustrations in a creation cycle, but the designer of the Gerona tapestry has created a meaningful pattern. The scene directly over Christ's head depicts the dove over the waters, a prelude to the first day of creation as seen at San Marco. The third person of the Trinity thus appears directly over the head of the second person of the Trinity. Framing the dove on either side are clearly labelled personifications of light and darkness. The separation of light and darkness, the first day of creation, is here physically separated by an intervening panel. Moving again to the left and right, we see a detailed illustration of the second, third, and fourth days of creation; at the left, the firmament has been placed in the middle of the waters and, at the right, the waters above are separated from the waters below; between them is a disk containing the sun, the moon, and the stars.

The last two days of creation are more extensively illustrated and occupy the remaining 180 degrees of the circle. The last two days are meant to be read in the same way as the first four days; that is, beginning with the creation of fish and fowl, a disproportionately large segment immediately beneath Christ. At the left is the creation of Eve and at the right Adam names the animals.

This seemingly haphazard and initially confusing arrangement reveals subtle correspondences of the type seen in the Flavius Josephus manuscript from St. Trond. Rather than arranging the series in either a clockwise or a counterclockwise fashion, the designer has chosen to place the thematically related scenes opposite each other. Thus, the two scenes picturing Adam, as well as the other segments depicting the firmament, appear opposite each other. The personifications of light and shadow are also mirror images. Finally, the remaining two scenes, the dove over the waters and

Fig. 5. Gerona, Cathedral Museum, Creation Tapestry.

Fig. 6. Gerona, Cathedral Museum, Creation Tapestry, detail.

the creation of fish and fowl, are opposite sides of the circle. While it may be purely coincidental, it is nonetheless worthwhile noting that both scenes illustrate birds placed over water. The arrangement of the Gerona tapestry is certainly not haphazard: still, it reflects yet another approach to the ordering of creation cycles.

Even more significant is the fact that the creation appears at the center of a cosmic scheme, thereby relating creation to other natural phenomena; the four winds, blowing horns, appear in the corners of the square surrounding the creation (fig. 6). The image at the bottom right is clearly labelled *AUSTER*, or east wind. The four corners of the outermost band of the tapestry purportedly once depicted the four rivers of paradise. Now, only Geon in the upper left survives.[44] The remainder of the outer border is equally revealing. Immediately above Christ and the dove over the waters is Annus, a personification of the year. Annus is surrounded by personifications of the seasons and the months. The cosmic and natural implications are obvious. God's creation flows to the four corners of the earth as evidenced by the winds and the rivers of paradise. The eternal calendar of the months, seasons, and year are almost part of a continuous cosmic process made possible by the creation. The Christ–Logos, as creator, appears at the center of natural history.

The arrangement becomes even more meaningful when, as de Palol has suggested, we envision the Gerona tapestry as a design originally planned for a dome.[45] If this were indeed the case, Christ would have appeared at the highest point and his creations would then radiate downward toward more earthly realms with the result that the physical hierarchy would echo and reinforce the thematic hierarchy. As the creation appeared at the center of church history in the two Flavius Josephus illustrations, so here the creation appears at the center of the natural world and its ongoing processes.

Three twelfth-century German Bibles illustrate another sort of problem in regard to images of the creation; for despite a common text, the Bible, and a similar format and choice of scenes, there are distinct differences among the three interpretations. The first of the group, the Walther Bible (Michelbeuren, Stiftsbibl., Perg. I, 6v) (fig. 7) probably made at the beginning of the second quarter of the twelfth century, has a full-page illustration of the six days of creation.[46] Beginning at the top, the days are read from left to right.

The illustration of the first day shows God accompanied by two other figures and pointing at an orb divided at its diameter into light and dark halves. The top, or light, segment depicts the dove over the waters; the rays extending from the dove's head suggest the creation of light. Scarcely visible in the darker segment of the circle is a devil between two dragons. The creation is thus viewed as a struggle in which the monster is vanquished, an idea reflected in the text of both *Jubilees*[47] and Ps. 73:12–15. The latter reads:

> Yet God my king is from old
> Working salvation in the midst of the earth.
> Thou didst divide the sea by thy might:
> Thou didst break the heads of the dragons on the waters.
> Thou didst crush the heads of Leviathan,
> Thou didst give him as food for the creatures of the wilderness.
> Thou didst cleave open springs and brooks;
> Thou didst dry up ever-flowing streams.[48]

At the top right, the three figures appear with a multicolored orb representing the separation of the firmament from the waters. On the third day, God stands before an orb containing the sun, the moon, and the stars. A nimbed figure appears to the right and left of the orb. The fourth day is represented by the creation of dry earth, trees, and seeds, while the fifth day shows the creation of birds and fishes. Both are standard illustrations, save that God is again accompanied by two nimbed personnages. The sixth day is unusual in the choice of scene—God addressing Adam and Eve; and, for the first time, God appears alone.

Thus, in five of the six scenes, God, the dominant figure officiating at the creation, is accompanied by two other figures. Visually, God is always the most prominent of the three because he appears *in toto*, while the other figures are partially obscured. On the basis of the strong literary tradition evidenced in such writers as Augustine, Ambrose, Bede and Rabanus Maurus, Adelheid Heimann has suggested that the three figures represent the Trinity taking part in the creation,[49] a comparatively rare visual image. The church fathers based their argument on the text of Genesis itself. The dove over the waters (Gen. 1:2)[50] is taken as the Holy

Fig. 7. Walther Bible, Michelbeuren, Stiftsbibliothek,
Perg. I, 6ᵛ.

Ghost. And, in verse 26 of the first chapter of Genesis, when speaking of the creation of Adam, the plural of the verb is used: "faciamus hominem ad imaginem, et sumilitudinem nostram."[51] According to the exegetes, this phrase suggests the union of Father and Son. Yet, strange to tell, it is only in the last scene of the Walther Bible, the one closest to the aforementioned text in terms of the narrative, that God appears alone. This inconsistency remains unresolved.

The second Bible in the group, the Admont or Gebhard Bible (Vienna, Nat. Bibliothek, Ser. Nov. 2701, 3v) (fig. 8), dates from around 1130.[52] It, too, illustrates the creation on a single page containing six scenes, some of which are partially damaged. Despite the similarity in format and style to the Walther Bible, there are distinct changes in the iconography. In the first scene, God sits on a rainbow and is flanked on either side by a winged figure. Under the feet of the figure at the right, the devil appears again. In essence, then, the illuminator of the Admont Bible has transformed the meaningful image of the Trinity into that of two accompanying angels. In this case, the number two is without significance as can be seen by the fact that the second and third scenes, similar in content to the Walther Bible, are each accompanied by four angels. One angel appears on the sixth day and none appears on the fifth day. The number of angels would thus appear to be without significance and unlike San Marco, the angels cannot be associated with the days. Yet it must be pointed out that the illuminator of the Admont Bible was not loathe to use personifications, as can be seen on the fourth day where earth is personified by a half-nude female and water by a nude male figure astride a large fish. These classical personifications, common in Carolingian art, continue to appear sporadically in Romanesque art.[53]

The Gumpert Bible (Erlangen, Univ. Bibl. 121, 5v) (fig. 9), the last and latest member of the group, was most likely completed before 1195.[54] The simple rectangles of the two previous manuscripts have been replaced by mandorla-shaped panels framed by a twisting vine decorated with leaves. This more graceful arrangement introduces naturalistic elements and reflects the transition from Romanesque to Gothic art. Unlike the Admont and Walther Bibles, the Gumpert Bible is meant to be read in vertical columns, from top to bottom and left to right. There are similarities to the Admont Bible in the first scene, save that the archangel Michael has

Fig. 8. Admont (or Gebhard) Bible, Vienna, Nat. Bibliothek, Ser. Nov. 2701, 3^v.

Fig. 9. The Bible of St. Gumbertus, Erlangen, Univ. Bibl., Ms. 1, fol. 5^v (cited as Gumpert Bible).

been added at the left; and in the third scene, the creation of earth and sea, the personifications appear again. Only one angel accompanies God on the second and fifth days. The fifth scene is unusual because animals appear along with birds and fishes as a simultaneous creation; normally the two events are separated. The creation of Eve, the sixth day, also departs from the norm because the scene is reversed; normally, Adam and Eve are at the right. There does not seem to be either an iconographical or a compositional reasion for this reversal.

Although the Gumpert Bible is clearly related to both the Walther and Admont Bibles, there is a unique additional feature. To the right of each of the six scenes is a narrow rectangular panel housing a scantily clad figure balanced delicately on a red disk. Save for the figure flanking the second day, all hold torches or lamps or, in the case of the fifth day, perhaps a candle. The figure adjoining the second day lacks an attribute, but eleven rays surround his head. The personification of light, or Lux, often has a torch or a flame as an attribute and the flames sometimes appear as a glory around the head. As we have seen at San Marco, light can also personify the days of creation. Heimann has therefore suggested that the figures personify the days accompanying God's creation.[55] Yet, here, each day is accompanied by only one figure, rather than a number denoting the particular day of creation as at San Marco. Since there are no other illustrations of this kind, it is difficult to arrive at a reasonable solution. Heimann's suggestion may be valid, but one is nonetheless forced to ask why the second day differs from the others and why there are minor differences in the clothing, attributes, and poses of the other five days.

I have chosen to discuss three manuscripts all having the same text, the Bible, and all having a similar format. All three come from the same geographical area and the same century. Indeed, the first two were probably made within the same decade. The analysis of the three creation illustrations suggests that some images, such as the devil on the first day of creation, are continued, while others, such as the Trinity or the so-called personification of days, are unique. These observations reaffirm the diversity of creation iconography and warn against broad generalizations even when epoch and provenance are similar.

Thus far, I have concentrated upon creation cycles in which the story is told in a consecutive, rather literal fashion, albeit with interpolations and inconsistencies. There is, however, another type of illustration that is transformed to the extent that it scarcely depends upon the Genesis text. This concept can best be illustrated by a series of eleventh-century Anglo-Saxon illuminations.[56] In a mid-eleventh century psalter (British Library, Cotton Tiberius C. VI, 7v) (fig. 10), there is an image of Christ appearing behind a large disk which must represent the cosmos. Only His head and hands are visible. Within the circle of the cosmos, the dove appears as the spirit over the waters, which are indicated by wavy

Fig. 10. London, British Library Cotton Tiberius C.VI, 7ᵛ.

Fig. 11. London, British Library Royal I.E., vii, 1ᵛ.

lines. The dove's head reaches into another arc which may perhaps be identified as earth. A scale hangs from a finger of Christ's right hand, while he holds a pair of dividers in the same hand. Two long horns protrude from his mouth.

The image immediately calls to mind two passages in Isaiah which are also quoted by Ambrose in his *Hexaemeron*. Isa. 40:22 says: "It is he who sits upon the circle of the earth."[57] In verse 12 of the same chapter, Isaiah says: "he who has measured the waters in the hollow of his hand, and marked off the heavens with a span, enclosed the dust of the earth in a measure, and weighed the mountains in scales and the hills in a balance."[58]

Heimann has pointed out that the manual of the Anglo-Saxon commentator, Byrhtferth, composed in 1011, is of even greater relevance because of the time and place of its composition.[59] Byrhtferth places great emphasis on the phrase from the *Wisd. of Sol.* 11:20: "But Thou hast arranged all things by measure and number and weight."[60] Further on in his text, Byrhtferth unites this statement with the concept of the Trinity, while insisting on the all-embracing unity of the creator.[61] Heimann thus concludes that the balance must denote weight, the dividers measure, and by process of elimination, the two horns must denote number.[62] She further suggests that, reading from the top downwards, the image can also be interpreted as the Trinity, with the creator as the first person, the two horns as the second person, and the dove as the third person. To my mind, this interpretation is incorrect because the creator has a cross-nimbus and this suggests that He is the second person of the Trinity, Christ–Logos.

Heimann also cites a copy of the Tiberius Psalter[63] illustration in a mid-eleventh-century Bible (British Library Royal I.E. vii, 1v) (fig. 11); without realizing that the illumination completely refutes her theory. At first glance, the copy appears to be similar to the Tiberius Psalter, except that the scale and dividers are clearly contained within the orb and the dove seems to be confined to the waters. But close examination reveals that wavy, flame-like lines emerge from the ends of the so-called horns. A similar image occurs in another Anglo-Saxon manuscript related to the Tiberius Psalter (Vatican, Reg. Lat. 12, 68v) (fig. 12).[64] A marginal illustration to Ps. 60, it, too, shows flame-like lines emerging from the horns. I wonder whether the so-called horns may be interpreted as torches or light, of the type seen in the Gumpert Bible. The

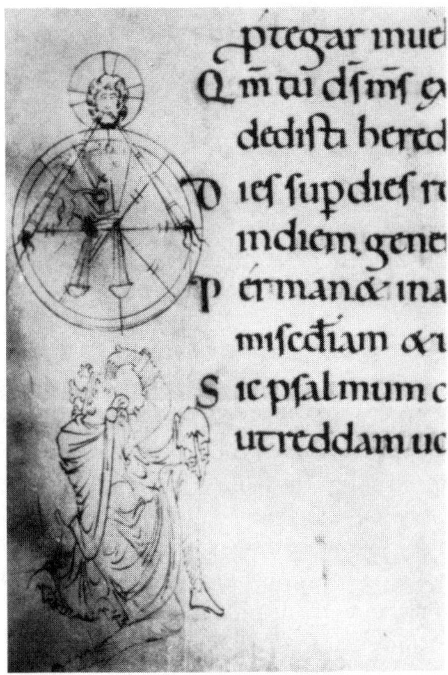

Fig. 12. Rome, Biblioteca Vaticana, Reg. Lat. 12, 68v.

Anglo-Saxon illuminations would thus allude to the first day of creation. As we have seen, light itself signifies the first day and the phrase: "God said, 'let there be light' and there was light" is consistent with this interpretation as is the dove over the waters. Rather than a complete cycle of the creation, only the first day is depicted and the creator is envisaged as an architect. Prov. 8:27–30 states:

> When he established the heavens, I was there,
> When he drew a circle on the face of the deep,
> When he made firm the skies above,
> When he established the fountains of the deep,
> When he assigned to the sea its limit, so that the waters
>   might not transgress his command,
> When he marked out the foundations of the earth,
> Then I was beside him as a master workman;
> And I was daily his delight, rejoicing before him
>   always.[65]

God is also mentioned in conjunction with the creation of the winds in Amos 4:13:

> For lo, he who forms the mountains, and creates the wind,
> and declares to man what is his thought;
> who makes the morning darkness,
> and treads on the heights of the earth.
> The Lord, the God of hosts is his name.[66]

Altough I believe this interpretation to be more correct than Heimann's, I am still troubled by the fact that the torches, or pipes, are placed in Christ's mouth; one normally associates this sort of image with personifications of the winds as seen, for example, in the Gerona tapestry (fig. 6). Robert Harris has cleverly suggested that the torches could also refer to the aforementioned Wisdom of Solomon.[67] In the sentence immediately preceding, ". . . thou hast arranged all things by measure and number and weight," it is stated: "Even apart from these, men could fall at a single breath when pursued by justice and scattered by the breath of power."[68] The wavy lines emanating from the pipes may thus refer to the creator's breath, and, hence, his almighty power. Here, we are perhaps dealing with the common medieval practice of transferring images so that one element of the personification of the winds is adapted to a new and different use.

The analysis of the Anglo-Saxon illustrations has raised another problem concerning the visual interpretation of creation. Here, the series of images is quite consistent, but the understandable desire to relate the images to a contemporary text, that of Byrhtferth, led Heimann to overlook the significance of the wavy lines emerging from the pipes. The Tiberius Psalter and the manuscripts related to it also clearly affirm that the opening chapters of Genesis are not the only biblical passages relevant to images of creation.[69]

For the most part, I have been discussing images of creation contained within one page of a particular manuscript. It is now time to return to Italy where extensive creation cycles were in vogue during the eleventh and twelfth centuries.[70] They appear in manuscripts, frescoes, ivories, and mosaics. The last two will be of concern here, for through an analysis of the first two days of creation, I wish to demonstrate how particular elements can be sub ject to varied interpretations even though the cycles may be related to each other in many ways. The four monuments of interest are an ivory in Berlin,[71] the series of ivories in Salerno,[72] and the mosaic cycles in both the Cappella Palatina at Palermo and in the cathedral of Monreale.[73] The interrelationships among these monuments and their sources have been the subject of extensive debate. An analysis of the first two days of creation will indicate the subtlety of these relationships and suggest the possibility of correspondence even among works of different media and scale.

The Berlin ivory (fig. 13), made in the ambient of Montecassino in about 1070, has a most unusual first day of creation. At the top of the small panel is a bust medallion of Christ-Logos, a Byzantine type; He is flanked by the letters *alpha* and *omega*. Two disks labelled *lux* and *nox* touch the medallion. Between the disks is the dove over the waters and immediately below the dove is a personification of Abyssus, a Byzantine motif that appears in Octateuch recensions of the creation.[74] Abyssus symbolizes the deep or chaos. The coeval Salerno ivory, on the other hand (fig. 14), simplifies the scene so that only *lux* and *nox* appear in labelled disks. The dove stands over the waters and the Christ–Logos is omitted.

The same scene in the Cappella Palatina, dating from about 1143 to 1166 (fig. 15), offers still another variant. Here, God the Father, with hand upraised in blessing, appears within a disk. The dove seems to be actually in the waters which extend upward towards the disk surrounding the creator. The immediately adjoining inscription reads: FIAT LUX ET FACTA EST LUX. The other two inscriptions refer to the dove over the waters and the creation of earth and sky.[75] Thus light is suggested by the rays and the inscription, but the personification of *Lux* and *nox* are omitted.

It has often been argued that the Monreale mosaic cycle, dating from the 1180s, is in large part based on the Cappella Palatina or that both cycles depend upon the same model.[76] Yet, the first image at Monreale is vastly different from Palermo (fig. 16). God appears in an orb and His hands extend downward towards the waters where the personification of Abyssus appears. The inscription simply states (in translation) that "in the beginning, God created heaven and earth."[77] There is absolutely no visual reference to light nor mention of it. The four Italian cycles, while sharing some elements, thus elicit different interpretations. The creator appears as God twice, as the Christ–Logos once, and is completely omitted

Fig. 13. Berlin-Dahlem, Skulpturenabteilung der Staatlichen Museen, Ivory, Creation Scenes.

Fig. 14. Salerno Cathedral, Museum, Ivory, First and Second Days of Creation.

in the Salerno ivory. Two have the personification of Abyssus while the other two lack it. Three refer to light either directly or indirectly, but Monreale does not. In other words, the first day of creation in Italian cycles offers conflicting information as to exactly what was created.

The second day presents similar problems which are best understood by beginning in reverse chronological order with Monreale (fig. 16). The mosaic depicts God seated on an orb and gesturing toward seven angels whose haloes have rays of light emitting from them. The inscription clarifies the image for it reads (in translation): "God created the light and called the light day and the shadow night."[78] The reference to light, omitted in the first panel at Monreale, appears here. The appearance of the angels is not surprising for we are immediately reminded of San Marco which suggested the Augustinian interpretation that the angels were created on the first day and that they symbolize light. Kitzinger has further suggested that the number seven signifies the seven days of creation in this context.[79] At Monreale, then, the creation of light is reserved for a separate scene, albeit one still referring to the first day of creation.

On the two ivories, light was created in the first panel. Yet, the second panels have an image related to Monreale, although in both cases the reference is to the second day of creation. On the Berlin ivory (fig. 13), Christ sits on an orb and five angels bow deeply before him; on the Salerno ivory (fig. 14), God stands and four angels bow before Him. Neither ivory has inscriptions or any other reference to light. Kessler has suggested a solution to the problem by pointing out that, although none of the church fathers refers to the creation of angels on the second day, certain of them do suggest that the firmament is the abode of angels.[80] For example, Walafrid Strabo states that the firmament is populated by angels.[81] Kessler concludes that the angels on the Berlin and Salerno ivories refer to the creation of the firmament, the activity of the second day. One still wants to know why five angels are represented in one instance and only four in the other. But, given their respective positions in the ivory cycles, the angels must be associated with the second day, rather than with the first day as at Monreale.

Finally, the Cappella Palatine (fig. 15) depicts a rather standard sort of image for the second day of creation. God is shown behind an orb containing the firmament and the separation of waters. Any

Fig. 15. Palermo, Cappella Palatina, Creation Scenes (Anderson).

Fig. 16. Monreale, Cathedral, Creation Scenes (Anderson).

reference to angels is omitted. The point here is simply that within the same cultural context, a shared image, such as angels, may be interpreted differently. These images suggest a vast knowledge on the part of both medieval craftsmen and their patrons, a knowledge based on both visual and literary sources. The Italian cycles amply illuminate this point.

In the foregoing discussion, I have barely skimmed the surface of illustrations of the creation. Rather, I have tried to illuminate their variety. In doing so, I have tried to suggest the methodological problems underlying the relationship between text and image. Several points emerge: (1) visual images tend to interpret, rather than simply illustrate; (2) the same text, such as the *Antiquitates Judaicae*, may engender different illustrations, although nothing in the text suggests a reason; (3) the creation cycle appears in a variety of contexts, such as the history of the church and the natural world; (4) similarity of format, locality, era, and style does not of necessity mean similarity of image, as seen, for example, in the German bibles; (5) images of creation need not always be based on the Genesis text, as witnessed by the Tiberius Psalter and its relatives; and, finally (6), as seen in the Italian cycles, a similar image—in this case, angels—may be interpreted in different ways.

Notes

Since this article was submitted in 1977, a new study, particularly useful for its copious bibliography, has been published: Johannes Zahlten, *Creatio mundi: Darstellungen der sechs Schöpfungstage und naturwissenschaftliches Weltbild im Mittelalter*. Stuttgarter Beiträge zur Geschichte und Politik, vol. 13. (Stuttgart, 1979).

1. For a collection of most of the significant monuments and brief comments concerning them, cf. J. van der Meulen, "Schöpfer, Schöpfung," *Lexikon der Christlichen Ikonographie*, vol. 4 (1972), cols. 99–123; C. Schmidt, *Die Darstellungen der Sechstagewerkes von ihren Anfängen bis zum Ende des 15. Jahrhunderts* (Hildesheim, 1938), an unillustrated list. For Italian works in general, cf. especially E. Garrison, "Note on the Iconography of Creation and the Fall of Man in Eleventh- and Twelfth-Century Rome," *Studies in the History of Mediaeval Italian Painting* 4 (Florence, 1961):201–10.

For German manuscripts, cf. most recently J. Zahlten, "Schöpfungsdarstellungen in Stuttgarter Handschriften," *Beiträge zum Kunst des Mittelalters, Festschrift für Hans Wentzel zum 60. Geburtstag* (Berlin, 1975), pp. 231–43. For a detailed account of the exegesis concerning creation, cf. "Création", in A. Vacant, E. Mangenot, and E. Amann, eds., *Dictionnaire de théologie Catholique*, vol. 3, pt. 2 (Paris, 1938), cols. 2034–201. Also useful are: F. E. Robbins, *The Hexaemeral Literature, A Study of the Greek and Latin Commentaries on Genesis* (Chicago, 1912); Y. M. Congar, "Le Thème de Dieu-créateur et les explications de l'hexameron dans la tradition chrétienne," *Mélanges Henri de Lubac* (Lyons, 1963), vol. 1, pp. 189–222; M.-Th. d'Alverny, "Le Cosmos symbolique du XIIe siècle," *Archives d'histoire doctrinale et littéraire du Moyen Age* 28 (1953):31–81.

2. Cf. the literature cited in the footnotes that follow.

3. "Et vereor ne occasione comperta scientiolam nostram leviter magis quam utiliter iactare velle videamur." *De Civitate Dei* 11.31, in *Corpus Christianorum, Series Latina* (Turnhout, 1953–) (hereafter cited as *CCSL*), 48:351.

4. For a thorough examination of the traditions, cf. C. A. Simpson and W. R. Bowie, "The Book of Genesis," in G. A. Buttrick, et al., *The Interpreter's Bible* (New York/Nashville, 1952), 1:439–65.

5. Gen. 1:9–11: "Dixit vero Deus congregentur aquae sub caelo sunt in locum unum et appareat arida. Factumque est ita. Et vocavit Deus arida terram, congregationesque aquarum appellavit maria. Et vidit Deus quod esset bonum et ait germinet terra herbam ficentem et facientem semen et lignum pomiferum faciens fructum iuxta genus suum cuius semen in semetipso sit super terram. Et factum est ita."

6. Gen. 1:24–27: "Dixit quoque Deus producat terra animam viventem in genere suo: iumenta et reptilia et bestias terrae secundum species suas. Factumque est ita. Et fecit Deus bestias terrae iuxta species suas et iumenta et omne reptile terrae in genere suo. Et vidit Deus quod esset bonum. Et ait faciamus hominem ad imaginem et similitudinem nostram; et praesit piscibus maris et volatilibus caeli et bestiis universaeque terrae omnique reptili quod movetur in terra. Et creavit Deus hominem ad imaginem suam, ad imaginem Dei creavit illum; masculum et feminam creavit eos."

7. Cf. footnote 6.

8. "Inmisit ergo Dominus Deus soporem in Adam, cumque abdormisset tulit unam de costis eius et replevit carnem pro ea; et aedificavit Dominus Deus costam quam tulerat de Adam in mulierem et adduxit eam ad Adam."

9. Cf. Footnote 6.

10. "Formavit igitur Dominus Deus hominem de limo terrae et inspiravit in faciem eius spiraculum vitae et factus est homo in animam viventem."

11. The Vienna Genesis (Vienna Nationalbibliothek, Cod. Vindob. theol. graec. 31) has been reconstructed with the suggestion that it once must have contained at least 96 pages with 192 illustrations. Unfortunately for our purposes, the surviving text begins with Gen. 3:4, the Fall of Man. On the Vienna Genesis, cf. W. von Hartel and F. Wickhoff, *Die Wiener*

Genesis, Beilage z. XV. u. XVI B. d. Jahrb. d. Kunsthist. Sammlungen d. A. H. Kaiserhauses (Vienna, 1895; reprinted in F. Wickhoff, *Römische Kunst* [Vienna, 1912]); H. Gerstinger, *Die Wiener Genesis*, 2 vols. (Vienna, 1931); E. Wellesz, *The Vienna Genesis* (London, 1960).

The Ashburnham Pentateuch (Paris, Bib. Nat. Nouv. Acq. Lat. 2334) is in such poor condition that it is extraordinarily difficult to reach any conclusions concerning its creation cycle. On the Ashburnham Pentateuch, cf. G. von Gebhardt, *The Miniatures of the Ashburnham Pentateuch* (London, 1883). B. Narkiss, "Towards a Further Study of the Ashburnham Pentateuch," *Cahiers Archéologiques* 19 (1969):48–60 subjected the manuscript to examination under ultra-violet light and suggested that four images of the creator appear on folio 1v.

12. K. Weitzmann, "Observations on the Cotton Genesis Fragments," in K. Weitzmann, ed., *Late Classical and Early Mediaeval Studies in Honor of Albert Mathias Friend, Jr.* (Princeton, 1955), pp. 112–31. He cites the earlier literature.

13. J. J. Tikkanen, 'Die Genesismosaiken von S. Marco in Venedig und ihr Verhältnis zu den Miniaturen der Cottonbibel," *Acta Societatis Scientiarum Fennicae* 17 (Helsingfors, 1889). Tikkanen did not believe that the Cotton Genesis could have been the direct model.

14. More recently, Weitzmann has provided additional evidence for the idea that the Cotton Genesis was the direct model for the San Marco mosaics. Cf. K. Weitzmann, "The Mosaics of San Marco and the Cotton Genesis," *Venezia e l'Europa: Atti del XVIII Congresso Internazionale di Storia dell'Arte, Venezia, 12–18 settembre 1955* (Venice, 1956), pp. 152–53. On the mosaics of San Marco, cf. primarily O. Demus, *Die Mosaiken von S. Marco in Venedig* (Vienna, 1935).

15. "Terra autem erat inanis et vacua, et tenebrae super faciem abyssi, et Spiritus Dei ferebatur super aquas . . ."

16. Cf. footnote 10.

17. There is some doubt as to whether the four rivers of paradise are original. They appear to be additions of the thirteenth-century mosaicist. Cf. Weitzmann, "Observations," p. 127, and E. Schlee, *Die Ikonographie der Paradiesesflüsse* (Leipzig, 1937), p. 8.

18. Cf. footnote 8.

19. John 1:1–3: "In principio erat Verbum et Verbum erat apud Deum et Deus erat Verbum. Hoc erat in principio apud Deum; omnia per ipsum facta sunt, et sine ipso factum est nihil quod factum est." For the Logos Creator, cf. also J. van der Meulen, "A Logos Creator at Chartres and Its Copy," *Journal of the Warburg and Courtauld Institutes* 29 (1966):82–100.

20. The Nicene Creed employs the word "homoousios" for this identity. For the Nicene Creed, cf., *inter alia*, A. E. Burn, *The Nicene Creed* (Oxford , 1909).

21. For a thorough study of the angels at San Marco, cf. M.-Th. d'Alverny, "Les Anges et les jours," *Cahiers archéologiques* 9 (1957):271–300.

22. Cf., for example, Heb. 1:7 and Ps. 103:4. Here, and in all follow-

ing citations, the numberings of the psalms is that of the Vulgate edition.

23. "Cum enim dixit Deus: 'Fiat lux' et facta est lux, si recte in hac luce creatio intellegitur angelorum, profecto facti sunt participes lucis aeternae quod est ipsa incommutabilis sapientia Dei, per quam facta sunt omnia, quem dicimus unigenitum Dei filium, ut ea luce inluminati, qua creati, fierunt lux et vocarentur dies participatione incommutabilis lucis et dei, quod est verbum Dei, per quod et ipsi et omnia facta sunt" (*De Civitate Dei*, 11.9 [*CCSL*, 48:329–30]). D'Alverny, "Les Anges," traces the possible sources of this passage.

24. "Qui vivit in aeternum creavit omnia simul" (*De Genesi ad Litteram* 2.5 f.; in J. P. Migne, *Patrologia Cursus Completus, Series Latina* (Paris, 1844–80) (hereafter cited as *PL*), 34.222 f. Cf. also C. O'Toole, *The Philosophy of Creation in the Writings of St. Augustine*, The Catholic University of America, Philosophical Series, 81 (Washington, D.C., 1944).

25. It must be pointed out, however, that elsewhere Augustine states that the same day is repeated six times because six is a perfect number; that is, the first number which is the exact sum of its factors: one, two, and three. Cf. *De Civitate Dei*, 11.30 *CCSL* 48:350). Elsewhere, he also suggests that the Creation is told in narrative form in the scriptures for the benefit of those who might not be able to understand the true account. Cf. *De Genesi ad Litteram* 4.33, 52; 5.3, 6. This particular aspect of Augustine's view of creation was not taken up by other medieval exegetes.

26. Cf. J. Garber, *Wirkungen der frühchristlichen Gemäldezyklen der alten Peters- und Pauls- Basiliken in Rom* (Berlin/Vienna, 1918); S. Waetzold, *Die Kopien des 17. Jahrhunderts nach Mosaiken und Wandmalereien in Rom* (Vienna, 1964), p. 55 f. Waetzold, *Die Kopien*, p. 57, refers to the first creation scene as Folio 23. The Vatican designates the folio as 25. In addition, Waetzold, *Die Kopien*, p. 57, believes that the first creation illustration depicts only Gen. 1:2–4. The presence of the sun, the moon, and the stars certainly indicates that the illustration is more extensive. For further problems concerning the interpretation of this image, cf. the following footnote.

27. There is some debate as to whether the lamb is original or a later addition. Cf. A. Weis, "Der Römische Schöpfungszyklus des 5. Jahrhunderts im Triclinium Neons zu Ravenna," *Tortulae: Studien zu altchristlichen und byzantinischen Monumenten*, Römische Quartalschrift für Christliche Altertumskunde und Kunstgeschichte, vol. 30, Supplement (Rome, 1966):330–316, esp. 309 f. For the text of Agnellus and its significance, cf. H. Gonin, *Excerpta Agnelliana: The Ravennate Liber Pontificalis as a Source for the History of Art* (Utrecht, 1933), pp. 68–70.

28. Cf. especially Weitzmann, "Observations"; and F. Bucher, *The Pamplona Bibles* (New Haven, 1970), 1:77 f.

29. For Carolingian creation cycles, cf. especially: W. Köhler, *Die Karolingischen Miniaturen*, vol. I: *Die Schule von Tours* (Berlin, 1930–33); H. Kessler, "Hic Homo Formatur: The Genesis Frontispieces of the Carolingian Bibles," *Art Bulletin* 53 (1971):143–60; and see H. Kessler, *The Il-*

lustrated Bibles from Tours (Princeton, 1977).

30. For a brief survey, cf. Robbins, *Hexaemeral Literature*, pp. 73-91. Also useful is H. Liebeschutz, "Kosmologische Motive in der Bildungswelt der Frühscholastik," *Vorträge der Bibliothek Warburg* (1923-24), pp. 83-148.

31. *cf.* P. Lauer, *Les Enluminures romanes des manuscrits de la Bibliothèque nationale* (Paris, 1927), pp. 81-82, plate 85(1); A. Heimann, "The Six Days of Creation in a Twelfth Century Manuscript," *Journal of the Warburg and Courtauld Institutes* 1 (1937-38):273. Heimann discusses the manuscript in the context of other manuscripts having personifications.

32. Ibid., p. 274.

33. "In virginem enim adhuc Evam irrepserat verbum aedificatorium mortis; in Virginem aeque introducendum erat Dei Verbum extructorium vitae; ut quod per eius modi sexum abierat in perditionem, per eumdem sexum redigeretur in salutem. Crediderat Eva serpenti: credidit Maria Gabrieli. Quod illa credendo deliquit, haec credendo delevit" (*Liber de Carne Christi* [Migne, *PL* 2.782]). For the relationship between Eve and Mary, cf. E. Guldan, *Eva und Maria, Eine Antithese als Bildmotiv* (Graz-Cologne, 1966).

34. This sort of representation is particularly common in the Gothic era and can be seen, for example, on the center door of the south transept at Chartres; cf. W. Sauerländer, *Gothic Sculpture in France, 1140-1270* (New York, 1972), plate 108. The original German edition, *Gotische Skulptur in Frankreich, 1140-1270*, was published in 1970 (Munich).

35. J. Meurgey, *Les Plus beaux manuscrits à peintures du Musée Condé à Chantilly* (Paris, 1930), pp. 8-11; S. Collon-Gevaert, J. Lejeune, and J. Stiennon, *Art roman dans la vallée de la Meuse aux XIe et XIIe siècles* (Brussels, 1962), pp. 229-30. For the English translation, see *A Treasury of Romanesque Art* (New York, 1972). (It should be noted that the pagination is different in the English translation.)

36. "Dixit autem Moses iste est sermo quem praecepit Dominus. Imple gomor ex eo et custodiatur in futuras retro generationes ut noverint panem quo alui vos in solitudine quando educti estis de terra Aegypti. Dixitque Moses ad Aaron sume vas unum et mitte ibi man quantum potest capere gomor et repone coram Domino ad servandum in generationes vestras." Cf. also John 6:30-36.

37. F. Röhrig, *Der Verduner Altar*, 2d ed. (Vienna, 1955), p. 71 and plate 22.

38. "Nec quisquam sumit sibi honorem, sed qui vocatur a Deo tamquam Aaron. Sic et Christus non semet ipsum clarificavit ut pontifex fieret, sed qui locutus est ad eum: Filius meus es tu ego hodie genui te quemadmodum, et in alio dicit, tu es sacerdos in aeternum secundum ordinem Melchisedech." Cf. also Heb. 7:1-25.

39. J. Stiennon, *Art roman,* loc. cit.

40. For a detailed analysis of this relationship, cf. A. Katzenellenbogen, *The Sculptural Programs of Chartres Cathedral: Christ, Mary, Ecclesia* (Baltimore, 1959.

41. P. de Palol, "Une Broderie catalane d'époque romane: 'La Genèse de Gérone'," *Cahiers Archéologiques* 8 (1956):174–214; 9 (1957):219–52; P. de Palol and M. Hirmer, *Early Medieval Art in Spain* (New York, 1967), pp. 174, 483.

42. DIXIT QUOQUE DS̃ FIAT LUX. ET FACTA ẼST LUX. Cf. de Palol, 'Une Broderie," p. 178. The inscriptions are based on the *Vetus latina hispana*; cf. de Palol, ibid., pp. 202–5.

43. Ibid., p. 178.

44. Ibid., p. 205 f.

45. Ibid., p. 194. Cf. also K. Lehmann, "The Dome of Heaven," *Art Bulletin* 27 (1945):1–27.

46. G. Swarzenski, *Die Salzburger Malerei von den Ersten Anfangen bis zur Blutezeit des romanischen Stils* (Leipzig, 1913), 1:67 f; vol. 2; plate 25 (84).

47. R. H. Charles, *The Apocrypha and Pseudepigrapha of the Old Testament* (Oxford, 1913), 2:1 f., esp. 20 (chap. 5, pp. 1–9). The angels were sent to earth and lusted after the women on earth. The Lord commanded that Noah bind up these angels in the depths of the earth in order to protect mankind whom He had created. Thus, the angels became demons after losing their first estate, given to them in the creation.

48. "Deus autem rex noster ante saeculum, operatus est salutes in medio terrae. Tu confirmasti in virtute tua mare, contribulasti capita draconum in acquis. Tu confregisti capita draconis, dedisti eum escam populis Aethiopum; tu disrupisti fontem et torrentes, tu siccasti fluvios Aetham."

49. A. Heimann, "Trinitas Creator Mundi," *Journal of the Warburg and Courtauld Institutes* 2 (1938–39):42–52.

50. "Spiritus Dei ferebatur super aquas."

51. "Let us make man in our own image, after our likeness."

52. Swarzenski, *Die Salzburger Malerei*, 1:71 f.; vol. 2: plate 27 (92). Cf. also O. Demus, 'Salzburg, Venedig, und Aquileja," in *Festschrift K. M. Swoboda* (Vienna-Wiesbaden, 1959); pp. 75–82; K. M. Swoboda, "Die Bilder der Admonter Bibel des 12. Jahrhunderts," in *Kunst und Geschichte: Vorträge und Aufsätze*, Mitteilungen des Instituts für Österreichische Geschichtsforschung, Ergänzungsband 22 (Vienna, 1969):41–54.

53. E. Panofsky and F. Saxl, "Classical Mythology in Mediaeval Art," *Metropolitan Museum Studies* 4 (1932–33):228 f.; E. Panofsky, *Renaissance and Renascences in Western Art*, Figura 10 (Stockholm, 1960).

54. Swarzenski, *Die Salzburger Malerei,* 1:129 f.; vol. 2; plate 30.

55. Heimann, "Six Days," p. 274.

56. A. Heimann, "Three Illustrations from the Bury St. Edmunds Psalter and Their Prototypes. Notes on the Iconography of Some Anglo-Saxon Drawings," *Journal of the Warburg and Courtauld Institutes* 29 (1966):39–59, esp. pp. 46–56. Although Heimann does not deal with the chronological problems, she does refer to British Library Royal I.E. vii, iv, and Vatican Reg. Lat. 12, 68v as "copies" of British Library Cotton Tiberius C.vi (cf. 53–54). Proposed chronologies of the manuscripts place all three around the middle of the eleventh century and no suggestion is

made concerning their exact chronology. Cf. F. Wormald, *English Drawings of the Tenth and Eleventh Centuries* (New York, 1953), pp. 68, 71, 79; M. Rickert, *Painting in Britain: The Middle Ages* (1954), pp. 44, 53.

57. "Qui sedet super gyrum terrae. . . ." For Ambrose, cf. Migne, *PL*, 14. 126.

58. "Quis mensis est pugillo aquas et caelos palmo ponderavit, quis adperdit tribus digitis molem terrae et libravit in pondere montes et colles in statera." For Ambrose, cf. Migne, *PL* 14. 127.

59. S. J. Crawford , ed., *Byrhtferth's Manual (A.D. 1011)*, Early English Text Society, 177 (Oxford, 1929).

60. Ibid., pp. 8–9. For the *Apocrypha and Pseudepigrapha*, cf. Charles, 1:553.

61. *Byrhtferth's Manual*, pp. 198–99.

62. Heimann, "Three Illustrations," pp. 48 f. The two passages cited by Heimann are separated by one hundred pages in the E.E.T.S. edition, as she notes on p. 48, footnotes 46 and 47. It must be pointed out, however, that, given this separation, it is difficult to view the passages as part of the same thought.

63. Ibid., passim, plate 11a.

64. Ibid., passim, plate 12b.

65. "Quando praeparabat caelos aderam, quando certa lege et gyro vallabat abyssos, quando aethera firmabat sursum et liberat fontes aquarum, quando circumdabat mari terminum suum et legem pinebat aquis ne transirent fines suos, quando adpendebat fundamenta terrae, cum eo eram cuncta componens et delectabar per singulos dies ludens coram eo omni tempore."

66. "Quia ecce formans montes et creans ventum, et adnuntians homini eloquium suum, faciens matutinam nebulam et gradiens super excelsa terrae, Dominus Deus exercituum nomen eius."

67. R. Harris, "The Marginal Drawings of the Bury St. Edmunds Psalter (Rome, Vatican Library MS. Reg. Lat. 12)," (Ph. D. diss., Princeton University, 1960), pp. 393 f.

68. Charles, *Apocrypha and Pseudepigrapha*, 1: 553.

69. For other types of schematic arrangement, cf. H. Bober, "In Principio, Creation Before Time," in M. Meiss, ed., *De Artibus Opuscula XL: Essays in Honor of Erwin Panofsky* (New York, 1961), 1:13–28; idem, "An Illustrated Medieval School-Book of Bede's 'De Natura Rerum,'" *Journal of the Walters Art Gallery* 19–20 (1956–57):65–97.

70. For a discussion of the Italian cycles, cf. primarily Garrison, "Note on the Iconography of Creation"; and O. Demus, *The Mosaics of Norman Sicily* (London, 1950), pp. 245 f.

71. H. Kessler, "An Eleventh Century Ivory Plaque from South Italy and the Cassinese Revival," *Jahrbuch der Berliner Museen* 8 (1966):67–95.

72. R. Bergman, "The Salerno Ivories," (Ph. D. diss., Princeton University, 1972). Of the earlier literature, the most comprehensive is A. Carucci, *Gli avori salernitani del sec. XII* (Salerno, 1065).

73. Demus, *Mosaics of Norman Sicily*, and E. Kitzinger, *The Mosaics of Monreale* (Palermo, 1960).

74. Cf., for example, Constantinople, Seraglio 6, 26v.

75. Demus, *Mosaics of Norman Sicily*, plate 26a.

76. Ibid., passim; Kitzinger, *Mosaics of Monreale*, passim.

77. The inscription can be seen especially clearly in the chromolithograph in D. B. Gravina, *Il Duomo di Monreale* (Palermo, 1859), vol. 2, plate 15-b.

78. Ibid., vol. 2, plate 15.

79. Kitzinger, *Mosaics of Monreale*, p. 54.

80. Kessler, "Eleventh Century Plaque," p. 81. He also suggests Jewish sources.

81. "De quibus dicitur Isa. XXXIV: 'Coelum sicut liber plicabitur'. Hoc firmamento discernit aquas superiores, id est populum angelorum, quibus non est necesse ut in lectione audiant Dei verbum" (Walafrid Strabo, *Glossa Ordinaria, Liber Genesis*, in Migne, *PL* 113. 73).

Comment

BY

David L. Simon

The interesting paper by Professor Dorothy Glass entitled "*In Principio*: The Creation in the Middle Ages" investigates Early Christian, Early Medieval and Romanesque representations of the first days of Creation. Professor Glass does not catalogue all illustrations of the *Hexaemeron*; rather, examples are chosen in order to discuss the relationship between word and image, to suggest a methodology for the study of such a relationship and to place illustrations of the Creation in the broader context of medieval thought. Professor Glass clearly shows that an artist or program designer selected from a variety of available images to produce representations that were interpretive, not merely illustrative.

Professor Glass has chosen to interpret Nature as symbolic, rather than to describe natural phenomena. That is just as it should be, for it is traditional to view the appearance of naturalistic elements in the visual arts as signaling the transition from Romanesque to Gothic art.[1]

Certainly this is not a new approach to the study of medieval art. Even while describing Gothic art, Emile Mâle classified the medieval view of the world and of nature as symbolic. Citing Honorious of Autun and Vincent of Beauvais, Mâle recognized that medieval theology relied on the premise that "God the Father created *in principio*, which is to say *in verbo*, that is by His Son. Jesus Christ is at once Creator and Redeemer."[2] It is for this reason that illustrations of the Creation appear in the context of all history, the history of the natural world and the history of the Church. The vital relationship between Creation and Salvation is a virtual leitmotif of the study of Genesis illustrations, from the Cotton Genesis recensions where the Creator is depicted as Christ–Logos to the illustration in the Paris *Antiquitates Judaicae* where the Virgin and

Eve are juxtaposed to each other.

Salvation imagery expressed through Genesis illustrations is particularly apparent in two eleventh-century manuscripts not discussed by Professor Glass, in MS Junius xi (Oxford, Bodleian Library, pp. 6–7) and the Bible of St. Hubert (Brussels, Bibliothèque Royale, MS II 1689, fol. 6v). Pamela Blum has recently studied the illustrations of the Junius Genesis where the six days labors are conflated into two miniatures, salvation symbolism unifying a compact illustrative program.[3] Her observations are based in part on the placement of the miniatures in the context of a poem recalling and elaborating on Genesis, in actuality two separate poems combined to read as one. What Blum discovered in this specific manuscript is precisely what Glass suggests is true of early medieval Genesis cycles in general, that the artist expresses ideas that go far beyond the theme of the text which his illustrations accompany.

In the Bible of St. Hubert, Genesis begins with a full-page monogram decorated with representations of the Christ–Logos and the Four Elements. Harry Bober has shown that the illustrations do not comprise a narrative account of the Creation, but a schema based on the study of numbers, measures, volumes and proportions that reflects the organization of the universe before Creation.[4] At the same time, certain features of the decoration refer to the Fall and Redemption. Thus the monogram is at once a history from before Creation and an anticipation of what is to come.

The Junius manuscript has been variously dated to the early or mid-eleventh century and Bober dated the Bible of St. Hubert to aobut 1070, although it has also been dated to the early years of the twelfth century. It is not surprising that Professor Glass does not discuss these examples since she is concerned with defining a method to approach the study of the visual image, not with compiling a catalogue of Genesis illustrations. However, what is of some concern is the implication that illustrations of the first days of Creation are lacking for the ninth through the eleventh centuries. Certainly the two eleventh-century examples discussed above, the three English eleventh-century representations examined by Glass herself, as well as those in Aelfric's Paraphrase of the Pentateuch and Joshua (London, British Library, Cotton Claudius B. iv) attest to the strength of the tradition of Genesis illustrations before the twelfth century. Also included in this list of eleventh-century representations should be that from the Coblenz Bible (Pommersfelden Schlossbibliothek, Cod. 333–334) and the elaborate cycles in the Roda and Ripoll Bibles, made in Catalonia and today preserved in Paris (Paris, Bibliothèque Nationale, Lat. 6) and Rome (Biblioteca Vaticana, Lat. 5729).

It is certainly true, however, that in the court centers of the Carolingian and Ottonian empires there seems to have been little interest in the representation of the first days of Creation, although full narrative accounts that begin with the Creation of Adam can be found in a series of large Carolingian bibles produced in the scriptorium at Tours. Herbert Kessler has demonstrated that the Tours artists had before them a very rich Cotton Genesis recension.[5] Why then was there no apparent interest in representing all the Creation events including those of the first days? And why is it that the first days of Creation were popular subjects during certain centuries and virtually ignored during others? These questions most be posed if we are to appreciate Creation imagery in the context of medieval thought. It is for the investigation of this problem that Professor Glass's paper has prepared us, and it is here that the importance of her contribution will be most appreciated.

Notes

1. Lynn White, Jr., "Natural Science and Naturalistic Art in the Middle Ages," *The American Historical Review* 52 (1947): 421–35; Marie-Dominique Chenu, "L'Homme et la Nature: Perspectives sur la renaissance du XIIe siècle," *Archives d'histoire doctrinale et littèraire du moyen âge* 28 (1952): 39–66; Max Dvorák, *Idealism and Naturalism in Gothic Art*, trans. Randolph J. Klawiter (Notre Dame, Ind.: University of Notre Dame Press, 1967).

2. Emile Mâle, *The Gothic Image: Religious Art in France of the Thirteenth Century*, trans. Dora Nussey (New York: Harper and Row, 1958), p. 29. (First published as *L'Art religieux du XIIIe siècle en France* [Paris: Colin, 1902].)

3. Pamela Z. Blum, "The Cryptic Creation Cycle in MS Junius xi," *Gesta* 15 (1976): 211–26.

4. Harry Bober, "*In Principio*: Creation Before Time," *De Artibus Opuscula XL; Essays in Honor of Erwin Parofsky*, ed. Millard Meiss (New York: New York University Press, 1961), 1: 13–28.

5. Herbert L. Kessler, "*Hic Homo Formatur*: The Genesis Frontispieces of the Carolingian Bibles," *Art Bulletin* 53 (1971): 143–60.

The Origin of the Fleur-de-Lis and the *Lilium candidum* in Art*

Robert A. Koch

Perhaps never has a secular symbol enjoyed such continuous popularity as the fleur-de-lis, emblem of the French kingdom. In the thirteenth century, it was also adopted as the emblem of the city of Florence, in a special, floriated design. The fleur-de-lis developed its heraldic form in the Romanesque period as a stylized flower of nature, I believe, as do a majority of scholars who have considered the matter.

Literature on the origin of the fleur-de-lis is vast, for the symbol is not just time-honored but, for the French, sacrosanct. (In fact throughout Europe and America it has become a hallmark connoting "superior quality" in a most vulgar commercial fashion.) While its legendary history begins as early as the fourteenth century, the first notable scholarly study was undertaken by Chifflet in 1658, with the title (translated from the Latin), *The True History, Botany and Heraldry of the French Lily.*[1] Subsequent studies include Montfaucon's *Les monuments de la monarchie françoise* in 1729; an article by Comte de Laborde, "Les fleurs-de-lis héraldiques et les fleurs-de-lis naturelles," in 1852;[2] and Leclerq in Cabrol's *Dictionnaire d'archéologie chrétienne,* in 1923.[3] Leclerq began his essay, written over half a century ago now, with the remarks: "The origin of the fleur-de-lis is currently one of the most difficult archaeological problems. . . . Some know nothing and tell us everything; others don't know much, and invent the rest."

Though the difficulty I fear is destined to remain, glimmers of new light have been shed recently in three articles: François Chatillon's "*Lilia Crescunt*";[4] James Johnson's "The Tree of Jesse Window of Chartres";[5] and Meredith Lillich's "The Choir Clerestory Windows of La Trinité at Vendôme."[6]

I should like to survey, for the first time to my knowledge, the cogent pictorial evidence as given on seals, coins, stained glass and other art media concerning the main scholarly problems posed by the fleur-de-lis: 1) Was it, as commonly assumed in earlier days, the *Lilium candidum,* the white lily, popularly called since the nineteenth century the "Madonna" or "Easter" lily? Or was it rather the blossom of the iris that was stylized to become the emblem? This seems to be the opinion most often encountered in recent literature. 2) At what time during the twelfth century, and why, does it become the official emblem adopted by the king of France? And, 3) What occasioned the adoption of exactly three fleur-de-lis for the royal armorial shield, the system called in heraldry "*France moderne?*"

Its age-old name of "lily flower" notwithstanding, there are modern theories which dissociate the origin of the device from *any* flower of nature. Leclerq, among others, felt that the transverse band could only be the guard of a sword, or halberd, or perhaps the linch-pin of an attack weapon. However, this would have been warlike and hence unseemly symbolism; moreover the very fact that the emblem was thought of and called a "lily" by writers of the High Middle Ages seems to rule out the weapon theory. I also view sceptically the conclusion of Bauerreis, in a book on the *Arbor vitae*: "In regard to the interpretation of the scepter lily and the heraldic lily, we are at least just as justified to see in it at its inception an abbreviation of a representation of a tree of life as we are to see it as a lily."[7]

As to our first problem, lily or iris blossom, it should be noted that the *Lilium candidum* has a long history of representation in ancient Near Eastern and Mediterranean art, whereas the iris, although it is also indigenous to the Mediterranean area, is not represented at all in ancient times, as far as I know. Also, the white lily, but not the iris, was of great medical importance to the ancients, and it appears in the earliest classical herbals—for example, the one of Dioskurides in the first century A.D., best known in the famous illustrated codex now in Vienna that was made in A.D. 512 for the Princess Anicia Juliana in Byzantium. Most important for our thesis, the lily was to be invested more than any other flower, including the rose, with profound religious Christian symbolism. Thus common sense dictates that the lily, since ninth-century Carolingian times, is the flower that appears as a simplified, three-petaled "fleuron" on kings's crowns and as a decorative but probably symbolic ornament on buildings. For example, the fleuron appears at the top of the gable of the temple-like enframement of a canon-table page in the Ebbo Gospel book, made in Reims before 823 (fig. 1). Note the transverse band or knosp binding the lower part of the three petals, and the two lateral ones curving sharply downward. Later, in the twelfth century, this type of fleuron is changed somewhat, though not fundamentally, to become the heraldic fleur-de-lis.

The fleur-de-lis in its most complicated form, as the heraldic emblem of Florence, is prominently represented on a shield in a painting by Roger van der Weyden, a fifteenth-century Flemish artist (fig. 2). A filament tipped with anthers has been added to either side of the upright petal (filaments being characteristic of the lily of nature and not of the iris). This is the fancy fleur-de-lis *fleuronné,* or *florencé.* A second characteristic of the heraldic fleur-de-lis, seen in the design on this shield, though not prominently so, is the tripartite foot below the knosp. In its originally simpler form it was probably intended to be an inverted, decorative reprise of the main theme above. The filamented fleur-de-lis, which was adopted as the emblem of Florence in 1252, had been invented in France, it seems, though it was not to be retained by the French kings. Roger van der Weyden's small icon-like depiction of the *Madonna and Child with Saints* was probably painted in 1450 when he visited Florence. A member of the Medici family probably commissioned it, as suggested by the presence of John the Baptist, patron saint of Florence, as well as the two name patron saints of the Medici family, the early Christian medical doctors Cosmas and Damian (the word "*medici*" meaning "doctors," whence the association). Though it is not documented, this picture bears further evidence that it was commissioned for an Italian, specifically a Florentine, because of the special design of the fleur-de-lis, and the fact that it is rendered in red, as distinct from the emblem of France, which is normally rendered in gold on a blue ground.

Prominent in the foreground of the painting, placed together in a vase as a cut-flower offering to the Madonna and Child, are the two blossoms of nature that we have discussed, the iris (the blue-and-purple species *germanica*), and the lily (species *candidum*). In the fifteenth century the iris could be a symbol of regality, because of the upright bearing of the blossom stalk and the beauty of the single blossom. In this painting it probably was selected by the artist to

Fig. 1. Ebbo Gospels. *Canon Table, Épernay, Bibliothèque de la Ville, Ms 1, fol. 11.*

underscore Mary's role as queen of the Christian heaven. Above all else, Mary was viewed as pure, and this aspect of her faultless being was symbolized by the stalk of white lilies that the artist includes. From the thirteenth century on, it was this flower, the *Lilium candidum*, that was virtually mandatory in a representation of the "Annunciation" as a symbolic indication that Mary remained a virgin at the incarnation of her son.

The iris of nature, as seen in this painting, does seem closer in design to the fleur-de-lis than the lily, which may in part, though only in part as we shall see, account for the fact that most recent writers state with no explanation that it was the iris that originally inspired the design of the fleur-de-lis. Allegedly it would not have been the blue *germanica* species found in Van der Weyden's painting but rather the yellow flag iris, botanically *Iris pseudoacorus*, which grows in fresh-water marshes, especially in northern Europe. Ancient legends concerning Clovis, founder of the Merovingian line of Frankish kings, also have played a role in associating the iris

Fig. 2. Roger van der Weyden, "Madonna and Child with Saints," Frankfurt a./M., Städelsches Kunstinstitut.

with the fleur-de-lis. It may have been Chéruel, in a mid-nineteenth-century dictionary entry on the *"lis"*, who first suggested that it was the yellow swamp iris that had been stylized as a fleuron, or three-petalled flower, by the Franks to recall their origin in the marshes.[8]

I shall return to the legend concerning Clovis's adoption of the fleur-de-lis at the end of the article. I would like to say, however, that I am quite convinced, for reasons that I have given, that it was not a species of iris but rather the white lily that inspired the fleuron of the early Middle Ages which became the fleur-de-lis proper.

To go further with this point, it should be noted that *Lilium candidum* was one of the most important commercial plants of antiquity, first cultivated, it is now believed, in Anatolia around 1500 B.C. It is to be found at about this same date in art; the nature-loving Cretans frequently represented it in fresco painting, possibly as a symbol of fertility and an attribute of the great Cretan snake goddess. The pulverized bulb was of pharmacological importance to the ancient Greeks, we learn from the herbal of Dioskurides; the Greeks marveled at the beauty of its blossom, which they associated with Hera and Aphrodite. (The Romans, similarly, linked the white lily with Juno and Venus.) A myth was created to explain the origin on earth of the noble *leirion* (lily) and simultaneously the origin in heaven of the starry Milky Way. In the sixteenth century, Tintoretto made a famous painting of the myth, a picture now in the National Gallery, London. Its story is as follows: Wishing to immortalize the infant Herakles, Zeus held the child to the breast of the sleeping Hera. After the child had stopped drinking, her milk continued to flow. The milk which spilled upward became the Milky Way, while the downward flow gave birth to lilies on earth. Tintoretto's painting was later taken down; however, in the Academy, Venice, a sketchy drawing of the entire composition by another artist shows the female personification of Earth, sprouting what are intended to be lilies.

The most compelling argument for the candidacy of the *Lilium candidum* as the flower which became the fleur-de-lis in the later Middle Ages is the attention paid to this Biblical flower by Christian authors, who find in it a supreme symbol of the Virgin Mary, and also of Christ. Walahfrid Strabo, abbot of the Reichenau monastery in the ninth century, seems to have been the first to write of the symbolism of the lily (together with the rose), in the verses at the end of his famous garden poem, the *Hortulus*. This was the first "horticultural work" to be written in the new Christian Europe. Later, in the twelfth century, the mystical meaning of the white lily was expounded in detail in the sermons of St. Bernard of Clairvaux, from one of which I shall quote presently. I think that it is not coincidental that apparently the fleur-de-lis was adopted by Louis VII as the royal emblem of France just at the time that Bernard, who was an intimate of the King, was so concerned with the symbolism of the lily.

There can be no question that the "lily" of the Bible, especially as mentioned in the Song of Songs, was the *Lilium candidum* for many medieval exegetes and for the artists. Furthermore, in the collective mind, as it were, of the later Middle Ages the emblematic fleur-de-lis was the white lily of nature in stylized form. Proof is to be found in the entry under *Lilium* in the fourteenth-century *Dictionary* of Petrus Berchorius (Pierre Bersuire). It reads in part:

> LILIUM is a medicinal herb, and beautiful. Generally can signify either Christ or Mary, or any just man. For Christ: *Song of Songs* 2: I am the flower of the field and the lily of the Valley. For Mary: *Song of Songs* 2: As the lily among thorns, so is my love among the daughters. And the rulers of France, Sicily, Hungary, and Navarre who wear the lily, and mainly the beatus Ludovicus (Louis IX) we honor as written in Hosea: "I will be as the dew: Israel shall spring as the lily. . . ."[9]

Accordingly, it is the *Lilium candidum* that appears in the beautiful woodcut illustration for chapter two of the Dutch blockbook *Canticum canticorum,* dating circa 1460 (fig. 3). Mary as the Church—the Bride in St. Bernard's interpretation—utters the words *"Ego flos campi, et lilium convallium;"* while the Bridegroom, at the left, appears to be uttering the words *"Dilectus meus mihi, et ego ille . . ."* ("My beloved to me and I to him who feedeth among the lilies"). The gender, however, seems to indicate that Mary the Bride makes both remarks that appear on the two banderoles. (As an aside, I am compelled to report that W. L. Schreiber, an illustrious cataloguer in the 1890's of the fifteenth-century blockbooks, made an amusing, but unconvincing, suggestion to explain the blockbooks's androgynous, female-appearing Christ figure with unusually long hair and a clean-shaven face. Schreiber attempted to explain this unusual figure by suggesting that it was a nun who painted the original manuscript model for the woodcuts. If we grant the existence of a manuscript model, which is unlikely in my opinion, why should the fact that a nun painted the model explain why Christ appears androgynous? Other medieval exegetes—for example

Fig. 3. Canticum canticorum, *Dutch Blockbook, Page 7, top.*

Fig. 4. Psalter and Offices of the Virgin, *"Annunciation," New York, Morgan Library, Ms 730, fol. 11 v.*

Rabanus Maurus in the ninth century—interpreted the speaker of the words *Ego flos campi* as the Bridegroom, Christ. But I do not need to get into this problem. Nor do I need to go into the botanical one of the correct identification of the Bible's *flos campi,* the flowers of the field of ancient and present-day Palestine. The best recent authority, Moldenke, in a monumental work entitled *Plants of the Bible,* believes that the Biblical flower of the field most probably was the anemone, which was one of the most colorful and ubiquitous of many flowers indigenous to the Holy Land.

Striking pictorial evidence to support the equation "fleur-de-lis equals *Lilium candidum*" is given in a late thirteenth-century French manuscript illumination (fig. 4). As I have mentioned, it was in the thirteenth century that a plant was introduced into the scene of the "Annunciation," and that plant, when identifiable and not abstracted, was the lily. Often Gabriel is shown holding the lily stalk, or else it is placed in a vase, near Mary, since the white lily symbolizes her purity. Sometimes three blossoms are shown, as we saw in the Madonna painting by Roger van der Weyden. These blossoms symbolize the threefold nature of her purity: a continuing virginity not only before, but during and after, the birth of her son. Inevitably, the number three brought thoughts of the Trinity to the mind of a pious observer at the time. Such is the case in this late-thirteenth-century "Annunciation," a very early representation of the scene in Western art, illuminated in Arras. The manuscript is now in the Morgan Library, No. 730. Unique in this miniature, as far as I know, the *Lilium candidum* of nature is stylized in white as the emblematic fleur-de-lis, thus proving rather conclusively my thesis.

I want to trace now what I have perceived to be the gradual transformation of the white lily in art, particularly on such art objects as the historically revealing seals and coins of the kings of France. These changed from a simple fleuron, or three-petaled flower motif, into the full-fledged, emblematic fleur-de-lis.

One of the very first representations of *Lilium candidum* in Christian art is to be found in the apse mosaic of the sixth-century church of Sant'Apollinare in Classe, Ravenna, depicting the "Transfiguration," with a bust of Christ situated on a huge jeweled cross set against a starry ground. Below, Saint Apollinaris stands in a terrestrial paradise of plants and animals. Fourteen clusters of white lily blossoms serve as punctuation marks between two groups of six sheep, symbolizing the twelve Apostles, aligned on either side of the saint. This is the *Lilium candidum*, stylized as a three-petaled fleuron in a design that is to remain in Western art for the next six hundred years.

We find it, in fact, six centuries later in another Italian apse mosaic, in the church of Santa Maria in Trastevere, Rome. Dating 1148, it is one of the earliest representations of the theme of the "Coronation of the Virgin" by Christ; it is also one of the first times in art that a flower—any flower—is connected with the Virgin Mary. Here the fleuron serves as a motif ornamenting her slippers. In addition, the white lily grows beside the throne as the old Byzantine flower of paradise in the sixth-century Ravenna mosaic. The lily occurs for the third time in this mosaic composition as an ornament on either end of the back of the throne.

Two years earlier, in 1146, Mary had appeared in French art on a seal created for the Chapter of Paris.[10] As Queen of Heaven Mary is shown wearing a crown adorned with what we may call the fleur-de-lis fleuron, given in triplicate to honor the Trinity. In 1195, fifty years or so, as we shall see, after the fleur-de-lis had been firmly established as the royal emblem of France by Louis VII, Mary again takes on the symbol of earthly royalty, the white lily; and in a seal prepared for the Cathedral Chapter of Notre-Dame in Reims, she is shown crowned and holding a scepter which terminates with a large heraldic fleur-de-lis.[11]

From the year 997 the seal of the son of Hugh Capet, King Robert the Pious, depicts him in half-length, wearing a crown with three fleur-de-lis fleurons, and he holds what is probably a fleuron in his right hand.[12] The attributes of royalty of Henry I of France, as held or worn by him on a seal that can be dated 1035, are not clear in the impression reproduced by J. Roman, though they seem to continue those of his father, King Robert: namely he holds a fleuron with three others ornamenting the crown.[13] A scepter has replaced the orb that King Robert held in his left hand and the King is depicted as a full-length, enthroned figure. This is the first appearance on a French seal of the so-called "majesty" type.

But another century was to pass before the fleur-de-lis appears on a French coin. This is a denier of Louis VI *"le Gros"*, who reigned from 1108 to 1137 as a good king, in the judgment of historians. (fig. 5). On the obverse of the coin is a church with three bells, while the reverse depicts a cross with four equal arms, with the

Fig. 5. Denier of Louis VI of France.

fleur-de-lis appearing between two of them. Why three should be the number of bells and two the number of lilies I am unable to answer, though there must have been a reason. When modern writers speak of the adoption of the fleur-de-lis as the heraldic emblem of the kingdom of France most impute the honor either to Louis VI, who rather timidly introduced it to this denier, or else to his son Louis VII, "*le Jeune.*" There is no question in my mind that it is to the younger Louis that the honor is due. His seal, for which I have been able to find a date as early as 1141, reveals in its iconography a compulsive interest in the fleur-de-lis as the royal symbol (fig. 6). It appears on his crown, again as a device held like a toy in his right hand, and finally as the terminal motif of the royal scepter. The regional coinage however remains, as with his predecessor, unspectacular and without special emphasis on the stylized lily.

Recently James R. Johnson has made an extremely important observation about the fleur-de-lis in an article on the Tree of Jesse window in the west façade of Chartres Cathedral.[14] The Jesse window comes into direct contact with the royal house of France, specifically Louis VII, in the 1140s, in that the royal fleur-de-lis is given in stained glass in a spectacularly monumental form. The "tree" is in fact composed of a vertical succession of giant lily blossoms, outlined in white, to serve as perches for the royal ancestors of Christ who are enclosed within the central petal of each

Fig. 6. Seal of Louis VII of France.

lily. Johnson believes that the window dates between the years 1146 and 1149, the years during which Louis VII led the Second Crusade. Saint Bernard preached the Crusade at Chartres in 1146, and the King took the cross from Bernard at Vézelay on Easter Sunday of that same year. It would be tidy to hypothesize, as have several scholars, that Louis le Jeune adopted the fleur-de-lis as the official insignia of the kingdom of France at this very moment. It would have been his shield and banner device for the crusade to the Holy Land; and thus the ancient Byzantine stylized white *Lilium candidum* might have returned home, so to speak, half a millennium later as the French fleur-de-lis. However, I can dispel this theory, since a seal attached to a document of 1141 indicates that Louis VII had adopted the fleur-de-lis at least five years earlier (see fig. 6). Johnson mentions the suggestion made long ago, as early as the seventeenth century, that the sudden interest in the fleur-de-lis by the two Kings Louis might have been as a rebus on their name, Louis, then spelled loys; thus "fleur-de-loys," or "flower of Louis." Further, in Chifflet's account of the history of the fleur-de-lis (see n. 1) we are told that Louis VII was called *Ludovicus Florus*. More likely, as Johnson has pointed out, political reasons may have been behind the adoption of the flower-of-the-lily by the Kings Louis in the twelfth century. As Capetian rulers of the Ile-de-France, they attempted a *renovatio* of the Merovingian and Carolingian empires, and theoretically they would have wished to adopt the fleuron for crown or scepter as did some of the earliest French kings. Montfaucon suggested long ago that the Frankish kings adopted the lily in imitation of Byzantine or other emperors, and he also believed that the jamb statues of St. Denis and Chartres represented Merovingian kings and queens with crowns *fleurdelisé*, an opinion that has been revived by recent scholars.[15] Adolf Katzenellenbogen, for example, believed that these could be double images, combining the kings and queens of the Old Testament with early rulers of France. There is an old French legend, which I shall recount presently, which holds that it was Clovis, founder of the Merovingian line of Frankish kings in the sixth century, who first adopted the fleur-de-lis as the symbol of his majesty. Although the legend cannot as yet be documented earlier than the fourteenth century, if it had been current in the twelfth we could have a fine explanation of the adoption, or re-adoption, of the fleur-de-lis by Louis VII in connection with his desire to associate himself with the Merovingian rulers. Also, for what it might be worth, Planché has pointed out that the name "Louis" is a modern version of the name "Clovis," and he calls our attention to the similarity of the words Clodovicus, Lodovicus, Lodowic, Ludwig, Louis, the "c" being dropped—as in Clothaire, Lothaire, Chilperic, Hilperic, and so on.

The design of the fleur-de-lis in the Chartres window reflects the elaborated one that was to become the emblem of Florence. This design, which I have discussed (fig. 2), first appears, it would seem, in France in the mid-twelfth century, and possibly for the first time in this very window at Chartres. On royal seals it makes its debut, apparently, in splendid isolation on a counterseal of King Philip II Augustus, son of Louis VII and one of the chief consolidators of the French monarchy.[16] The seal dates from the first year of Philip's reign, 1180. His queen, Elizabeth of Hainault, adopts it for her own seal (fig. 7). She is shown as a standing figure, holding in her right hand an elegantly designed and oversized fleur-de-lis as her royal emblem. Elizabeth is crowned with the simple fleur-de-lis, which also appears at the end of the scepter, a continuation of the tradition of its originator, Louis VII.

No one has suggested a reason for the appearance of the filaments,

Fig. 7. Seal of Elizabeth of Hainault, Queen of France.

Fig. 8. Gold Florin of Florence, reverse, fleur-de-li

a fancy addition to the design of the fleur-de-lis rarely to be found in French royal heraldry after the thirteenth century. It could be that the idea of showing two of the six filaments with their golden anthers—a very prominent feature of *Lilium candidum* in nature—was inspired by contemporary, i.e., twelfth-century, Biblical exegesis on the lily. The most famous reference to the lily in the Bible of course was the *lilium convallium* in the Song of Songs. The most famous exegete of the Song of Songs was Bernard of Clairvaux. He wrote of the lily's golden anthers as symbolizing one aspect of Christ, a flower that issued from the roots of Jesse. In connection with the Chartres window, Johnson quotes the following passage from Bernard's seventieth sermon on the *Canticum canticorum*:

And consider how close is the analogy between the truth

> of God and the lily of the valleys (i.e., *Lilium candidum*). . . . From the center of this flower there springs a number of little golden rods . . . which are surrounded by the petals of a dazzling white, beautifully and fittingly arranged in the form of a crown. You have here symbolized the gold of Christ's divinity.

Still, until someone produces a documented or at least cogent explanation for the elaborated design of the fleur-de-lis *fleuronné* we should not assume that special significance was attached to it. If so it surely would have been mandatory in royal French heraldry, probably from its inception in the twelfth century and certainly consistently so thereafter.

The story of the adoption of the fleur-de-lis by the Florentines in the thirteenth century is an interesting one. It would seem that the fleur-de-lis first appeared in Florence on a silver coin, the *grosso*, shortly after 1220. This was called a *fiorino* which, like the device of the lily (*fiore*) which it bore, was a play on the name of the city. The famous gold florin, one of the earliest gold coins struck in western Europe, made its appearance in Florence in the year 1252. On the obverse is the figure of St. John the Baptist, patron of the city, while on the reverse is the lily (fig. 8). The gold florin, which continued to be struck for almost two centuries, until the year 1422, is the most important coin historically of all of the many which bore the fleur-de-lis. With a value of 240 pennies, it was quickly adopted as the coin by which transactions were consummated throughout the Western world. With the same two images the gold florin was struck in other cities in Europe in the fourteenth century, for example in Avignon by the anti-popes John XXII and Urban V. After the thirteenth century, as I have mentioned, the fancy, Florentine-type fleur-de-lis appears but rarely as a symbol of the monarch in France. However, there are interesting French coins that clearly show the influence of the lily as it appeared on the florin. These coins are from the reign in the mid-fourteenth century of Jean II "*le Bon*."[17] Briefly, the story behind the adoption of the fleur-de-lis as the emblem of Florence is as follows: according to legend, Santa Reparata, a virgin in Cappadocia, was believed to have appeared in the battle for Florence on October 8, A.D. 405, in which the leader of the Goths, Radagasius, was defeated. Reparata carried a blood-red banner which bore the device of a white lily. Henceforth the white lily became the city's device, and Reparata was regarded as its patron saint from 680 until 1298. *Il Primo Popolo*, the First Democracy, was established in Florence in 1250. One of its initial acts was to give the city its coat-of-arms, the lily, though with a color change from white to red which came about for the following reason. In 1251, when the war for control of Tuscany began, the Florentine Ghibellines committed an open act of treason by joining the enemies of their native city. What irked these noblemen was the triumph of democracy in their home town. Challenging them, the democracy abandoned the white lily on a red field to the noble traitors, reversed the color scheme, and declared their emblem to be the red lily on a white field. Readmitted to favor in 1252, the Ghibellines returned to Florence, and the gold florin was issued.

I wish to turn now to the last of the three scholarly problems concerning the fleur-de-lis that I posed at the beginning of this lecture: When, and why, were exactly three fleur-de-lis chosen for the royal armorial shield of France, the system called in heraldry *France moderne*? The first French monarch to employ *France moderne* with regularity was Charles VI, who reigned from 1380 to 1422. He issued a gold *écu* in 1389 on the obverse side of which is a shield with three fleur-de-lis, and above the shield a crown *fleurdelisé.*[18] The reverse has a fancy cross within a quatrefoil, with eight more lilies worked into the design. This *écu à la couronne* was to become the standard French gold coin for more than two hundred years.

In his *Histoire de la maison royale,* Pierre Anselme states that the first example of a field of three fleur-de-lis on a royal emblem appeared on a seal of King Philip III, son of Louis IX, in 1285.[19] Princes of the royal house of France also used the reduced field of three, for example Pierre d'Alençon, fifth son of St. Louis. His equestrian seal on a chart dated 1287 shows a field of fleur-de-lis carpeting the horse's robe, while *France moderne* appears on his shield.[20] The seal of his wife, Jeanne de Chatillon, dates from the year of their marriage, 1271. She is shown standing beneath an arch, the shield of her husband attached to a column at her right while opposite, at her left, are the armorial bearings of her own family.[21]

Although any number of fleur-de-lis designs could appear on a shield, especially favored were six and ten, owing to the fact that these numbers neatly fitted the available space in three diminishing rows. The number of lilies on the royal shield seems to be arbitrary until the time of Charles VI in the late fourteenth century, when *France moderne* was adopted once and for all. We can be certain that when the number of lilies was three, symbolism was intended, if not from their first appearance on a royal shield, at least by the time of Charles V in the third quarter of the fourteenth century. The symbolic meaning, of course, was inevitably associated with the Holy Trinity. A document from the year 1376 clearly spells this out. It is the charter founding the Monastery of the Holy Trinity of Limay, near Mantes, by Charles V in February of that year. The large initial letter K of the charter, for Karolus, depicts the monarch kneeling in profile, offering the charter to four Celestine monks (fig. 9). Above them is pictured the Trinity, while over the head of the king two angels hold the crown and the shield of France with three fleur-de-lis. The character says that the three gold fleur-de-lis on the azure shield are the mystic emblem of the Holy Trinity. We read further that since power, wisdom and benevolence are attributes of the three persons of the Trinity, so the three lilies on the shield of France express the power of arms, knowledge of letters, and clemency of princes, and that the majesty of the king of France is only a reflection of divine majesty. This interesting document was given rather obscure publication in France in 1857.[22]

In the fourteenth century the fleur-de-lis appears on the royal shield of England. Edward III contested the right to the French throne of the first Valois, Philip VI; and Edward claimed it for England in 1339 in right of his mother, Isabella of France. In so doing he quartered the fleur-de-lis of France on the royal shield of England which previously had consisted solely of three lions. The lilies were to remain for centuries, and were finally dropped by George III in 1801.

Of the coins issued during the reign of the Valois Philip VI, from 1328 to 1350, one is of special interest in connection with the adoption of *France moderne*. It is the *ange d'or* issued on January 27, 1341, depicting a crowned angel supporting a shield with the three lilies (fig. 10). This is the first appearance of *France moderne* on royal coinage, and it was evidently issued as propaganda to support the claim of the house of Valois as the legitimate successors of the Capetians to the throne of France. The image on the coin encapsulates the pseudo-historical story of the revelation by an angel to a monk,

Fig. 9. Initial Letter "K" in a Charter of 1376 of King Charles V of France

Fig. 10. Gold Ange d'Or of Philip VI of France

and thence to King Clovis, of the fleur-de-lis as the new insignia for the royal arms. According to different legends, it replaced either the crescent moon or the toad, both of which had been the prior emblems of Clovis. The new insignia enabled the first Merovingian king to win an important battle, and it converted him to Christianity.

François Chatillon discusses the legend as it is recounted in a rhymed Latin poem, perhaps for the first time between between 1328 and 1335, a few years before the *ange d'or* was designed.[23] The poem tells of the foundation of the Abbey of Joyenval, near Paris, in the thirteenth century, and it begins with the story of Clovis and the fleur-de-lis: "This is the way whereby three lily flowers were revealed to a certain hermit. . . ." The Clovis story is retold later in one of the early universal histories, the *Mer des histoires*. The edition printed in Paris in 1488 by Pierre le Rouge contains a full-page woodcut which depicts in detail the entire legend (fig. 11). The composition is divided into two parts: at the left is the dénouement in which Clovis is baptised by Bishop Remigius (St. Remi) at Reims on Christmas Day in the year 496, thus making as it were a Christian nation of the pagan Franks. On the right is the battle at Tolbiac (the site is a fifteenth-century invention), when Clovis defeated Caudat, king of the Alemani, by virtue of his new fleur-de-lis insignia. In the background above is the prelude: Queen Clotilde, who had been converted earlier, implores Clovis to abandon his pagan gods and take up Christ. This he does, after winning the battle; and later he is baptised at Reims with chrism sent down by a dove from heaven. This detail is shown in the upper right corner of the woodcut, together with the motif that we saw on the coin, an angel holding a shield with *France moderne*. Here a monk receives it and passes it on to Clovis to exchange for the three toads, which are to be seen on his breast.

The same story had also been told earlier, in 1371, by Raoul de Presles in the preface of his translation of St. Augustine's *Civitas Dei* into French, addressed to King Charles V. The best known manuscript was made in 1445 for Bishop Jean Chevrot of Tournai, counselor of Duke Philip the Good of Burgundy. Philip later acquired the manuscript, and today it is in the Bibliothèque royale in Brussels.[24] It has an original and unusually interesting title-page miniature (fig. 12). At the left, St. Augustine reads his book to eleven ecclesiastics and doctors, while at the right stands King Clovis, above whom in the sky are the dove with the consecrated oil and the angel bearing *France moderne* on a shield. François

Fig. 11. Mer des Hystoires *(Paris, 1488), woodcut depicting legends of King Clovis.*

Fig. 12. Cité de Dieu, *Brussels, Bibliothèque Royale, Ms 9015, frontispiece, fol. 1.*

Chatillon quite reasonably supposes that Raoul de Presles made a pilgrimage to Joyenval (which owned relics of Clovis's wife, the sainted Clotilde) to the Premonstrants, who were under the rule of St. Augustine. Here de Presles would have learned details of the Clovis story for his *City of God* preface.

In conclusion, I want to summarize my answers to the three main issues that scholarship has raised concerning the fleur-de-lis. In this endeavor I have tried to assemble the most important visual, art historical evidence available to art historians—much of it collected here for the first time.[25] 1) I believe that the fleur-de-lis as the heraldic charge of the kingdom of France evolved from the stylization of a flower. This flower, I believe, was the *Lilium candidum* and not the yellow flag iris (*Iris pseudoacorus*). 2) The emblem appears to have been adopted officially as the royal symbol of France by Louis VII as early as 1141, when he used it with compulsive abandonment on his official seal. 3) The fleur-de-lis in triplicate for the royal armorial shield was probably adopted for the first time in the decade before 1341, in connection with a legend. This said that God gave the insignia to Clovis, who became the first Christian king of France upon his baptism at Reims at the end of the fifth century.

Notes

*In converting the lecture into this somewhat shortened essay I have omitted a number of supportive examples of objects of art, but there is no change in content.

1. *Lilium francicum veritate historica, botanica, et heraldica illustratum* (Antwerp, 1658).
2. *Revue archéologique* 9 (1852):355–65.
3. Vol. 5 (1923), p. 2, cols. 1699 ff.
4. *Revue du moyen-âge latin* 11 (1955):89 ff.
5. *Speculum* 36 (1961):1 ff.
6. *Journal of the Society of Architectural Historians* 34 (1975):238 ff.
7. Romauld Bauerreis, *Arbor vitae* (Munich, 1928), p. 138.
8. A. de Gubernatis, *La mythologie des plantes* (1882), 2:201.
9. *Dictionarii . . . Petri Berchorii* (Venice, 1583), 2:408.
10. M. Lawrence, "Maria Regina," *Art Bulletin* 7 (1925):150 ff., fig. 19.
11. *Catalogue of Seals in the Department of Manuscripts, British Museum,* vol. 5 (1898), pl. VI, no. 18376.

12. J. Roman, *Manuel de sigillographie française* (1912), pl. III, 2.
13. Ibid., pl. IV, 1.
14. Bernard de Montfaucon, *Les monuments de la monarchie françoise* (Paris, 1729), 1:xxxiii.
15. Cf. n. 5 above.
16. Reproduced in J. Johnson, "The Tree of Jesse Window at Chartres," *Speculum* 36 (1961): opposite p. 11.
17. J. Lafaurie, *Les monnaies des rois de France* (1951), e.g., nos. 307, 307c, pl. XIV.
18. J. Porteous, *Coins in History* (1969), p. 123, fig. 131.
19. Cited in M. Lillich, "The Choir Clerestory Windows of La Trinité at Vendôme," *Journal of the Society of Architectural Historians* 34 (1975):248–49.
20. Ibid., fig. 7.
21. Ibid., fig. 8.
22. *Bulletin du Comité de la Langue . . . de la France* 4 (1857):239 ff.
23. Chatillon, "Lilia crescunt," pp. 89 ff.
24. MS. 9015–6.
25. For invaluable suggestions I wish to thank Dr. Adelaide Bennett of the Index of Christian Art, Princeton University, and Prof. Wesley O'Neill.

Comment

BY

François Bucher

These comments offer a catalogue of types of medieval representations of Nature, with the purpose of providing a background for Professor Koch's paper.

The medieval perception and representation of the physical world was more intricate and more subtly rubricated than all later approaches to the visible environment in the history of Western art. The classical, especially the Roman, use of plants and living beings in a non-symbolic context was shifted to the ornamental sphere, as in the capitals of Reims Cathedral and Altenberg with their botanically identifiable flora, or to the powerful portraits of Bamberg, Naumburg and, for instance, of Rudolf of Habsburg in the Dome of Speyer (c. 1258) which are suffused with idealized realism. Medieval landscapes *per se* are rare and far between. They were created for the Umayyad Mosque in Damascus by Byzantine artists (c. 715), they adorn the *Carmina Burana* of c. 1220 in Munich (Staatsbibl. Lat. 4660), King René's *Book of Love* (c. 1457) and, most splendidly, the *Très Riches Heures* presented to Duke Jean of Berry between the years 1413–16. Generalized landscapes are present in the Bayeux Embroidery and later in the works of some Italian artists such as Ambrogio Lorenzetti's frescoes in Siena of 1337–40. In addition there were many outdoor themes with and without figures in the painted cycles on the walls of castles, ecclesiastical palaces, and city halls, and above all of the burghers' houses. Illustrations of the chase were especially popular from the large fourth-century mosaics at Piazza Armerina to those in the Chambre du Cerf in the Avignonese Palace of the Popes.[1] Among the most engaging preserved outdoor scenes are those of about 1410 found in Torre dell'Aquila in the Trento, where the occupations of the months are transformed into frolicsome games of elegant courtiers. In spite of major losses of secular examples, these private, often lighthearted works were but a very small fraction of the total output of medieval art dealing with topics taken from nature. More usually the artists turned to selected aspects of the visible world to illustrate through them more central concerns ranging from salvation to political power.

In an earlier essay I listed some of these themes in which elements of nature as specific iconographic types clearly served to enrich the particular moral, political or symbolic ideas and endeavours of patrons.[2] The use of objects or living beings from the physical environment for a specific purpose falls into the following categories:

1. Didactic

a. Botanical sketches from Dioskurides of Anazarba's first-century compilation of plants to the botanically accurate, but more symbolic Mille Fleurs tapestries discussed by Robert A. Koch.[3]

b. Zoological themes ranging from the tense, abstract symmetry of animals in conflict in the Migration arts and in Hiberno-Saxon manuscripts to the pseudo-scientific *Physiologus* which spawned the bestiaries. The beasts are shown in conventionalized environments and the morally enlightening text demonstrates that they are instruments in the net of God's perfect scheme. Thus the Basilisk, which frizzles up humans by a mere glance, is conquered by the weasel because "God never makes anything without a remedy."[4] Functional zoological texts such as Frederick II's *De arte venandi cum avibus* with highly accurate images are even rarer than animal studies by some artists and sculptors such as Pisanello.

c. Geographical treatises and planimetric views, from those found in the books of the *Agrimensores* to the late thirteenth-century Hereford *Mappa Mundi* and panoramas in Gothic chronicles, are never more than theoretical or semi-accurate.

d. Medical and other scientific manuscripts use the human figure to illustrate anatomy, the setting of bones, bandaging, and the astrological influence of planets upon organs. Other, sometimes excellent, picture cycles deal with mining, bathing, building, chess, armour and other practical activities or devices.

2. Schemata

An extensive imagery, still largely unexplored by art history, is contained in tables and schemata which included hierarchies of observable facts, musical proportions, humours, elements, theological constructs, alchemical stages of enlightenment, health charts, and many others. Since their purpose is an abstract analysis of universal forces, laws or "facts," they offered the artist an opportunity for surprisingly lively and sometimes, I think, unsupervised pictorial comments. A complex but standardized example is offered by the early thirteenth-century stained glass cycle of the South transept rose in Lausanne Cathedral which includes humanoids living in distant regions of earth.[5]

3. Narrative

a. Most interesting are Calendar Landscapes or the Labors of the Months which were often attached to the zodiac. Frequently lacking in moral intent, they constitute the major visual source for the study of an unbiased medieval interpretation of immediate surroundings and of the complex stratification of society, proving, among other items, interest in and respect for the peasant.

b. An overwhelming number of religious, and fewer literary and historical narratives use nature mostly as a necessary prop. Exceptions to the standardization of specific themes are found in pictures of the Garden of Eden, for instance in Ferentillo, in the representation of David with allegorical personifications (Paris, Bibliotheca nationale Ps. Gr. 139), the ninth-century Utrecht Psalter and its copies, and some imperial portraits. Roman aerial perspective from a brown foreground to a blue distance or even an impressionistic background are reintroduced in Carolingian and in some Ottonian illuminations. In the fourteenth and fifteenth centuries exceptionally clear observations of gardens or panoramas begin to appear within iconographically fixed environments, as in the Rhenish *Hortus Conclusus* panels, and in the Italian religious pageants most splendidly exploited by Giotto, Francesco Traini and the sculptor Lorenzo Maitani in Padua, Florence, Pisa and Orvieto.

c. The visionary landscape was used for representations of the Heavenly City, the *Fons Vitae*, Ottonian Evangelists in ecstasy, the unearthly visions of St. John which led to the powerful Beatus manuscripts, and finally the strange visions in Hildegard of Bingen's *Liber Scivias* (Lucca, Bibliotheca Statale, c. 1220 A.D.).

4. Symbolic, Emblematic, Occult

A beginning of the exploration of medieval perception of nature as a vehicle for highly complex ideographs has been undertaken in J. Huizinga's and E. Panofsky's studies on the late Middle Ages.[6]

Innumerable representations of objects, ranging from birds to planets and from realistic renderings to nearly total abstraction such as in coats of arms or books dealing with the occult, have yet to be deciphered. A small lion hit by the tail of a comet shown in a 15th century single leaf woodcut in the National Gallery in Washington for instance, represents nothing less than the hoped-for demise of the House of Burgundy. The lore found in marginalia or figurated initials of manuscripts from the twelfth century onward contains precise and largely unexplored information on topics from simony to clerical homosexuality.[7]

The complexity of just one of these emblemata, the fleur-de-lis of France, is analyzed in the essay of R. A. Koch. How many layers of thoughtful emotions were triggered by the lily and its transferral from the realm of martyrs and saints and other religious iconography to the royal standard?[8] Or did the three lilies in the azure field of "France moderne" become as debased as a coin? Why was the lily chosen instead of the lion of Burgundy or the wolf of Orléans, or even the original animistic and alchemical toad which adorned the legendary armorial shield of Clovis before he replaced it with a lily? How deeply did the mystical emblem, which was often connected with the *arbor vitae*, color public reaction toward the rulers?

One final question must still be answered: How deeply did the constant submission of nature to a higher moral order hinder an unbiased analysis of visible phenomena? The creation, cosmography and the cycles of time were personified and subjected to God-given, geometrically perfect heavenly mechanics and the consonance of the music of the spheres. Dorothy Glass's "*In Principio*: The Creation in the Middle Ages" and Sonia Simon's "Carolingian Astronomical Illustrations"[9] show that the weight of symbolism and the trust in navigationally useless, anthropocentric stellar images, in short pictures which need not confirm physical evidence at all, may have prevented the need for widely based accurate observations. Surrounded by scientific emblemata, it is difficult for twentieth-century intellectuals to sympathize with the medieval view of man and nature as a complete microcosm existing in the center of the universe and embedded in the perfect design of God's Providence. In the last analysis, this is a cocky and not entirely unenviable anthropocentric stance.

In his recently published essay, "Jan van Eyck and Adam's Apple," James Snyder[10] proved that the fruit proffered to Adam by

Eve in the Ghent altar is neither a *malus* (apple), pomegranate, Sinaasappel (orange) nor a lemon as had been suggested, but is in fact the Portuguese citrus fruit *Pomum Adami* which van Eyck observed while on a diplomatic mission for Philip the Good to Portugal in 1428–29.

A medieval viewer might have felt uneasy about the botanical accuracy of the fruit. For in finally identifying Adam's Apple "scientifically" and thus making it a strictly Mediterranean fruit, van Eyck exemplified the growing conflict between faith and scientific observation which is, to this day, called reason. It was the tension between these two fundamentally different views of the world which was to destroy the sophisticated innocence governing the attitudes toward nature in medieval thought and visual arts.

Notes

1. For literary equivalents see Marcelle Thiébaux, "The Mediaeval Chase," *Speculum* 42 (1967): 260–74.

2. F. Bucher, "Medieval Landscape Painting," *Medieval and Renaissance Studies* 6 (1968): 119–70.

3. R. A. Koch, "Flower Symbolism in the Portinari Altar," *Art Bulletin* 46 (1964):70–77, and Adele Coulin Weibel, "Mille-fleurs in French Tapestries," *Detroit Institute of Arts Bulletin* 36 (1956–57).

4. T. H. White, *The Bestiary,* 12th ed., (New York, 1960), pp. 168–69.

5. Ellen Beer, *Die Rose der Kathedrale von Lausanne, und der kosmologische Bilderkreis des Mittelalters* (Bern, 1952). The humanoids shown are the Tetracolus, Ceffus, Pigmei, Cynomologi, Epiphagi, Sciapodes, Gangaridae, Satyri.

6. J. Huizinga, *The Waning of the Middle Ages* (London, 1924), and E. Panofsky, *Early Netherlandish Painting* (Cambridge, 1958).

7. Lilian M. Randall, *Images in the Margins of Gothic Manuscripts* (Berkeley, 1966).

8. Prudentius (c. 348–405) and Sigebert of Liège (c. 1030–1112) describe saints walking among lilies. Venantius Fortunatus (c.530–609) also characterizes the lily as the most outstanding flower. See Bucher, "Medieval Landscape Painting," pp. 123, 134–35.

9. Professor Sonia Simon's paper was among those read at the present

conference, "Nature in the Middle Ages," but not included in this volume.

10. J. Snyder, "Jan van Eyck and Adam's Apple," *Art Bulletin* 58 (1976): 511–15. This paper was among those read at the present conference, "Nature in the Middle Ages," but not included in this volume.

Aristotle's Concept of Nature: Avicenna and Aquinas

James A. Weisheipl, O.P.

The word "nature" in English today is used in all sorts of loose ways. Nature lovers think of the great outdoors, naturalists immediately think of minerals, plants or animals, while philosophers commonly think of some "universe" out-there, a meaning more or less synonymous with that of the Greek word κόσμος a beautiful appearance attractive to behold. The dictionary meaning refers to a thing's essential quality or innate character without explanation or examples. And lawyers today have a great deal to say, positively or negatively, about what is called "the natural law," without having much to say about what is "natural." All of these uses can be traced back to ancient usage, but none of them focuses on the precise philosophical meaning from which all other uses of the term derive. The ancient Greek philosophers, all the early Fathers of the Church, and the medieval scholastics were very much concerned with the precise meaning of the term "nature," precisely because they eventually had to discuss the two "natures" in Christ in theology. Renaissance humanists often distinguished between Nature with a capital "N," meaning God, and nature with a small "n," meaning the universe created by God. Strangely, even in this context the dynamic character of ancient usage was commonly accepted as well known to all those brought up in the scholastic tradition. Our own thoughts about nature have to a large extent been molded by the mechanistic philosophy predominant since the seventeenth century. It is hard for us to avoid thinking in clear and distinct mechanical terms. If we wish to appreciate what the word "nature" meant during the Middle Ages, however, we must put aside for the moment any mechanistic notions we have about the universe. We must go back to a richer philosophical language, one teeming with "principles," "causes," and ultimate goals. This philosophical language is difficult for us moderns to grasp, precisely because it is non-mechanistic and apparently foreign to our "scientific" minds.

In this paper we will attempt to reach back to a Greek conception of nature as it was clarified by Aristotle and then try to see what Avicenna and Aquinas made of it in the Middle Ages. Briefly, we will see that although both Avicenna and Aquinas accepted Aristotle's definition of nature and thought of themselves as faithful followers of Aristotle, it was Avicenna who failed completely to appreciate the Aristotelian conception, and ended by defending a real Platonism which was influential throughout the Middle Ages. Therefore in the thirteenth century we have again the radically different mentalities of Plato and Aristotle in a Christian arena.

The Greek word corresponding to "nature" is φύσις, from which we derive the English words "physics," "physical," "physician," and the like. In Greek antiquity, the word φύσις had a very precise meaning in a highly technical philosophical language. It meant "a *source* or *principle* from which movement and possession proceed." In the Latin Middle Ages, the word *natura*, or English "nature," also had a precise philosophical meaning derived from Greek thought. Sometimes the Greek word φύσις and the Latin *natura* were used in the static sense of "cosmos" (κόσμος) as we sometimes use the term "nature" today. But more often than not, something more is implied, namely, a rich source of dynamic activity and achievement, as when we say "Let nature take its course," or "The wound will heal by nature," meaning "by itself."

Considering the difficulties of modern readers of medieval literature, I would like to convey some idea of this precise sense of nature as the source, or origin, or principle of clearly recognizable movement and characteristics in every created thing. It has become difficult for us moderns to think in non-mechanistic terms, so as to be able to grasp the non-mechanical richness of Greek philosophy and the even richer philosophy of the Middle Ages. But even as foreigners of sorts, it is still possible to see how far our notion of nature has been impoverished, as it were, by a merely mechanistic outlook on the world.

In this paper I would like to do three things. First, I would like to explain something of Aristotle's philosophy of nature, because both Avicenna and Aquinas tried to be Aristotelians. Second, I would like to show that Avicenna and Aquinas differed in their Aristotelianism, and that Avicenna indeed was really a Platonist in his philosophy. And third, I would like to indicate some of the consequences of this difference for the thirteenth century. What I am about to present will not be easy to comprehend because it is philosophical and technical, but I shall try to keep it as simple as possible, even at the risk of over-simplifying.

I

First let us consider what Aristotle himself thought the word φύσις signified and what he himself tried to do in his natural philosophy. Briefly, Aristotle tried to restore to dignity the ancient, pre-Socratic quest for some rational explanation of the way things are in the world we live in. He tried to restore natural philosophy as a truly "scientific quest," in the face of Plato's opinion that such investigations were useless myth-making.

First let us be clear about our definitions. Aristotle was very much concerned about the meaning and origin of words. The word in question here is φύσις in Greek, or "nature" in English. One entire book of Aristotle's *Metaphysics* is really a philosophical lexicon in which the meanings of certain words are traced etymologically and philosophically. Discussing the word φύσις, Aristotle explains that the word originally meant "the genesis of growing things—the meaning which would be suggested if one were to pronounce the υ of φύσις long."[1] That is to say, the word is probably derived from φύω, which has υ long in most of its forms, so that the connotation of φύσις is that of a begetting process, specifically the process of growth. It is impossible to convey this sense in English in any one word, but in Latin it seems that *natura* originally signified *nativitas*, or "birth." In his *Encyclopedia of Religion and Ethics*, Hastings says, "Fundamentally *natura* signified 'birth' as in Terence (*Adelphi* 126, 902), that is, the process by which living objects come into being."[2] For Aristotle, then, φύσις originally meant the very *process* of growing. But very early in Greek thought, the word was applied to the *origin* of growing things. From this meaning it is an easy step to thinking of "nature" as the *principle* of *all* movement and rest, as Aristotle defines the term throughout his works: "Nature is the principle and cause of motion and rest in those things, and those things only, in which she inheres primarily as distinct from incidentally." This is the Loeb translation of a highly technical definition involving the distinctions *per se* and *per accidens*. *Per accidens* means 'incidental" or "concomitant" to what we are really talking about *per se*. Thus the Oxford translation by Hardie and Gaye of this same technical definition reads: "Nature is a source or cause of being moved and of being at rest in that to which it belongs primarily (*per se*) and not in virtue of a concomitant attribute (*per accidens*)."[3] In other words, we start with some definite characteristic (i.e., typical and normal) movement or achievement in mind and we apply the word φύσις to its origin, indicating that we are not concerned for the time being with what may incidentally be associated with it. For example, if a statue falls to the ground and breaks, it does so not because it is a statue by Michelangelo, but because it has weight and is made of breakable material. We are not concerned about what may be incidental to the point under discussion, but are concerned only with a specific natural motion and its *per se* principle or source, leaving aside everything that may be irrelevant to that motion and termination, such as, Who made it? Why? or any monetary value.

The wise men of Greece before Socrates were φυσιολόγοι; that is, they were concerned with φύσις as "the primary material out of which any natural object is made."[4] Aristotle notes that some have called it fire, others earth, others air, others water, others something else of the sort, and some named it more than one of these, and others all of these.[5] The important point is that the pre-Socratic search for the "nature" of things was a search for the active principle or source (ἀρχή) out of which all things were formed. It was not simply a search for the one and the many, but a search for the ultimate explanation of the cosmos in terms of nature, an *active* principle of movement and becoming. As a young man, Socrates himself was a φυσιολόγος in search of the ultimate principle of all physical things, but he soon despaired of ever finding any such principle and turned his quest to ethical values.[6]

Aristotle made a tremendous advance over the pre-Socratic φυσιολόγοι by respecting the evidence of the senses, that is, by inquiring about the source of things, or substance (οὐσία) as perceived in sense experience. For him, a tree is essentially and substantially a tree and not just one of the four elements making up a tree. The "man" we perceive in human experience is totally and substantially a man, and not just a juxtaposition of atoms or prior natures such as one of the four elements; nor is he a bio-chemical organization of genes, nervous systems and a brain capacity. When a man dies, a "substantial" change has taken place; his substance, his essence, his nature is no longer there. In other words, for Aristotle, the word φύσις belongs primarily to the total composite "man" and not to the anterior elements that are in him, or out of which he may be composed. Thus the total composite "man" essentially and substantially has a "nature" called "human," which is a primary and *per se* principle of motions and characteristics proper to man. That is, the word φύσις belongs primarily to the *form* which gives the substantial essence (οὐσία) to bodies, and not to one of the anterior elements postulated by the φυσιολόγοι.

The earliest philosophers wanted to restrict the term φύσις to one or more of the elements, but Empedocles, who was quoted by Aristotle on this point, acknowledged that men do in fact give the name φύσις even to the total composite.[7] It is really this latter sense of φύσις that Aristotle develops in his philosophy of nature. Consequently, he frequently attacked the pre-Socratics because they considered only the underlying *matter* to be "nature," or substance (οὐσία) and failed to distinguish between "first matter" (or *primary matter*) and "second matter," which is the total composite of matter and form.[8] The problem was that the pre-Socratics had been unable to explain the possibility of true substantial change, a concept denoted by the Greek word γένεσις. Aristotle was the first to recognize the reality of substances that could really change. That is, he was the first to explain the possibility of γένεσις, or "substantial" change, and thus recognize as true "substances" those which appeared to be such in human experience. This he did by perceiving the fundamental difference between potency and act, applying the word *potency* to the ultimate, radical possibility of change, called "matter," and the word *act* to the first, immediate actuality of that potency. He called this actuality 'form," or that which makes a thing to be what it is *by definition*. Aristotle's explanation of substantial change allowed him to justify and develop the more commonplace use of the term "nature" φύσις as the specifying form of bodies that manifest characteristic activities and appearances. But we must keep in mind that this substantial form of a thing is really a principle (ἀρχή), a dynamic source of characteristic behavior and properties, be they human or inhuman. It is "by an extension of meaning" from this primary sense of φύσις that every essence has come generally to be called "a nature."[9] Thus we can even talk about the "nature" of triangles, although triangles have no behavior whatever. St. Thomas calls this an extension of meaning "secundum quamdam metaphoram,"[10] that is, "something of a metaphor."

In Book Delta of the *Metaphysics*, Aristotle presents all of these distinctions without proof or elaboration. In that passage he is concerned simply with classifying the various meanings of the term φύσις and in pointing out its primary meaning. Aristotle's own position in the history of Greek thought, however, is clearly marked out by this passage we have been examining. It was mainly in Books 2 and 8 of the *Physics* that he fully justified and elaborated his conception of nature as an intrinsic principle, either active (formal) or passive (material), of movement and rest.

In a famous passage in the *Laws,* Plato accused his predecessors and contemporaries of impiety and of leading young men away from the gods.[11] All other philosophers, he says, teach that this beautiful universe, the regularity of celestial movements, and the human soul arise "not because of mind, nor because of any god, nor by art, but as we may say by *nature* and *chance*."[12] Even the playwright Aristophanes had occasion to refer to this last state of affairs, for in his play *The Clouds* we read, "Zeus is dethroned and Vortex (δίνη) reigns in his stead."[13] Plato observed that all things which come about in the universe are the result either of art (τέχνη), nature (φύσις), or chance (τύχη).[14] But the ancient φυσιολόγοι, and even Plato's own contemporaries, attributed the origin of the universe and all its phenomena to "nature" (φύσις), which was thought of as a blind, material element operating by chance. Plato then asks, how it was that "nature" in the first place acquired movement and force to produce the order of the universe? How, he asks, can soul (ψυχή) be the result of material φύσις, since intelligence must be anterior in order to direct growth and order?[15] If φύσις means "the first source" (ἀρχή), then the term should not be applied to fire, air, or earth, but to Soul (ψυχή).[16] For Plato it is Soul (God) which is the first source of all being and becoming, the ruler of the heavens, the law-giver.[17] The ancient philosophers who attributed all phenomena to "nature" were accused by Plato of derogating from the rights of God, who is the true Nature, unseen by the senses of the body, but perceived by the intellect.[18] In his explanation of the material world, Plato gave to art a preeminence over nature and chance. That is to say, Plato insisted that the material universe is a product of the art of God. And even Aristotle himself employed this explanation in his early work *De philosophia*, where he represents the world as produced "by the very perfect art of God."[19]

Plato, however, did not use the term φύσις consistently throughout his works, for sometimes he opposed two classes of being, φύσις and intelligence,[20] and sometimes he attributed the traditional role of φύσις to Soul, maintaining that the use of the term to designate material elements must be absolutely condemned.[21] In fact, however, it must be admitted that Plato did not develop a doctrine of 'nature"; rather, he replaced the prevailing theory of nature with a theory of Soul.[22] His concern was to show that all material reality proceeds from divine intelligence, which necessarily must be anterior to the world. Further, in the course of developing his arguments against his adversaries, he argued that all corporeal movement without exception depends upon the influence and direction of the Soul, which permeates space.[23] Furthermore, both in the *Republic*[24] and in the *Timaeus*,[25] Plato insisted that the philosophy of nature can be no more than a "likely story," deserving only of opinion (δόξα) and belief, but not science (ἐπιστήμη).[26] In other words, Plato denied the status of true 'scientific" knowledge to any theory of the natural world. For him, ultimate understanding of the phenomenological world was to be sought in mathematics and dialectics, which alone deserve the name of "science." Hence we can say that for Plato, "nature" is not the primary concept in the explanation of the physical world or of physical reality, but rather the divine Soul, which produces the world and directs movement by *art*—the art of emanation, reflection, and participation.

Undoubtedly Aristotle had in mind Book 10 of the *Laws* when he developed his own doctrine of 'nature" in Book 2 of the *Physics*. The threefold division of causes into nature, art, and chance, which was Plato's point of departure for attacking his adversaries, is also Aristotle's starting point for rehabilitating the naturalist theories of the φυσιολόγοι in the face of Plato's criticism. Whereas Plato, insisting on the priority of Soul, had rejected the idea of nature and attributed most of the characteristics of φύσις to Soul, Aristotle tried to maintain *both* the priority of Soul and the reality of "nature" as a primary, spontaneous source of characteristic movement and rest.

The Aristotelian conception of "nature" must be understood, therefore, in contrast to both art and chance. We have already seen that this tripartite division was commonplace at the time of Plato. By art, Aristotle meant any production by human intelligence, or anything produced by the mind acting upon reality.[27] The term encompasses not only pictures, statues, machines, and other works of human craftsmanship, but every result of human interference, such as pushing, pulling, throwing, twirling, holding, and so forth. In other words, a stone thrown into the air would not be considered to move upwards *naturally,* but to move as the result of art (τέχνη). Admittedly, not every human action on the physical world can properly be called "artistic," or "intelligent," in Aristotle's sense. One need only understand that there are phenomena in the world that *can be accounted for* as the work of man. Basically it is a question of giving a rational account of motion, and of observing that some motions can be accounted for by human activity.

Besides these activities, however, there are many other phenomena in the world that are the result of mere chance (τύχη), or accident. Chance is the irrational element in the world. After a chance event has occurred, the phenomena can be explained rationally as the concurrence of such and such a factor, usually two or more. But the event itself, the accident, is unintended, unexpected, unpredictable. Just as in human experience many things happen merely by chance, so too in the physical world many events are the result of two factors, each of which has its own history. But every result of chance presupposes factors that have an individual history, a make-up and intelligibility proper to each. That is to say, every chance event presupposes *nature.* Everything incidental or concomitant and accidental, everything *per accidens*, presupposes something *per se*, something intended, rational, and *given* in the world. That ultimate "givenness," that ultimately intended and rational drive is what Aristotle calls "nature" (φύσις). In other words, once we have excluded everything that can be explained by art or by chance, we are still left with phenomena that can be explained in no other way than by"nature," some source which is ultimately *given* in human experience. This "ultimately given" in human experience is what is studied in natural philosophy, sometimes called *scientia naturalis.*

That is to say, all these phenomena we call "natural" in the universe can be traced back to some ultimate and primary principle we call the "form" of the thing, the "nature" of the thing. This "form" is an active, dynamic *source* of what is actually observed in human experience. Besides "form," however, we can and must recognize the potentiality for form. This potentiality we can call "matter" (or ὕλη). Thus for Aristotle the word "nature" can be used in two senses. In the sense of "form," it is active, dynamic, and spontaneous. It explains what is specific, characteristic, and formally recognizable in different natures we observe in the world. But there is also another sense of φύσις, as when we apply it to what is potentially so, or material. In other words, even when we have excluded everything that comes about by human art or by chance, there are not only "formal" principles of motion toward a term and the possession of that term, but also the real "ability" (material capacity) to have that form, as the seed and the ovum are only potentially a man before they are united in the embryo. That "ability" or "potentiality" can also be called "natural" when it specifically belongs to the thing under consideration.

In the Middle Ages, the scholastics developed to a considerable extent this twofold meaning of the word "nature" as an active and as a passive principle. "Nature" as matter, or *natura secundum materiam,* signified not only the pure potentiality of first matter, but also all passivities of bodies which require a natural agent to actualize them. These too can be studied and understood as proper to each body. "Nature" as form, or *natura secundum principium formale,* signified the active and spontaneous source of all characteristic properties and behavior; ultimately this active source (or principle) was considered to be the so-called "substantial form" which functions through active qualities, such as hot and cold, heavy and light, dry and moist, etc. In all scholastic terminology, nature regarded as "matter" is equivalent to *principium passivum, receptivum,* and *materiale,* while nature regarded as "form" is equivalent to *principium activum* and *formale.* This equivalence is consistently observed not only by authors of the thirteenth century, notably by St. Thomas and St. Albert, but also by authors of the fourteenth and later centuries.[28] Everyone accepted Aristotle's definition of the term "nature" as a principle of motion and rest, and everyone knew that in its formal sense it is an active, spontaneous, given source of classifiable activities and properties. In the Middle Ages, nature was not thought of as a machine, but as a principle that can be studied and understood rationally in a scientific way.

St. Thomas lays down the general principle that natural bodies have within themselves an innate principle of movement precisely to the extent to which they have motion: inasmuch as they spontaneously *move*, they have an *active* or formal principle. And inasmuch as they must *be moved*, they have the *passive* principle, which is matter.[29] Experience alone can indicate whether bodies act spontaneously or are being acted upon by an external force. The study of such principles was called natural philosophy, or the science of nature. It was taught in all the universities in Europe and every schoolboy knew Aristotle's definition of "nature" by heart—though, of course, not every school boy understood the full implications of Aristotle's philosophy of nature.

II

Much of medieval thought was molded by the thought of Avicenna, whose works came into the Latin West in the twelfth century. These works were translated into Latin at the same time as the translations of Aristotle's own writings came into the West from Greek and Arabic. It was all part of "the new learning" that excited Latin scholasticism and molded its thought about God, man, and the universe.

Avicenna in his *Sufficientia*[30] and Algazel in his paraphrase *Maqâcid el-falâcia*[31] (both of which were translated in the twelfth century) propound the theory that in natural movement the "form" is the *mover* of the body which it informs. That is, Avicenna, followed in a fuller way by Averroës, thought that the form is the mover (*motor coniunctus*) accompanying the body which it moves. That is to say, if "nature" taken strictly and formally applies primarily to *form*, then substantial form ought to be the primary cause, or "mover," responsible for the body's activity. Modern historians of medieval science often attribute this view to Aristotle himself. But the Aristotelian answer to this view is obvious: If the natural form moves the body which it informs, then what is the difference between living and non-living things? For Aristotle and St. Thomas no such distinction can be drawn in non-living things between form as "mover" and body as "moved," for each non-living body is a quantified whole which is infinitely divisible, having no "first" which can possibly be the "mover". But it is only by one actual part moving another actual part that living organisms can exercise self-motion.[32]

It is important to note that for Aristotle, "nature" is only an active *source* of movement; it is nothing more than a *source*, a *principle*, an (ἀρχή). It is not an *efficient cause* of the body's natural motion, whether that motion be growth, decay, alteration, or simple local motion. This distinction is a difficult one to grasp, even for us, but it is of fundamental importance both for us and for the ancients, because much of medieval physics depends upon it. If nature as a "form" is also an efficient cause or self-mover (a *motor coniunctus*) accompanying the body it moves, then there is no way to explain the difference between living and non-living bodies. By definition, a living body is one that moves itself by means of its parts; it is, by definition, a self-mover, an efficient cause of *some* of its motions, notably of walking, flying, swimming, crawling, and other similar motions where one part moves another. It is characteristic of all animals that they can move themselves from one place to another. But a non-living thing simply moves *of* itself and not *by* itself. A stone simply falls to the ground, if there is no obstacle; it does not move itself to the ground. It is not a self-mover. A non-living thing, such as a stone, simply has no *first part* by which that part could possibly be the first mover or efficient cause of its motion. Further, every material thing is continuous; that is, it is quantitatively divisible into an infinite number of divisible parts, none of which is the first or ultimate part. Whatever is moved must be moved by another, but it is impossible to account for the movement by an infinity of firsts or by the absence of a first; therefore non-living things cannot move themselves.[33] For Aristotle as well as for St. Thomas, the "form" is not the mover, but is only the *source* of necessary and spontaneous movement. The whole matter is succinctly expressed by St. Thomas when he says:

> Just as other accidents follow upon the substantial form, so does being in place, and consequently motion toward that place; not however in such a way that the natural form is the mover (*motor*), but the mover is the generator which begot such a form upon which that motion follows.[34]

It is precisely in this distinction between matter and form that one can see most clearly the different conception of Aristotle's φύσις expressed by St. Thomas and Avicenna. For St. Thomas, matter and form are not two things making up a third, but simply passive and active principles of one single composite. For Thomas, matter and form are not two *quods* (things, each with its own existence), but two *quos* (principles, neither of which has existence of itself). Further, he held that each natural body is an *unum per se*, an undivided unity, having only one existence, namely, the existence (or *esse*) of the composite. For Avicenna, on the other hand, and for his many followers in the Middle Ages, matter and form are two things, two *quods*, two partial substances somehow making up a thing, each having its own peculiar existence. His was a pre-Cartesian Cartesianism, which has continued to plague Aristotelianism throughout its long history. For Avicenna, therefore, the form of an inanimate body can be called a "mover" of the body it accompanies. Even Duns Scotus, following Avicenna, describes nature as an active principle which, in a sense, moves itself to activity.[35] The common example he gives is hot water in the process of cooling off: the natural form of water moves the water to cool in the absence of heat.[36] Such a conception of nature as an efficient cause of natural motion is possible only by conceiving form as a reified thing, a *quod* in its own right, a part having an actual existence and activity of its own. This is not Aristotle's concept of "nature" as form. Nor Aquinas's. But much of medieval thought in physics, metaphysics, and theology depends on Avicenna's view of nature as an active source of self-movement. The view of St. Thomas is very different. For Thomas, "The natural form is not the motor, but the motor (efficient cause) is the generator, which gives such a form upon which such motion follows."[37] Once that nature is in existence because of some efficient cause, then it does whatever comes naturally to it spontaneously, immediately (*statim*), and automatically (*in promptu*), provided there is no obstacle. Contrary to the opinion of many modern historians of medieval science, Aristotle and Aquinas did not require a resisting medium to be overcome for the possibility of motion.[38] Nature as form simply acts spontaneously whether there is a resisting medium or not.

The first basic difference, then, between Avicenna and Aquinas concerning Aristotle's notion of nature is that Avicenna conceives the form of bodies as an efficient cause responsible for the natural movement of bodies. For Aquinas, on the contrary, the form of bodies is not an efficient cause, but only a principle *by which* bodies move naturally and spontaneously, the efficient cause of that motion being outside that body, namely, the agent which produced it in the first place.

Here we must observe carefully that for St. Thomas, the animal, which is the efficient cause of its self-movement, is a self-mover only with regard to certain kinds of motion. There are other motions, such as falling down, or growing up, or even the beating of the heart, for which the animal is not responsible (that is, not an efficient cause). All such motions are natural in the primary sense of active and formal; they are spontaneously given in nature. And all of these must be brought into existence *in the first place* by another, the true efficient cause, which ultimately is God, the First Mover.

This, then, is the first peculiarity of Avicenna's notion of nature. He conceives "form" as an active efficient cause accompanying the body it moves, giving it the power to move itself. But this position fails to account for the difference between living and non-living things. This is a direct consequence of Avicenna's conception of "form" as a *res*, a thing having *esse* in its own right. This peculiarity of Avicenna's natural philosophy indicates a deeper and more radical difference between Avicenna and St. Thomas. This second difference lies in their explanations of substantial change in the world of nature.

The pre-Socratic φυσιολόγοι always had a problem regarding the possibility of substantial change. It is the problem of γένεσις, the problem of coming-into-being and passing-away. How can one substance become another kind of substance? How is it possible for water to become air, or a non-living thing become living? Either the form of the second substance already exists in the first or it does not. If it already exists, then it does not *become* a new thing: *quod est, non fit.* If, on the other hand, it does not yet exist in the first, then where does it come from? It cannot come from itself, for then it would already be; and it cannot come from nothing, for from nothing, nothing can come: *ex nihilo, nihil fit.* Aristotle solved this ancient dilemma with his famous distinction between potency and act, whereby the new form is seen to exist only potentially in the old.[39] In order for the potential form to become actual in the new, there is required an efficient cause actualizing the potentiality of matter.

Avicenna faced the same problem,[40] but he never grasped Aristotle's solution embedded in the concept of the pure potentiality of prime matter. For Avicenna, natural agents can only *dispose* the matter of the subject to be capable of receiving the new form. But from whence comes this new form? Avicenna could see no way out but to postulate a separated *dator formarum*, a giver of forms. This *dator formarum,* for Avicenna, was an immaterial substance, the tenth intelligence in the emanation of all intelligences from God, which somehow instilled or implanted a new form in matter already disposed.[41] There is no such thing as a *dator formarum* in the whole of Aristotle's doctrine. It was invented by Avicenna to explain, among other things, the possibility of substantial change in nature. Many Christians identified this *dator formarum* with God in their inability to explain substantial change. In other words, for Avicenna, the natural agency of fire is sufficient to dispose water to become warmer and warmer. At a precise moment in time, when the water was sufficiently hot, the *dator formarum* would infuse into the water the new form of air to replace the form of water, thus producing a substantial change. As Avicenna points out in his *Metaphysics,*[42] natural agents do nothing more than dispose a substance to be able to receive the new substantial form from the giver of all forms, the *dator formarum*.[43]

This, however, is not the only function of the *dator formarum* in the Latinized philosophy of Avicenna. It is also the "agent intellect" by which the human mind knows all reality.[44] This agent intellect is immaterial and separated from all matter, and therefore one for all mankind. The individual human mind, while capable of knowing all reality, of itself has no form or concept of anything. The new form or concept is infused in the mind by the "agent intellect" when the mind is disposed toward it and therefore in some way conjoined to it. In other words, just as Avicenna was unable to explain substantial changes in nature, so he was unable to explain intellectual abstraction in knowledge. According to Avicenna, human teachers and books can only dispose the mind to be receptive of new concepts from the *dator formarum*, the "agent intellect." It was Avicenna's basic inability to explain how the potential can become actual that made him postulate an extrinsic *dator formarum* to explain the works of nature.[45] Many Christians, including William of Auvergne, later bishop of Paris, and Roger Bacon, identified this agent intellect with God, the First Light "who illumines every man who comes into this world" (John 1:9). Such a Christian conception of Avicenna's teaching was compatible, in a way, with St. Augustine's theory of divine illumination. This is the kind of adaptation that Gilson has called an *Augustinisme avicennisant* in his various writings.

For St. Thomas, there is no need for a *dator formarum* in order to explain knowledge or substantial change. For him, both are simply the work of nature. Just as each man has his own "possible intellect" by which he thinks, so each man has his own "agent intellect" by which he can abstract and think. These are two powers of the human soul (*potentiae animae*), and they are the work of nature as an active, formal principle within man, from which necessarily and immediately these two powers flow, as all other proper attributes. The "agent intellect," which is an active power in man, illumines the world of experience whereby the mind can perceive the universal truths found in experience. For Thomas, the mind, or intellect by which we think, (the *intellectus possibilis*), is basically a passive power of the human soul, just as the eye is a passive power of the animal soul. And just as the objects of vision are actualized by physical light, so objects of the mind are actualized by intellectual light, that is, by the agent intellect (the *intellectus agens*). When the eye sees, the visible object is actually seen. So too when the mind knows, the intelligible object is actually known. There was no need, either for St. Thomas or for Aristotle before him, for a separated *dator formarum* (or agent intellect) to explain human knowledge.

Similarly, in the case of natural events, Thomas's view was that fire is sufficient in itself not only to dispose water to its boiling point, but even to the point of becoming another substance, namely, air. There was no need for him to invoke a *dator formarum,* since nature itself can be credited with substantial changes—real efficient causality—in the world. The great irony of Avicenna's view is that he conceives "nature" as an efficient cause of the body's own motion, and yet refuses to allow "nature" to be an efficient cause of changing another body. Consequently the second point of difference between Avicenna and Aquinas is that Avicenna explains all substantial changes in terms of a *dator formarum*, a celestial force existing apart from nature, while Thomas explains them in terms of "nature" as an active source of natural motion and an efficient cause of substantial changes.

The third point of difference between Avicenna's and Aquinas's conceptions of "nature" may be seen in their treatments of the problem of determinism and indeterminism. For Avicenna, the whole of reality, immaterial and material, emanates from the First Intelligence in a necessary hierarchical procession from the highest to the lowest by a necessity of nature (*necessitate naturae*), and the lowest is governed in all its activities by the higher.[46] That is to say, just as the *dator formarum*, the lowest of the celestial intelligences, bestows substantial forms in the world of nature, so too all natural activities are guided by the position of the stars and higher intelligences. There is no room in Avicenna's universe for *chance events* as far as the influence of the stars is concerned. There is even a serious question as to what man's freedom of will entails in Avicenna's teaching. Moslem fatalism played too strong a role in his whole philosophy to allow for true freedom of the human spirit, but I do not wish to discuss this point here. My main concern is Avicenna's understanding of the world of inanimate nature and man's place in it.

In Aristotle's natural philosophy, chance (τύχη) plays a most important role, because φύσις, as he understood it, is always determined to one effect, the same effect, the same behavior. Nature, for Aristotle, is "determined," "directed" or "intended" for a definite end (final cause), which it actually does attain "for the most part" (*ut in pluribus*) as we observe from experience. Chance, however, is precisely that event in the universe which is not and cannot be *intended* by any nature. The monstrous birth, for example, is not intended by any nature; it is the freak phenomenon when things do not go right in nature. Thus, for Aristotle, the chance event cannot have a *per se* cause; it is not the type of thing that can be intended by nature. If it were intended, it would be "natural" and happening "for the most part," according to Aristotle's definition of the term.[47] The chance event is beyond the intentionality of nature (*praeter intentionem naturae*). The coincidence of two or more natural intentionalities produces the chance event, the accident of nature, the unexpected, the unintended. Aristotle was not a determinist in the sense of being a fatalist in his natural philosophy. A universe without chance events would not be an Aristotelian universe, but a Stoic or Moslem universe or possibly a mechanical universe. It would certainly not be the universe as Aristotle saw it.

For Avicenna, however, terrestrial events are ruled by the stars. What may appear to be a chance event in the sublunar world is foreseen and produced by the souls of celestial bodies and their intelligences.[48] For Avicenna, the nature and position of the stars impose an inescapable physical causality on the whole sublunar world to such an extent that it is difficult to see how even the free will of man escapes its all-embracing determinism.

That the stars exert some causality in the world cannot be denied, since the sun and moon are numbered among the stars. St. Thomas observed that the sun affects the activity of all plants and animals and even held that it causes the generation of smaller living things through spontaneous generation; in the same way, the moon causes the tides, and certain conjunctions of the stars affect the atmosphere and thereby even some of man's bodily disposition. But for Thomas this is still the realm of nature.[49] Nature as a passive principle is susceptible to certain influences of higher forces, and consequently what is produced is "natural." But even within the whole realm of the physical universe, many events are contingent and even come about by chance. St. Thomas, as every Christian must, specifically exempts the human will from celestial influences, but he goes further and insists on the reality of chance events in the universe. He held that there are many chance occurrences that cannot be accounted for by the stars or even by higher created intelligences. These are all those future contingent events that depend solely on the free will of God in his divine providence.[50]

In other words, the third difference between Avicenna's and Thomas Aquinas's conceptions of nature is that Avicenna's universe is fatalistic and deterministic, allowing no room for chance occurrences, whereas Aquinas taught that the indeterminism of chance is the spice of nature, allowing natures to be what they are and to operate as they are determined to operate, but with the door left open to chance.

Briefly, then, we may say that both Avicenna and Aquinas accepted Aristotle's definition of "nature" as a principle of motion and rest within bodies. They both acknowledged "form" as an internal, dynamic principle of movement. They both acknowledged "matter" as an internal, passive principle of movement and rest. But they both held radically different views of the natural universe. Avicenna makes the active form an *efficient cause*, a self-mover, in natural movement. Aquinas makes the active form a mere *principle* of spontaneous motion. Avicenna requires a *dator formarum* to account for substantial change. Aquinas rejects outright the need for any *dator formarum*, and holds that natural bodies are capable of changing other bodies substantially. Finally, Avicenna's natures are governed by fate, while Aquinas allows both nature and chance to operate in the world of creatures. In other words, we might say that Avicenna underestimated the power of "nature" in the universe and attributed its main functions to celestial forces, whereas Aquinas acknowledged the dynamic role of nature as the instrument of God. For Thomas, God works through true secondary causes. If the secondary cause is a necessary cause or principle, such as "nature," then whatever results from it is truly necessary and determined. But if the secondary cause is free, such as man's free choice, then whatever comes from it is free and undetermined. Thomas does not allow the intermediary of "Fate" to govern the universe by supranatural forces. The whole realm of terrestrial and celestial bodies constitutes the total reality of "nature" and its laws. Thus in Thomas's universe there is no room for a goddess called "Fate" intermediate between God and his creatures.

These three major differences between Avicenna and Aquinas could be multiplied and expanded if we were to include psychology, ethics, and metaphysics within our scope. But the differences which we have considered in this paper are fundamental in their significance and cannot be fully appreciated without considering also their implications.

III

The contrast between Avicenna and Aquinas in the Middle Ages is basically the contrast between Plato and Aristotle in antiquity. There is irony in this pairing, because both Avicenna and Aquinas thought they were commenting on Aristotle. The history of medieval thought is full of commentators on Aristotle whose inspiration came from Avicenna and his neo-Platonism, rather than from the truer Aristotelianism of Averroës, Albert the Great, and Thomas Aquinas. It is perhaps not necessary to do more than mention here the phenomenon of so-called "Latin Averroism"—perhaps better called an "Averroist Aristotelianism"—in which even Averroës is seen to depart sometimes from the sound principles of Aristotle.

It is more important in this paper to see that Avicenna's influence in the West was the influence of Avicennian Platonism in the Middle Ages. This can be seen most clearly in three respects within the realm of natural philosophy.

First of all, in Avicenna's Platonism there is a bifurcation, or separation of man from nature—a pre-Cartesian dualism between spirit and matter, between mind and body. The intelligence of man illuminated by the separated agent intellect is somehow set apart and divided from nature. There is, as it were, a philosophical gulf between man's Ego on the one hand and "nature" on the other. Man is somehow a mere spectator in the world of nature and not really a part of it. Rather, his intellect belongs to the realm of the *dator formarum*, which is distinct from "nature." In Avicenna there is always a gulf between celestial forces (of which the *dator formarum* is a part) and the forces of individual natures moving and acting in a determined way. The heavens are governed by fate, and the stars rule the activity of nature. The important point is that Avicenna draws a line between the celestial and terrestrial world and places man partly in the celestial. For Aquinas, on the other hand, man is part of nature and continuous with it. There is no bifurcation between the celestial and terrestrial; there is no *dator formarum* to explain natural changes in the terrestrial world, and earthly changes are not explained by the stars. For Aquinas, nature is simply the principle of motion and rest in material bodies; and there are many kinds of motion, just as there are many kinds of natures both active and passive, formal, and material. Thomas does not deny that there are intelligences governing celestial motions, but these intelligences belong to the realm of metaphysics, and hence their reality must be demonstrated in natural philosophy. The realm of nature for Aquinas is in a certain sense autonomous and real—and man is part of it. In other words, for Aquinas, man's nature is continuous with the realm of the world, animate and inanimate, even though he occupies a unique part of it.

Second, Avicenna's bifurcation, or division of man from nature, rests on a bifurcation within man himself. It rests on the questionable gulf within man between his body and his mind. By denying that the agent intellect is a power within man's soul (a *potentia animae*), he was logically compelled to introduce a duality of mind and body. Such a dualism, of course, strikes at the very heart of man's unity. For Aquinas, as for Aristotle, man is an *unum per se*, but a highly complex one. The complexity of human nature for Aquinas is radically unique. As soon as the human soul informs the embryo, a most extraordinary unity is achieved, a unity of a unique *esse* with a unique, individualized matter as the principle of individuation. But the *esse* in question is more than just an existence; it is a *rational existence* with all that this implies, namely, a spiritual intellect and a free will. Man is not one of the separated substances of which Avicenna speaks. He is rather a unique creature composed of a rational intellect and a free will concretized in a unique body by a unique *esse*, which belongs to the individual person. All of this is summed up in his human *person*, his personal existence as a man distinct from all other men. The uniqueness of an individualized, personalized *esse*, which is the existing man in the world of nature, is in one sense uniquely simple: undivided in itself and distinct from everyone else. But in another sense it is highly complex, and its historical development to maturity is also complex, taking place over a long period of time. Such a conception of the concrete man recognizes the dignity of the individual human person. Two elements are involved in this conception: (1) the recognition of man as specifically distinct from both animals and angels, and (2) the recognition of the unique *esse* by which man exists in reality and for all eternity. This Thomistic conception of man is very different from Avicenna's Platonic conception, according to which the divine element in man is the light of the *intellectus agens* coming to him at the end of a long and necessary emanation of intellects from the unity of God, conceived as the First Intellect.

A third consequence of the topic we have been considering is really a corollary of what we have already seen. It has to do with the *way* human life should be lived to the full in order to reach true human happiness, which for all the philosophers consists in some kind of contemplation. Contemplation for Avicenna consists in an escape from the world of "nature" to the light of the agent intellect. But for Thomas Aquinas contemplation consists in seeing *through* "nature" to the Author of nature. Platonic mysticism is an escape from the materiality of nature, a flight from the world. But Aquinas sees the sanctity of all nature and embraces it as a means to God. The flight from nature is, in Aquinas's view, unrealistic, for man cannot escape from nature; he *is* a nature and he belongs to the world of nature. If such is the case, the view of human nature offered by St. Thomas is clearly more realistic and more inclusively human and personal than that offered by the Platonism of Avicenna.

In the Middle Ages there was an axiom, of uncertain origin, accepted by everyone: *Opus naturae est opus intelligentiae.* "The work of nature is the work of intelligence." Both Platonists and Aristotelians could accept the axiom, but each party saw it from different points of view. The Platonically minded philosophers would by-pass the works of nature to contemplate the divine intelligence, which alone for them was really real. The Aristotelian minded philosophers, on the other hand, would embrace nature as the work of God and the means of attaining Him. There can be no question that the full Aristotelian concept of "nature" as the internal, dynamic principle of all natural phenomena was obscured from Avicenna by his essentially Platonistic suppositions, but was clearly grasped by Aquinas, who consequently never lost sight of man's place in the world of nature.

Notes

1. Aristotle *Metaph.* 5. 4. 1014b17-18.

2. *Hastings' Encyclopedia of Religion and Ethics* (Edinburgh, 1917), vol. 9, s.v. "Nature."

3. Aristotle *Phys.* 2. 1. 192b21-23. This definition is repeated more or less complete in various works of Aristotle: *Phys.* 3. 1. 200b12-1; 8. 3. 253b5-6; 8. 4. 254b16-17; *De caelo* 1. 2. 268b16; 3. 2. 301b17-18; *De anima* 2. 1. 412b15-17; *De gen. animal.* 2. 1. 735a3-4; *Metaph.* 6. 1 .1025b20-21; 9. 8. 1049b8-10; 12. 3. 107017-8; *Ethic. Nic.* 6. 4. 1140a5-6; *Rhet.* 1. 10. 1369a35-b1.

4. Aristotle *Metaph.* 5. 4. 1014b27-28.

5. Ibid. 1014b32-35.

6. See Plato *Phaedo* 96E-100C.

7. H. Diels, *Die Fragmente der Vorsokratiker,* 5th ed. (Berlin, 1934-38), 31 B. frag. 8. For an exegesis, see John Burnet, *Early Greek Philosophy*, 4th ed. (London, 1945), pp. 205-6, n. 4.

8. Aristotle *Metaph.* 1. 3. 983b6-19; 1. 7. 988a18-22; 7. 3. See also St. Thomas, *In VII Metaph.*, lect. 2, nn. 1281-93, where he develops this idea very fully.

9. Aristotle *Metaph.* 5. 4. 1015a11–12.

10. St. Thomas, *In V Metaph.*, lect. 5, n. 823.

11. Plato *Laws* 10. 884A–913D.

12. Ibid., 889B.

13. Aristophanes *Clouds* 828, the idea being that Zeus no longer reigns supreme by his art, but now something belonging to creatures is to be credited for its activity. See also Diogenes Laertius *Lives* 9.31–34, trans. and ed. by A. R. Caponigri (Chicago, 1969), pp. 69–79; H. Diels, *Doxographi Graeci* (Berlin, 1929), pp. 142–43; and J. Burnet, *Early Greek Philosophy*, pp. 338–39, 341–47.

14. Plato *Laws* 10.888E. Plato implies that this division was employed also by his adversaries; cf. also 889C.

15. Ibid., 891B–982A.

16. Ibid., 892C.

17. Ibid., 898D-E.

18. Ibid., 898D-E.

19. V. Rose, *Fragmenta*, Bibl. Teubneriana (Leipzig, 1886), frag. 21.

20. Cf. *Apologia* 22C.

21. Plato *Laws* 10.892B–C.

22. A. Mansion, *Introduction à la Physique Aristotélicienne,* 2nd ed. (Louvain, 1945), p. 83.

23. Plato *Laws* 10.899D ff.

24. Plato *Republic* 7.522A ff.

25. Plato *Timaeus* 27D ff.

26. J. A. Weisheipl, "The Concept of Scientific Knowledge in Greek Philosophy," *Mélanges à la Mémoire de Charles De Koninck* (Québec, 1968), pp. 487–507.

27. Plato seems to have been the first to apply the word "art" to the activity of divine intelligence in the world. But in the present context, which is the context of human language, Aristotle means to discuss only the work of human intelligence.

28. See, for example, St. Thomas, *In II Phys.,* lect. 1, n. 4; *De pot.*, q.5, a.5; q.5, a.5 ad 12; *Sum. cont. Gent.,* III, c. 23; *In I De caelo*, lect. 16, n. 13; III, lect. 7, nn. 5–9; *In VII Metaph.*, lect. 8, n. 1442z; Gualteri Burlaei, *In Physicam Arist. Expositio et Quaest.*, II (Venice, 1501), fol. 36ra.

29. St. Thomas, *In II Phys.,* lect. 1, n. 4. Since, in the last analysis, the whole of nature must be brought into existence and directed by God, "tota irrationalis natura comparatur ad Deum sicut instrumentum ad agens principale," as Thomas frequently reminds us (e.g., *Sum. theol.* I–II, q.1, a.2; also I, q.22, a.2 ad 4; q.103, a.1 ad 3; I–II, q.6, a.1 ad 3; *In IV Sent.*, dist.5, q.1, a.2; *Sum. con. gent.*, I, c. 44. For this reason Thomas can even define "nature" as the "ratio artis divinae, indita rebus, qua moventur ad suos fines" (*Sum. con. gent.*, III, c.3). Consequently, since all "nature" *as such* is devoid of reason and freedom, it should be classified with passive powers rather than active in the sense that "nature" does not have dominion over itself, as neither do brute animals. It is in this sense of the *passive*

voice that the passage from St. Thomas *In V Metaph.*, lect. 14, n. 955, interpolated into the Leonine text of *In II Phys.*, lect. 1, n. 4, should be understood: "Gravitas enim in terra non est principium ut moveat, sed magis ut moveatur." (See exegesis in my *Nature and Gravitation* [River Forest, 1955], pp. 25-26, n. 78.) Similarly St. Thomas frequently uses the passive voice to describe animals that in fact move themselves and others:". . . creaturae irrationales, quae tantum aguntur, et non agunt" (*Sum. theol.* I, q.103, a.5 ad 2, etc.). By such considerations, however, Thomas in no way wishes to deny the dynamic reality of "nature" as an *active* and *formal* principle of natural characteristics and movement toward a proper goal.

30. See H. A. Wolfson, *Crescas' Critique of Aristotle* (Cambridge, 1929), pp. 672–75; also B. Carra de Vaux, *Avicenne* (Paris, 1900), pp. 184–85. The late-fourteenth-century Jewish philosopher Crescas also followed this Arabic tradition: cf. Wolfson, ed., *Critique (Or Adonai)* prop. 17, pp. 296–99.

31. J. T. Muckle, ed., *Algazel's Metaphysics* (Toronto, 1933), pp. 30–31; 99–102. Concerning the nature of the *Maqâcid*, see D. Salman, "Algazel et les Latins," *Archive d'hist. doctr. et litt. du M.-A.* 10 (1935):103–27.

32. Cf. Aristotle *Pys.*, 8. 4. 225a5–19; St. Thomas, *In VIII Phys.*, lect.7, nn. 6–8; *In VII Phys.*, lect.1, n. 2. The basic error of Avicenna is his conception of "form" as a *thing* (*res*) in its own right; see St. Thomas, *Sum. theol.* I, q.110, a.2; *Sum. con. gent.*, III, c.68; also P. Hoenen, *De origine formae materialia* (Rome, 1932). In animate activity the whole subsistent being is responsible for the subsequent movement which it accomplishes through various organic parts. Since inanimate things have no organic parts, they cannot move themselves.

33. Note that for St. Thomas this principle is demonstrated by Aristotle with a *propter quid* argument because it contains the proper cause of the conclusion. This is against Averroës who says that the proposition "Omne quod movetur ab alio movetur" belongs to the class of demonstrations *signi*, or *quia*, in which a conditional clause is used. William A. Wallace has given an excellent analysis of this argument in his "The Cosmological Argument: A Reappraisal," *Proc. Am. Cath. Phil. Assoc.* 46 (1972):43–57. See also my "Principle *Omne quod movetur ab alio movetur* in Medieval Physics," *Isis* 56 (1965):26–45, where I had not yet realized the full import of Thomas's argument.

34. "Sicut alia accidentia consequuntur formam substantialem, ita et locus, et per consequens moveri ad locum: non tamen ita quod forma naturalis sit motor, sed motor est generans, quod dat talem formam, ad quam talis motus consequitur" (St. Thomas, *In II Phys.*, lect 1, n.4).

35. Joannis Duns Scoti, *Comm. in II Sent.*, dist.2, q.10, in *Opera Omnia*, ed. L. Wadding (Paris, 1893), 2:523–46.

36. See Roy R. Effler, *John Duns Scotus and the Principle "Omne quod movetur ab alio movetur,"* (St. Bonaventure, 1962). All of Scotus's attacks on the validity of the principle must be seen within the context of the Averroist interpretation, which he unconsciously assumes to be Aristotelian.

37. This became the terminology of the Thomistic school as expounded by Domingo de Soto, *Super Octo Physicorum Quaestiones,* 2d ed. (Salamanca, 1551), super II, q.1, fol. 31v–34r; super VIII, q.3, fol. 104r–v; Joannes a S. Thoma, *Cursus Philosophicus Thomisticus,* ed. B. Reiser (Turin, 1933), II, q.23, a.1 ad 3; Cosmo Alamano, *Summa Philosophiae (Physica),* P. II, q.34, a.2 ad 4, ed. B. Felchlin and F. Beringer (Paris, 1890), 2:103a.

38. See my specialized study "Motion in a Void: Aquinas and Averroës," in *St. Thomas Aquinas 1274–1974: Commemorative Studies* ed. A. A. Maurer (Toronto, 1974), pp. 467–88.

39. Concerning the difference between Aristotle and the pre-Socratics on this point, see F. Solmsen, *Aristotle's System of the Physical World: A Comparison with His Predecessors* (Ithaca, N.Y., 1960).

40. Here we are not interested in Avicenna's personal philosophy, which must be studied in Arabic, but with his philosophy as it was known to the Latin West and to St. Thomas in particular. For a summary of Avicenna's doctrinal impact on the West, see E. Gilson, "Avicenna en Occident au moyen âge," *Archives d'hist. doctr. et litt. du M.-A.* 44 (1969):89–121. For his influence on St. Thomas, see Georges C. Anawati, "Saint Thomas d'Aquin et la Métaphysique d'Avicenne," *St. Thomas Aquinas 1274–1974* ed. A. A. Maurer, (Toronto, 1974), 1:449–65.

41. See Aimé Forest, *La Structure métaphysique du concret selon saint Thomas d'Aquin* (Paris, 1931), pp. 226–31.

42. Avicenna, *Metaphysica,* tr. IX, c.5, in *Opera Omnia* (Venice 1508), fol. 105va-b. Cf. St. Thomas, *Sum. con gent.*, II, c.76; III, c.65 and c.103.

43. Ibid.

44. For a thorough development of this, see E. Gilson, "Les Sources gréco-arabes de l'augustinisme avicennisant," *Archives d'hist. doctr. et litt. du M.-A.* 4 (1929):5–149.

45. See A. Forest, op. cit., p. 228.

46. Avicenna, *Metaph.* tr. IX, c.4, *Opera omnia,* fol. 105ra–vb.

47. Aristotle *Phys.* 2. 6. 198a5–13.

48. Avicenna, *Metaph.* tr. IX, c.4.

49. St. Thomas, *In VI Metaph.,* lect. 4.

50. The difficult problem of how God knows future contingent events and causes them freely is beyond the ken of natural philosophy, and even metaphysics can do no more than present the *mystery* in terms of what we are humanly certain. Even the theologian can do little more than clarify the clear facts of revelation and help indicate the precise point of the real mystery of faith, the mystery of divine predestination working in the human free will freely. For a thoroughly orthodox presentation of the traditional Catholic position, one should study Thomas Bradwardine's *De causa Dei contra Pelagium* (London, 1618).

Comment

BY

William A. Wallace

Father Weisheipl has given us a comprehensive and accurate summary of Aquinas's concept of nature and how this differs from Avicenna's. He focuses attention on three differences, the first being how these men conceive nature as a cause of natural motion, and the second and third, how they see heavenly bodies and intelligences effecting substantial change and determinism within the sublunary world. In my comments I will focus only on the first of these. I shall do so by raising the question of how influential these alternative conceptions were in later centuries, and particularly how they influenced the rise of modern science.

More to the point, I should like to ask whether the view of nature embraced by Galileo has more in common with that of Avicenna or that of Aquinas, and this in the context of his famous discussion of falling bodies. You may recall that in the *Two New Sciences* Galileo justifies his definition of natural falling motion as uniformly accelerated on the basis that nature always employs the simplest and easiest means, one wherein the velocity of motion increases uniformly with time of fall.[1] From this text it would appear that Galileo saw nature as the cause, the determining factor that serves to explain falling motion. However, in a passage much quoted by historians of science, when later Sagredo raises the question whether the new discoveries reported in the discourse reveal the cause of natural acceleration, Galileo has Salviati reply that seeking this cause is not really worthwhile; it is sufficient to investigate the properties of falling motion, whatever its cause might be.[2] Some historians interpret this latter statement as Galileo's rejection of causal explanation—the beginning for them of the modern era, as opposed to that of medieval science—although in this interpretation they take no account of Galileo's earlier statement about nature.[3] Now it seems to me that we should accord Galileo some measure of consistency: if we attempt to reconcile his two statements, it then is of capital importance whether nature is a cause and, if so, in what way.

We know that Galileo studied and taught at Pisa between 1581 and 1591, so it should not be difficult to ascertain the concepts of nature that were current at that time. In his notebooks dating from the Pisan period, Galileo in fact references two Spaniards, Domingo de Soto and Benito Pereira, both of whom discuss nature extensively in their commentaries on Aristotle's *Physics.*[4] Soto composed his commentary at Salamanca around 1545, and in it he explains the definition of nature in very much the way Father Weisheipl has described Aquinas's teaching.[5] This is not surprising, for Soto was a Dominican and a Thomist. In light of Father Weisheipl's paper, however, we may ask whether Soto knew anything about Avicenna. The answer is, yes, he did, for Soto quotes Avicenna and raises an objection to the definition of nature based on Avicenna's text. This objection raised difficulties that very much puzzled sixteenth-century thinkers.[6] The problem is that the heavens seem to be natural bodies, and their motion seems to be natural also, as coming from nature. But no active principle moves the heavens from within, since they are moved actively by intelligences, which are extrinsic principles; nor does their motion have an internal passive principle, for this could only be their matter, and matter naturally tends to rest, whereas the heavens appear to move eternally. Since a natural motion must derive from internal principles, either active or passive, and neither of these can be found in the heavens, their motion is not natural in Aristotle's sense. Soto goes on to mention also Avicenna's opinion that Aristotle is wrong in holding that nature is so obvious as not to require demonstration.[7] Neither of these positions is directly pertinent to our discussion, but they bear witness to the facts that Avicenna's opinions were known in the mid-sixteenth century, and that they were discussed, though the opinions dealt with here are not the identical points treated by Father Weisheipl.

Pereira's textbook on natural philosophy was published at Rome in 1576, and, perhaps because Pereira was a Jesuit professor at the prestigious Collegio Romano, it exerted a great influence in

Italy to the end of the century.[8] Pereira had read Soto, of course, and he likewise gives evidence of acquaintance with Avicenna's views.[9] He discusses nature under the title, *De forma ut est natura*, which seems to accent nature's role as a formal principle, and possibly even as an active principle, of natural motion.[10] Pereira is not as Thomistic as was Soto, for in many of his teachings he favors the interpretations of Averroës and of Scotus, both of whom were popular in northern Italy at the time of his writing. Indeed, when discussing the motion of the heavens, he aligns Scotus with Avicenna in holding that Aristotle's definition of nature does not fit the heavens, though he himself prefers to follow Aquinas in saying that it does.[11] But on the problem discussed by Father Weisheipl, namely, whether nature is an active principle of the motion of the elements, Pereira is in a quandary. He does not have a definite answer, but it seems probable to him that the position of Averroës and Scotus (he does not mention Avicenna here) is correct: the elements are not moved by the generator, but they move themselves, and thus nature is an active principle within them.[12] Pereira notes, however, that he does not agree with Averroës that the medium is necessary for falling motion, nor does he think that Scotus explains himself very well; so he defers his own treatment of the problem to the time when he will write his own book on the elements—a work which unfortunately never did find its way into print.[13]

As I said earlier, Galileo mentions Pereira in his notes written at Pisa, and there is evidence that Galileo may even have copied portions of those notes from Pereira's text.[14] Not all is there, however, and so I have been tracking down other sources of Galileo's notebooks. Recently I have discovered some interesting parallels between them and *reportationes* of lectures given at the Collegio Romano around 1590 by other Jesuit professors.[15] One of these men—Muzio Vitelleschi—turns out to be significant for our purposes.[16] In his physics lectures Vitelleschi has an extensive treatment of nature and the causality it exercises in all forms of natural motion.[17] Since Galileo seems well acquainted with the positions Vitelleschi takes on other matters, I would be surprised if the latter's explanations did not match Galileo's at the time he was studying philosophy, and later teaching, at Pisa. Vitelleschi, I should note, is more consistently a Thomist than was Pereira, but there is some ambivalence in his exposition, which I will now detail for you briefly.

The passages of interest occur in a disputation on Aristotle's second book of the *Physics* that inquires "Whether any cause is included in the definition of nature, either universal, or accidental, or efficient?"[18] Vitelleschi replies with seven propositions, as follows: 1) the universal cause, as such, is not contained under the definition of nature; 2) no accidental principle is there contained; 3) nor is any efficient cause, precisely as it is efficient and acts on others; 4) nor is the final cause, as such; 5) nor is generation; 6) nor privation; 7) nor any composite. Of these seven points only the first three need concern us, as pertinent to Father Weisheipl's paper.

The first proposition, that the universal cause as such is not included under the definition of nature, Vitelleschi says is directed against Philoponus.[19] Now this is an interesting observation, for if we consult Philoponus's commentary on the *Physics* we find that he is dissatisfied with Aristotle's definition of nature, and emends it considerably.[20] Philoponus's revised definition is the following: "Nature is a kind of life or force that is diffused through bodies, that is formative of them, and that governs them; it is the principle of motion and rest in things, and in such things alone, in which it inheres primarily and not incidentally."[21] As seen from this definition, Philoponus conceives nature as a type of *anima mundi*, an enlivening force operative throughout all of creation and accounting for its spontaneous movements. Whether Philoponus would equate this force with God is not clear from the text, but in his reply Vitelleschi appears to do so. The Universal cause of all things is God and God is not a principle of motion in himself. Or perhaps you mean, he goes on, that the heavens are the universal cause? His answer to this is that the heavens do indeed have a nature, but they are not said to be natural because of the motions they effect in the sublunary region; rather this is because of motions that are properly their own.[22]

Vitelleschi's second proposition, viz., that accidental principles are not included under the definition, is directed, he says, against Albert the Great, who taught that motive qualities are nature because they are primary, i.e., they are the immediate and proximate principles of natural motion. Vitelleschi replies that when "primary" is used in the definition of nature it does not mean proximate; rather it means basic, as opposed to instrumental. Accidents such as motive qualities, however, are instrumental principles, and so they do not fit the definition.[23] At this point, however, he raises an objection that is somewhat illuminating. The objection is that if water vapor moves upward it would seem to do so naturally, since its motion is from an intrinsic principle; but such a motion can be explained only by the *levitas* of the vapor, and this is something accidental. The motion cannot come, moreover, from the substantial form of the vapor, for this is the form of water, and its natural motion is downward. To resolve the difficulty Vitelleschi maintains that the upward motion of the vapor, in such a case, can be natural only *secundum quid*, because it comes from an instrumental principle, *levitas*, that has a natural inclination upward. Absolutely and *simpliciter*, on the other hand, the movement must be violent, for it is not consonant with the nature of water, which has a natural inclination downward.[24]

This leads directly to Vitelleschi's third proposition, with which I will conclude: No efficient cause, precisely as efficient and as acting on another, is included in this definition.[25] Vitelleschi has a long exposition of this, which I will have to skip so as to come quickly to an objection similar to that of the water vapor. The objection proceeds as follows: Fire goes upward naturally, just as it heats naturally; but natural motions come from nature; so the form of fire must be nature with repect to both these motions. But in the case of the second motion, heating, nature acts as an efficient cause; therefore it must so act in the first case, that of upward motion. Vitelleschi's reply is too complex to summarize in brief compass, but again it focuses on the ways in which things are said to be natural, as in the previous reply where he qualifies some motions as natural *simpliciter* and others as natural only *secundum quid.* Some motions are called natural, he now says, when they produce effects that are recognizably such as proceeding from an efficient cause; it is in this way that fire heats the cold object with which it comes in contact. Other motions are natural when they proceed from a passive instrumental principle, such as *gravitas* or *levitas*, which bring about the motion of the heavy and light object respectively, but do not produce effects in another object, as does an efficient cause.[26] So nature is truly a cause, and sometimes it produces effects in another, and thus can be called an efficient cause; but it is not always an efficient cause, and particularly not in the case of upward and downward motion, and thus efficiency is not a proper attribute and so should not be included in nature's definition.[27]

The foregoing clarification of the types of causality involved in natural motion may prove helpful for understanding Galileo's apparently inconsistent use of causal terminology in the passages referenced from the *Two New Sciences*. When referring to nature as the determining factor that explains how bodies fall Galileo clearly had in mind an internal cause, a fundamental principle from which their motion proceeds. In substantiation of this I would call attention to his explicit citation, in his notes on motion written around 1590, of a passage from Aristotle saying that the natural character of a motion requires an internal, not an external, cause.[28] Like his contemporaries Galileo probably identified this internal cause with the substantial form of the falling body. Whether he saw this form, and the accidental form of *gravitas* associated with it, as an active principle or as a passive principle is problematical: he might have seen either of them in Platonic or Avicennian fashion, following Philoponus, as a kind of natural *vis*, or he might have viewed them, as did Aquinas and Vitelleschi, as merely passive principles. Regardless of how he decided this particular option, however, it seems quite unlikely that Galileo would have labelled either form, as natural and internal, the proximate *efficient* cause of the body's fall. In the context of the question raised by Sagredo, on the other hand, the causes mentioned by Salviati as explaining the body's acceleration (viz., its nearness to the center of gravity and the actions of the medium on it) are all extrinsic to the body and are thought of affecting it in some efficient way.[29] By Galileo's day much ink had already been spilled on identifying such agents that affect natural fall, all to no avail. Thus it was far from revolutionary for him to have Sagredo reply that further discussion of external causes was not really worthwhile. Suffice it to know that the motion proceeded from nature as from an internal cause, and then go on to investigate the properties of the resulting motion as *natural*, regardless of what its proximate efficient agents might be.

My comments, as you can see, lend themselves to ready development into a separate lecture on Galileo. It is not my intention to do that. But the foregoing observations may show that the different understandings of Aristotle's concept of nature found in Avicenna and Aquinas are of more than antiquarian interest. Indeed, they have considerable bearing on the rise of modern science.[30]

Notes

*Research on which this paper is based has been supported by the National Science Foundation (Grant No. SOC 75-14615), whose assistance is gratefully acknowledged.

1. *Le Opere di Galileo Galilei*, ed. Antonio Favora, 20 vols. in 21 (1890–1909; reprint ed., Florence: G. Barbera Editore, 1968), (hereafter cited as *Opere*), 8: 197. For an English translation see Galileo Galilei, *Two New Sciences*, trans. with Introduction and notes by Stillman Drake (Madison: University of Wisconsin Press, 1974), p. 153.

2. *Opere*, 8:201–2; trans. Drake, pp. 157–59.

3. See, for example, Drake's n. 12, p. 159; also his Introduction, pp. xxvii–xxix.

4. *Opere*, 1:24, 35, 144–46. Since presenting this paper, the author has published an English translation of these materials under the title, *Galileo's Early Notebooks: The Physical Questions: A Translation from the Latin, with Historical and Paleographical Commentary* (Notre Dame, Ind.: University of Notre Dame Press, 1977). The references to Soto and Pereira are to be found on pp. 35, 54, 208, and 210 of this translation.

5. Dominicus Sotus, *Super octo libros physicorum Aristotelis quaestiones* (Salamanca: Andrea a Portonariis, 1555), fols. 29v–33v. This is the second edition, which is more widely diffused than the first; there are no significant changes in this particular question, viz., Lib. 2, q. 1: Utrum diffinitio naturae sit bona.

6. Ibid., fol. 31r; see also fols. 29v and 32v.

7. Ibid., fol. 33v.

8. Benedictus Pererius, *De communibus omnium rerum naturalium principiis et affectionibus* (Rome: Franciscus Zanettus, 1576).

9. Pereira makes frequent reference to Soto's commentary throughout his work; in his treatment of nature he mentions Avicenna on pp. 249 and 253.

10. Lib. 7, De forma ut est natura, pp. 242–70.

11. Ibid., pp. 249D, 251A, and 253B.

12. Ibid., p. 262B.

13. Ibid., p. 263B–C; see also p. 260B. Pereira probably treated the mover of the elements in his lectures on the *De caelo*, but no section entitled *De elementis* survives in the *reportationes* of these lectures preserved in the Oesterreichische Nationalbibliothek, Cod. Vindobon. 10509. However, he does have a disputation *De elementis* in his course on the *De generatione*, Cod. Vindobon. 10470, fols. 167–73, and this includes a discussion of their motive qualities, but not how these influence the local motion of bodies.

14. Galileo's answer to the question, *An mundus potuerit esse ab aeterno,* in *Opere* 1:32–37, parallels very closely Pereira's treatment of the same ques-

tion in *De communibus*, pp. 505–12, and could have been copied from it. See *Galileo's Early Notebooks* (n. 4), pp. 49–57; also the commentary on pp. 260–62. Galileo apparently extracted also a portion of Pereira's treatment of the cause of acceleration in free fall; see *Opere*, 1:318, 411.

15. See my essay, "Galileo Galilei and the *Doctores Parisienses*," in R. E. Butts and J. C. Pitt, eds., *New Perspectives on Galileo,* University of Western Ontario, Philosophy of Science Series (Dordrecht, Holland: D. Reidel Publishing Company, 1978), pp. 87–138.

16. Muzio Vitelleschi taught logic at the Collegio Romano in 1588–89, natural philosophy in 1589–90, and metaphysics in 1590–91; he was also prefect of studies in 1605–6, and later served as general of the entire Jesuit order. See R. G. Villoslada, *Storia del Collegio Romano dal suo inizio (1551) alla soppressione della Compagnia di Gesu (1773),* Analecta Gregoriana vol. 66, (Rome: Gregorian University Press, 1954).

17. These are preserved in the Staatsbibliothek Bamberg, Cod. 70 (H.J.VI.21), which also contains Vitelleschi's lectures on the *De caelo*, both given at Rome in 1589–90.

18. This is but one of many disputations included in the lectures, which expose the text of Aristotle and then raise questions relating to its understanding. The titles of disputations relating to the subject of nature include the following:

> De definitione naturae
> An in definitione naturae contineatur causa aliqua universalis vel accidentalis vel efficiens
> An secundum Aristotelem natura sit solum principium passivum, an solum activum, an utrumque
> Quinam motus et respectu cuius principii sint a natura
> An possit demonstrari naturam esse
> An materia vel forma vel utraque sit natura
> Cuinam forme conveniat ratio naturae

19. "In secundum librum Physicorum, disputatio secunda," Cod. Bamberg. 70, fol. 112r.

20. A Latin translation of Philoponus's commentary on the *Physics* was published at Venice in 1539, and another translation in 1554. For a detailed analysis of Philoponus's analysis of falling motion, based on the Greek text, see Michael Wolff, "*Fallgesetz und Massebegriff*: Zwei wissenschaftshistorische Untersuchungen zur Kosmologie des Johannes Philoponus," *Quellen und Studien zur Philosophie*, 2 (Berlin: Walter de Gruyter & Co., 1971).

21. "Natura est quaedam vita sive vis quae per corpora diffunditur, eorum formatrix et gubernatrix, principium motus et quietis in eo cui inest per se primo et non secundum accidens." (Aristotle, *Physicorum libri quatuor, cum Ioannis Grammatici cognomento Philoponi commentariis, quos . . . restituit Ioannes Baptista Rosarius* [Venice: Hieronymus Scotus, 1558], p. 67, col. b).

22. Cod. Bamberg. 70, fols. 112r–v.

23. Ibid., fol. 112v.

24. Ibid.

25. "Causa efficiens ut efficiencs est et agit in aliud non continetur in hac definitione . . ." (ibid., fols. 112v–113r).

26. There is a sense, however, in which the falling object alters the resistance of the medium through which it falls, and so produces an effect "in another object," namely, in the medium. For an explanaton of this phenomenon and how Vitelleschi uses it to account for acceleration in free fall, see my "Causes and Forces in Sixteenth-Century Physics," *Isis* 69(1978): 400–412. It is noteworthy from the examples given, moreover, that Vitelleschi does not limit the exercise of internal efficient causality to living beings alone, but sees nature as operating efficiently even in some instances of non-living phenomena, such as that of flame heating a cold object.

27. Cod. Bamberg. 70, fol. 113v.

28. "Aristoteles, 7 Phys. t. 10, inquit, ad naturalitatem motus requiri causam internam, non externam, motus" (*Opere* 1:416). Cf. another notation: "Quae sursum moventur, magis violenter quam naturaliter ascendunt: nam ascensus externam habet causam, descensus autem internam" (*Opere*, 1:417).

29. *Opere*, 8:202; trans. Drake, p. 159.

30. In the broader context of the role of causes in scientific explanation generally, as I have stressed in my work on that subject, much harm has been done by philosophers who focus on efficient causation to the exclusion of other types of causal explanation. The history of science is replete with explanations made through final, formal, and material causes, most of which have proved easier to discover than those through efficient agents, particularly when the latter are conceptualized as forces, occult or otherwise. It is to Galileo's credit that he did not show such a narrow preoccupation, but based his *nuova scienza* on principles broad enough to include even those of Aristotelian natural philosophy. See my *Causality and Scientific Explanation,* 2 vols. (Ann Arbor: The University of Michigan Press, 1972–74), passim.

An expanded version of these comments, with an appendix containing the Latin text of Vitelleschi's commentary cited above, and locating the comments in the context of the early development of Galileo's science, now appears as Essay 13, "Galileo and the Causality of Nature," in the author's *Prelude to Galileo: Essays on Medieval and Sixteenth-Century Sources of Galileo's Thought.* Boston Studies in the Philosophy of Science, Vol. 62 (Dordrecht-Boston: D. Reidel Publishing Company, 1981), pp. 286–99.

The Analytic Character of Late Medieval Learning: Natural Philosophy without Nature

John E. Murdoch

It has been almost twenty years since the late Ernest Moody published a seminal article on the history—and at the same time the historiography—of medieval philosophy. Entitled "Empiricism and Metaphysics in Medieval Philosophy,"[1] it addressed itself to the question of how, as a philosopher as well as an historian, one should most properly view the history of philosophy in the fourteenth century, a particular area of scholarship in which Moody was a universally acknowledged master. That it was problematic just how one *should* view this segment of philosophical history arose not simply from the fact that the history of medieval philosophy was—and still is—very much "in the making," but also from the verdict of "guilty" that so many historians had brought in for the judgment of fourteenth-century philosophy in the Latin West. Compared to the thirteenth century, it was held to be a period of scepticism, destruction, and decline.[2]

In Moody's eyes, this was a judgment that came about as much from not putting the right questions to the relevant historical evidence as from not sufficiently knowing or appreciating this evidence in the first place. However, because what Moody maintained as a remedy to this historiographic situation—a situation, he believed, largely of error—is extremely important for the whole history of medieval philosophy, it will be beneficial to look at the crux of what he said in some detail.

One should first note, he claimed, that the basic attitude of the Church and its theologians in the thirteenth century toward philosophy was anti-metaphysical and that "for this reason, the actual development of scholasticism toward an empiricist conception of philosophy was a fulfillment, rather than a failure, of the scholastic enterprise."[3] Secondly, this "fulfillment" came to pass through an "internal criticism" during the later thirteenth and early fourteenth centuries of the "metaphysical claims of the Greek and Arab philosophies which had been introduced from the East." This was a key event in medieval philosophical history. To quote Moody *in extenso*, it was key because:

> . . . this epistemological and logical criticism of metaphysics . . . transformed the whole character of philosophy from its Greek form—primarily cosmological and speculative—to forms which became characteristic of the philosophies of the seventeenth and eighteenth centuries—essentially *critical*. This transformation of the *form* of philosophical inquiry, from the speculative to the analytic, seems to me to be the most significant fact, for the history of philosophy, in the scholastic period. For better or for worse, it gave a new character and direction to all later philosophy, of which we have not yet seen the end.[4]

To express the opinion of at least one other historian of late medieval philosophy and science, I am myself not just willing, but even anxious, to go on record as saying that I believe that Moody is right in maintaining this transformation of the form of philosophical inquiry from the speculative to the analytic. In point of autobiographical fact, over the past years I have been rather preoccupied with this transformation, especially in the realm of natural philosophy or science. But this preoccupation has not been with convincing myself of the fact of this transformation but rather with what it amounted to. If it is true that fourteenth-century philosophy was analytic when viewed against the more speculative background provided by thirteenth-century philosophy, just *how* was it analytic? What characteristics made it so and just how were these characteristics exhibited in detail in fourteenth-century learning, in theology and science (if it is proper to distinguish such a discipline in this period) as well as in philosophy? I have on earlier occasions set forth at least some of the results of this preoccupation and, as the first words of the title of my presentation today undoubtedly suggest, I shall be setting forth a few further results now.

But before I proceed to that, it will be useful to say something more of Moody's thesis, something more in particular of the "background" he gives for it. Thus, in trying to explain why historians *could have* regarded the fourteenth century in philosophy as a period of decline, he claims that they reached this conclusion by focusing their attention not upon the crucial internal criticism of Greek and Arab metaphysics that occurred at that time, but rather upon the problem of the "*uses* made of philosophical ideas and language in the internal development of Christian theology" during the thirteenth century (his italics).[5] If this is one's focal point, then, because the developments that occurred in response to *this* problem "found their most adequate expression in the thirteenth century," that century will turn out to be the "high point" in one's overall view of medieval philosophy. Hence, Moody concludes:

> . . . by this criterion the fourteenth century will appear as an age of decline, because philosophy in the fourteenth century withdrew itself from the kind of questions which are of interest to theology and thereby ceased to be of value as a medium of expression for theology. The development of empiricism meant that the orientation of philosophy was no longer toward theology but toward positive science.[6]

I have troubled to quote Moody at length again because it is here that I find reason for some disagreement with his claims. For it seems to me that fourteenth-century philosophy did not withdraw itself from theology and from the questions of interest to it. Fourteenth-century philosophical developments were, I think, of considerable use to fourteenth-century theology. If anything, it was perhaps more of a "two-way street" between these two disciplines in the fourteenth century than it was in the thirteenth. By this I do not simply mean that a lot of philosophy proper was done by theologians in theological works. That occurred throughout most of medieval philosophy and the fact that there may have been more of such a phenomenon in the fourteenth century is not especially crucial. I have in mind instead three other phenomena that seem to me to speak for the intimacy of the relationship between philosophy and theology in the fourteenth century. First, the widespread utilization of methods and techniques of analysis developed in philosophical contexts in dealing with essentially theological problems. Second, the direct relevance of philosophical problems and the results reached in their resolution to theological concerns, even major theological concerns. If it is true, for example, that the new area of importance for fourteenth-century theology was that of justification, grace, and predestination, then the philosophical deliberations over the logic of future contingent propositions surely was a phenomenon of relevance. Alternatively, an intensifying of philosophical investigations of the infinite went hand in hand with the continued theological interest in the problem of the possible eternity of the world. Third, it was even true that attention paid to a theological issue—such as that of the Eucharist—had repercussions in philosophy. Thus, the separation of philosophy from theology in the fourteenth century was not nearly so great as Moody's remarks might lead one to believe.

This is my first suggested qualification of Moody, but there is yet another point at which his contentions stand in need of some revision. It is that he places too much emphasis—or so I believe—upon the role of empiricism in fourteenth-century philosophy. It is essentially this which leads him to conclude that the orientation of philosophy was then "toward positive science." What he means by this is made explicit:

> Aristotelian dynamics was criticized by Jean Buridan, and a functional mathematics, applicable to the cinematic analysis of local motions and of the acceleration of falling bodies, was developed by Heytesbury, Swineshead, Dumbleton, and Nicole Oresme.[7]

But the irony of the fact is that by far the major share of the fourteenth-century developments in science of which Moody here speaks were not accomplishments due to a rising empiricism. True, empiricist *epistemology* was dominant in the fourteenth century. But this did not mean that natural philosophy then proceeded by a dramatic increase in attention being paid to experience and observation (let alone anything like experiment) or was suddenly overwrought with concern about testing or matching its results with nature; in a very important way natural philosophy was not about nature.[8] On the contrary, its procedures were increasingly *secundum imaginationem* (to use an extremely frequently occurring phrase) and when some "natural confirmation" of a result is brought forth, more often than not it too was an "imaginative construct."[9] To be even more specific, what one finds as a dominant feature of fourteenth-century natural philosophy—especially at Oxford, but so too in the dissemination of the ideas and methods of *Anglicana* at Paris—is the extension of the application of logic and logico-mathematical techniques in not just resolving, but even in creating and then resolving, problems in natural philosophy. Ironically, in the sentence directly following those I have just quoted from Moody, he himself notes the substantial fourteenth-century developments in formal logic and "semantics."[10] But he did not sufficiently emphasize that the "positive science" of natural philosophy of which he had just spoken was very intimately bound up with these logical developments, far more, I believe, than they were with the shift to an empiricist epistemology. A sampling of just how this was so will be made clearer, I hope, in some of what I shall have to say in what follows.

In point of fact, a good number of the conclusions I have come to in earlier attempts at discovering just what the fourteenth-century transformation from the speculative to the analytic amounted to have made the preponderant role played by logic and logical techniques more apparent. This is no place to restate—or even to summarize—these earlier conclusions. Let it be sufficient to say that these conclusions as a whole served to underline the importance of new *methods* (in both philosophy and theology) as characteristic of this transformation, of the creation, development, and application of what I have called (with purposeful ambiguity) new "languages of analysis."[11] The kinds of "languages" I have in mind were—to cite but several examples—the language of *proportiones*, the language of intension and remission, the language of first and last instants, or of beginning and ceasing, and the theory of supposition. Thus, the language of *proportiones* was used most notably to elicit the relations obtaining between varying velocities and the varying force-resistance pairs that function as the causes of these velocities, but found application in treating other problems in philosophy, medicine, and even theology as well.[12] Alternatively, the language of intension and remission supplied the fourteenth-century scholar with a way of handling or measuring variations in qualities or forms. It allowed him to describe, for example, the distribution of heat throughout a body, whether this distribution was uniform, uniformly non-uniform (in medieval terms uniformly difform), or non-uniformly non-uniform (difformly difform) from one degree (*gradus*) to another; and even to describe what was involved should it be *imagined* that one such distribution changed into another.[13] Since the language of first and last instants or beginning and ceasing and the theory of supposition will receive further attention in what I shall say in a moment, their identification can be omitted for the present.

In place of further details about the "mechanics" of these so-called analytical languages, I should like to note that each of them—with the possible exception of that of *proportiones*—had a strong logical input, if not in the conceptions it utilized, then in the way in which it was applied in solving problems. The theory of supposition was, naturally, part of medieval logic itself. Today I want to say something more about this logical input, not simply in these "languages," but as it is found in fourteenth-century natural philosophy as a whole. Such an "input" has, of course, long been regarded as part of what scholasticism, as a method, was and, perhaps, still is. But in referring to it now as part of the fabric of late medieval thought, I do not have in mind the increased logical "neatening up" of how the fourteenth-century scholastic presented his arguments, whether this occurred by a more frequent display of any number of techniques and conceptions found in Aristotle's logic or by the increased application of the medieval doctrine of *consequentiae* in carrying out the philosophical enterprise. Rather, I have in mind three other things: (1) the metalinguistic treatment of problems, (2) the application of the doctrine of supposition, and (3) the impact of the tradition of solving sophisms. Let me postpone further specification of what was involved in each of these logical techniques or conceptions until I come to explain by example just how they were applied and say by way of introduction that, in choosing these examples, I will limit myself to the late medieval investigation of a single kind of "entity": indivisibles. Temporal indivisibles or instants; spatial indivisibles or points; indivisibles of a motion, called *mutata esse* or *mota esse*; and even intensive indivisibles, the degrees or *gradus* of a quality that is capable of becoming more or less intense (or remiss) in a subject.

Lest it be thought that this is an inconscionably narrow area to which to restrict oneself, a word should be said about the importance of indivisible entities of all sorts in Aristotelian physics. Indeed, anyone who did Aristotelian physics on the basis of Aristotle's work of that name was bound to deal with such entities in coming to grips with any number of problems. For the later books of the *Physics* deal with motion, and, as Aristotle says at the very outset of his investigation of this topic, with all those things that are necessarily involved in or follow from motion; that is, with what it is to be continuous, with how the infinite presents itself in the continuous, and with place, void, and time as the presumably necessary conditions of motion.[14] But in analyzing each of these things (with the exception of the void), especially as they relate to motion, indivisibles of one sort or another constantly enter into the argument. Thus, if, as the medieval scholastics, we take Aristotelian physics to be a "science" concerned with *all* of the kinds of things we find treated in the work entitled *Physics* (and not merely with what we might, using modern science as our guide, select from that work), then indivisibles assume a most important role in natural philosophy. And the scholastics realized this only too well, particularly in the fourteenth century. They then went much beyond Aristotle in developing the conceptions, questions, and arguments he had initially raised and, more than that, in seeing implications and tangential problems that he did not raise. Moreover, they often developed particular aspects of all of this into whole separate treatises which then subsequently took up a life and formed a tradition of their own. This, then, is the kind of literature I shall be drawing my examples from today.

The particular example I shall first deal with from this literature is not, however, one that had an especially strong "Aristotelian background." It is that of the question of the *existence* of indivisibles. The scholastics themselves recognized that Aristotle had not taken special care to treat this question directly,[15] but had devoted his attention instead to problems and arguments involving indivisibles in one way or another, most notably to the task of proving that no continuum could be composed of indivisibles.[16] But in the fourteenth century there was little, if any, hesitance to treat the question of their existence. The most fundamental piece of literature addressing the question was most likely the first part of William of Ockham's *De sacramento altaris* (an instance, we might note in passing, of the occurrence of a theological context for the determination of a philosophical question).[17] I have termed Ockham's treatment of this question "most fundamental" not on the basis of its philosophical competence (although, like most all of Ockham's work, it is impressive in that), but rather because (again like so much of Ockham's writings and contentions) of the decided influence it is observed to have had. Put briefly, it provided a thesis and a way of investigating the question of the existence of indivisibles that had to be taken into account in almost all subsequent late medieval treatments of the issue.

Ockham's general view was that indivisibles do not exist at all. To take the particular kind of indivisible with which he begins his inquiry, points are not things (*res*) in any proper sense. One may think that they do exist as things since they serve as the termini of lines, but this is an error. All we have, or need, are finite lines of this or that length, not "real" points somehow separable from such lines and functioning as their termini.[18] And the same stricture against existence as a thing must be said of lines and surfaces (since they too are, respectively, indivisible in the dimensions of breadth and depth or just depth). Thus, in the final analysis, only bodies exist as things, divisible in all dimensions, and it is as a "function" (to use an anachronistic term) of these bodies that we are able to speak of those indivisible entities termed surfaces, lines, or points. That is to say, it is because this or that body is of such and such a finite shape that we are allowed to speak of the indivisible surfaces that limit it or render it finite. And the finite surfaces and lines thus derived allow us to treat, respectively, of indivisible lines and points.[19]

This may initially sound as if what Ockham maintained was basically empiricist in nature and may even remind one of attempts by mathematicians at the beginning of the present century to give an empirical grounding to geometry.[20] Indeed, Ockham's thesis is related to his empiricist or, better, particularist ontology, but to make this into the fundamental characteristic of what he has done ignores just how he went about establishing and confirming this thesis and what else he believed he had accomplished with it.

He begins his investigation by running through the traditional contexts and arguments that were often held to account for the existence of indivisibles or points, and shows that none provides adequate grounds for such a position. (Included are such contexts as a point being an accident inhering in some subject, existing because it belongs to some genus, or because it is needed to account for the continuation or the division of continuous magnitudes.)[21] He then goes on to show *per rationes theologicas* that points need not exist, his fundamental ploy being to maintain that, *sub potentia Dei absoluta*, God can very well create a line without its terminating point.[22] But by far the most extensive and most important part of Ockham's examination of the problem is devoted to its metalinguistic treatment. That is to say, he refrains from talking about the entities presumably involved in the problem before him, but examines instead the propositions that speak of such entities and the terms within these propositions that in some way stand for such entities.

Ockham approaches this by saying that there *is* a sense in which a point is a *res*, an *aliquid*. This is so not in spite of the fact that there are no things such as points in nature, but rather because this is just another way of expressing that fact. That is, we can admit that a point is a thing, an *aliquid*, if we consider 'point' as a *term* in a language (either mental, written, or spoken). If we do this, then we can see that the term '*punctus*' has no "real counterpart," that it denotes nothing among the individual substances and qualities that populate the real world, that it doesn't have a real definition (*definitio quid rei*). But we can also see that it does have a nominal definition (*definitio quid nominis*), that is, a definition that explicitly states whatever the term '*punctus*' connotes or stands for implicitly, and this nominal definition shows us how a point is something.[23] To be more specific: to give the nominal definition of the term 'point' is to say that the term 'point' signifies the same thing as the phrase 'a line of such and such a length'. This is but standard procedure; it fits, Ockham notes, with the "rules" for the nominal definitions of other terms.[24] Furthermore, if, following Ockham, we do the same thing with the indivisible entities line and surface, instants, and *generationes* or sudden *mutationes*, we then have a "metalinguistic translation" of the fact that only bodies and time intervals exist as things. There are no indivisible entities as individual, separately existing, things.

But Ockham's metalinguistic move has other consequences as well. Hence, he tells us, whenever the term 'point' occurs in a proposition or *oratio*, then the *oratio* is a *locutio figurativa*, not one that functions *secundum proprietatem sermonis*.[25] Still, such *orationes* or propositions can be conceded once we realize that (to return to our example) the term 'point' is being used in place of its nominal definition, in place of a phrase equivalent to it. Moreover, we concede that such figurative propositions *should* be utilized *causa brevitatis*, a factor that explains why they occur in Aristotle and other *antiqui*.[26]

Secondly, this metalinguistic analysis takes adequate account of the other distinctions and conceptions that are traditionally connected with points. It explains, in other words, just what is involved in the most important propositions in natural philosophy in which the term 'point' appears. It tells us what is really at stake, for example, when it is said that a point is a privation, that a point enters into the *ratio* or definition of a line, or into the standard, Aristotelian definition of continuous magnitudes.[27] And the same thing can be done for such terms as '*instans*', '*mutatio subita*', and so forth. This in turn means that we can translate or reduce all propositions speaking of indivisibles in Aristotelian natural philosophy into others in which indivisible terms such as 'point', 'line', 'instant', etc., do not occur (although it would be incredibly cumbersome to do so).

Ockham concludes his account of the problem of the existence of indivisibles by noting that it is a problem that is far more difficult to resolve than such issues as the composition of continua out of indivisibles where more straightforward and more understandable mathematical arguments usually do the yeoman duty. Here, more subtle arguments are involved, arguments "which mathematicians and others less competent in metaphysics and logic are not able to comprehend."[28] But just how far Ockham was himself prepared to carry his "metalinguistic elimination" of indivisibles in the course of doing natural philosophy in his other works is apparent when we see that just such an approach is utilized in these other works in doing away with such terms as 'instant' and 'first acquired part' in his account of what the continuity, and the *velocitas* and *tarditas*, of motion amounts to.[29]

I have thus far spoken only of Ockham's analysis of the problem of the existence of indivisibles. Yet this was not merely a "one-man" thing: what he accomplished in this analysis was most influential. Thus, we find his successor at Oxford, Thomas Bradwardine, adopting his conclusions—though largely without the metalinguistic analysis—at the end of his *Tractatus de continuo* where he raises the question of the reality of the indivisibles he has been dealing with in the first 141 conclusions of the *Tractatus*. "There are no surfaces, lines, or points at all," Bradwardine concludes, and then adds the equally Ockhamist corollary that "a continuum is neither continued nor rendered finite by such [indivisibles], but by its very self."[30] Somewhat later at Paris we find the likes of Jean Buridan, Gregory of Rimini, and Albert of Saxony clearly supporting Ockham in their definitions of a point.[31] And still later we even learn of Ockham's influence through the historical remark that there are some thinkers who will not admit terms involving"indivisibility" into their logical expositions of certain propositions.[32]

On the other hand, Ockham is also "present" when fourteenth-century scholars such as William Heytesbury, Albert of Saxony, and Nicole Oresme expressly stipulate that there are not such things as instants and indivisible points, but that because they are so prevalent in Aristotelian natural philosophy (especially in what the fourteenth century developed out of this natural philosophy), we must concede them *secundum imaginationem*. Such a concession avoids an unnecessary prolixity of speech.[33] Ockham himself may as well have uttered such words.

Yet if we now set Ockham aside and turn our eyes to at least one other area in fourteenth-century natural philosophy in which indivisible entities were so prevalent, we shall find the metalinguistic approach again to be a most frequent tool for analysis. This other area turns away from the problem of the existence of indivisibles and concentrates on their necessary occurrence *in* continua (be these continua of space, time, or motion, no matter). Here there is an immense amount of late medieval literature. For example, beginning with Aristotle himself,[34] we meet with an amazing number of questions and treatises dealing with the composition of continua out of indivisibles[35] or—adding something totally new to Aristotle—with the question of whether there are more indivisibles in a whole continuous magnitude than in its half and the sub-question following from this of whether one infinite can be greater than another.[36] The metalinguistic component really comes to the fore, however, in another aspect of the fourteenth-century analysis of a continuum: its infinite divisibility. Almost all medievals agreed with Aristotle's opinion that all continua are infinitely divisible into always further divisible parts (that between any two points in a line, for example, there is always another).[37] But how can one most clearly and most rigorously establish that this is so and show just what this infinite divisibility entails? This was somewhat more problematic in the fourteenth century than for Aristotle himself, because there were then certain scholastics (in the minority to be sure) who maintained that continua were infinitely divisible but infinitely divisible *into indivisibles* and, furthermore, that *all* of these indivisibles could be designated or known. Aristotle would have denied that all of the points in a continuous line (for example) could be simultaneously actualized (since such would involve that the infinite division of a continuum be completed), but these renegade scholastic "indivisibilists" argued that there was nothing wrong, in effect, in assuming that they all were so actualized, an assumption that was "guaranteed" by invoking God (his *potentia absoluta* again) as the actualizer, designator, or knower.[38]

Given such a situation, the question then became: how are *all* these points related to the initial point (for instance) of the continuous line to which they belong?[39] The question was answered, again, by metalinguistic analysis, but this time not simply by treating terms and propositions in place of the events and entities of which they spoke, but by doing so by means of the medieval logical doctrine of suppostion.[40]

This is no place to explain even the barest details of this doctrine.[41] Let it be sufficient to say that supposition dealt with the question of what entity or entities terms within, and only within, propositions stood for (*supponit pro*). Furthermore, just what these terms within propositions stood for could be made to vary by the presence of this or that "logical word" (such words as 'all', 'some', 'not', etc.) in the proposition in question or even by the variant position of the same logical word or words in the proposition. The matter before us will provide an example of how this works.

The procedure was roughly this: Take the following two different propositions: (1) 'between the first point of a line and every other point known by God of the same line, there is a mean point'; (2) 'there is [some one] mean point between the first point and every other point perceived by God of the same line'. The first proposition is true, but the second is false. This is so because, in the first proposition, the term 'mean point' has a type of supposition called "merely confused" (due to the fact that the logical term 'every' precedes it in the proposition), while this same term 'mean point' in the second proposition has a supposition called "determinate." But given what merely confused supposition and determinate supposition mean and what logical procedures are licit or not licit when one or the other occurs with respect to a term like 'mean point', this entails that in the second proposition we can "descend" from the term 'mean point' to the specification of either 'this [particular] mean point' or 'that [particular] mean point' or 'that other [particular] mean point', etc. But this means that the second proposition is false because there is no one, no this or that, particular mean point that falls between the initial point of the line and *all* other points in the line. On the other hand, in the first proposition, the term 'mean point' has merely confused supposition which means that one *cannot* disjunctively descend to 'this or that [particular] mean point'—which represents what as a matter of fact is the case, namely, there is no one mean point between the initial point of the line and all others. Hence, the first proposition is true.[42]

In fourteenth-century terms, what had been accomplished with this analysis was the creation of a way to distinguish clearly between two different kinds of infinite divisibility, the one involving always further divisible parts and constituting true continua, the other resolving a continuum into an infinity of indivisibles and hence not yielding proper continuity (at least for most scholastics). Moreover, by this procedure it was seen that these two kinds of divisibility were not merely distinct, but that one could not make a valid inference from the one to the other, in particular from the "true" one to the "false" one as some thinkers had maintained.[43] But the point to note in the present context is that these fourteenth-century scholars were able to formulate this distinction clearly by viewing the problem metalinguistically, hence allowing its rephrasing in terms of a standard, universally accepted, logical distinction between kinds of supposition. At the same time, they also formulated a more rigorous notion of how the initial point of a continuous line serves as its limit: it now only precedes all, the total infinity, of points in the line, but precedes no one of them.

All of this represents but one phase of how the use of logical conceptions made fourteenth-century natural philosophy more analytic. But metalinguistic analysis was even more rampant in the late medieval investigation of yet another problem relating to the infinite divisibility and limiting of continua. Here, unlike the issue we have just examined, there was a definite passage of departure in Aristotle. The context is that of the continuity of motion and the problem that of order within such continuous motion. Briefly stated, in Book VI, chapter 5, of the *Physics*, Aristotle addressed himself to the question of whether there is a first element, a "primary when," at the *beginning* of a continuous change or motion and whether there is such a primary element for the *completion* of such a change, a moment when it is first true to say "this change is now over."[44] Let us call this problem and others related to it "limit decision" problems. Now Aristotle's reply to the particular limit decision problem he had posed was that one should deny that there is a "primary when" at the beginning of a continuous change, but affirm that there does exist one at its end that signifies that the change has been concluded.[45] It would be interesting and historically valuable to go into Aristotle's arguments as to why he believed one must come to this decision and into the ramifications he saw as attendant upon it, but for our purposes we need only note that this chapter in Book VI of the *Physics* (and certain passages in chapter 8 of Book VIII as well)[46] were absolutely crucial for a large body of scholastic literature that carried the problem of the limits of continua a good deal beyond what one had in Aristotle.

There was considerable interest in the problem raised by this passage in the *Physics* already in the thirteenth century. Roger Bacon, for example, saw a relevance of some of what Aristotle had maintained to the problem of the transmutation involved in the Eucharist.[47] But it is the fourteenth century when we are witness to whole treatises dealing with the problem. When we look at this literature we find scholars setting down into summary, almost axiomatic, form much that was involved in the problem initially set by Aristotle. Thus, we first notice that the word *instans* is used in place of Aristotle's "primary when" (τὸ ἐν ᾧ πρώτῳ). Furthermore, in terms of this new vocabulary, these treatises tell us that we can then distinguish between two ways in which a continuous change may begin: either by there being a first instant of the existence (*primum instans esse*) of that change, or a last instant of the non-existence (*ultimum instans non esse*) of that change immediately prior to its existence (which is what Aristotle meant in denying a "primary when" for the beginning of a continuous change). Similarly, there are two ways in which a continuous change may end: either by there being a last instant of its existence (*ultimum instans esse*) or a first instant of its non-existence (*primum instans non esse*) immediately upon completion of the change (which is what Aristotle meant by affirming a "primary when" at the conclusion of a continuous change). They had, I think it fair to say, sharpened Aristotle by thus translating his limit decision for a continuous change into the claim that there was a last instant of its not being at its beginning and a first instant of its not, or no longer, being at its termination, thus making it quite clear that the change in question was *extrinsically* limited in both directions. (Such a double extrinsic limit for a continuous change might be diagrammed as in figure 1.)

The fourteenth-century treatises and questions in which all of this was summarily presented were most often entitled *De primo et ultimo instanti*, that of Walter Burley the most popular among

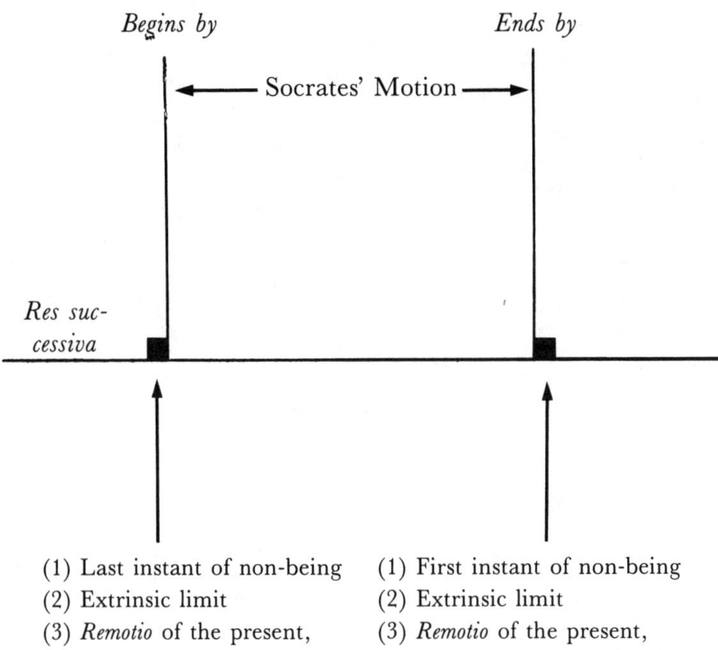

Figure 1

them.[48] But it was not simply a translation of Aristotle's results to which thirteenth- and fourteenth-century scholars devoted themselves in this whole literature. They also extended and scholasticized the "limit decision problem" by stipulating what kinds of things had what kinds of "beginning and ending" limits: *successive* things which have their parts not all at once but one after another (a category in which Aristotle's example of continuous motion or change naturally falls) or *permanent* things the parts of which all do exist *simul*. Successive things (like a run made by Socrates, for example) and permanent things whose existence depends on successive things (for example, the truth of the proposition 'Socrates runs') are extrinsically limited at both ends just as Aristotle had maintained (see Figure 1). But the limit decision for permanent things was more problematic. A permanent thing that lasts through a time interval—such as Socrates' existence or Socrates' being white—

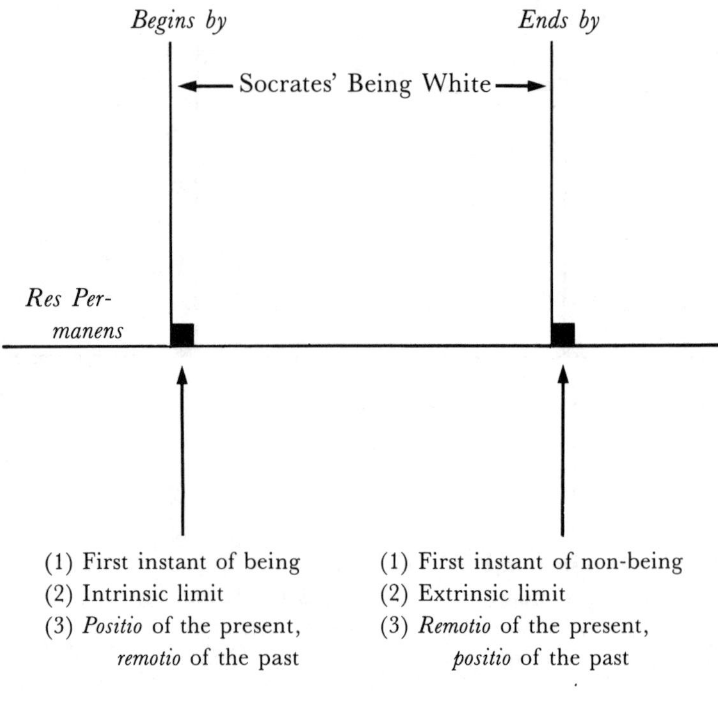

Figure 2

was limited by there being a first instant of existence at its beginning and a first instant of its non-existence at its termination, thus yielding an *intrinsic* beginning limit and an *extrinsic* terminating one (see figure 2). And this was extended to include limit decisions for other special categories of permanent things, for example, those that exist for but a single instant.[49]

Several things should be noted about all of this before we proceed further. First, we should realize that what is really crucial to the problem being investigated is the absolute continuity of *time*. Even when one is not dealing with successive things like continuous motions, it was still problematic to set the appropriate limit of a permanent thing because its existence necessarily occurred within or against the continuous "background" of time. Secondly, we should make note of the fact that in the kind of literature we have been sampling, the scholastics were debating the question and stating their conclusions in what we would today call the "object language"; they were speaking about limits *in re*.

But this kind of treatment of the problem is not our major concern. It is rather to follow out another development of this "limit decision" literature, to examine what one historian has labeled the *logical* phase of the problem, a phase to be distinguished from the *physical* one we have just mentioned.[50] Here we have to deal with quite another class of literature, not totally distinct from such physical discussions as that of Burley's *Tractatus de primo et ultimo instanti*, but surely distinct enough to be easily discriminated in any number of ways. It is the literature of "beginning and ceasing," of *de incipit et desinit.*[51]

Although there is literature belonging to this new category from the twelfth century onward, it is, unfortunately, a literature whose history harbors a fair number of gaps (and which, even more unfortunately, the primary sources may not allow us ever to eliminate). What these gaps or missing pieces are can be brought out if one begins by dividing this *incipit/desinit* literature into three segments: (1) that which is almost purely logical, (2) that which is logical plus physical, the two strands not, however, being integrated, and (3) that which reveals the logical quite thoroughly integrated with the physical. I should caution that, although these three segments appear in chronological order, this certainly does not mean that there was no temporal overlapping, that, in particular, an earlier segment did not continue to appear long after the birth of one of its successors. I might also mention that all three segments of this *incipit/desinit* literature contain sophisms as part of the way in which they deal with the problems at hand, but, this notwithstanding, the segments do possess basic features that make them quite distinct. But let me try to show that discriminating these three segments is a reasonable way to interpret the historical picture and at the same time to reveal what the gaps are in this picture.

The first segment is constituted of logical treatises that were written in the twelfth and early thirteenth centuries. (All anonymous, I shall ignore just which treatises these were; they have all been edited by L. M. De Rijk and, relative to our *incipit/desinit* problem, analyzed by Norman Kretzmann.)[52] As Kretzmann has clearly established, the main point for us to note in this literature is that the terms 'incipit' and 'desinit' contain "covert references" to the past or future or to negation and therefore confuse or stymie inferences made from propositions in which these terms occur. However, relative to the historical story that is before us, the important thing to indicate is that, when some such proposition as 'Socrates begins to be white' (*Sortes [Socrates] incipit esse albus*) is treated as problematic in this literature, the point is not the problem of there being (or not being) a "first element" in the process of becoming or being white, that is, Aristotle's limit decision problem is not at issue.[53] What is more, as far as I can see, all of the examples or sophisms treated in this literature are consistent with a "discrete" or non-continuous time or process of change in time. (And then, of course, the limit decision problem would no longer really be so problematic.)[54]

The second segment of our *incipit/desinit* literature is also made up of logical treatises, all apparently written in the thirteenth century. First, the tracts on syncategorematic terms (that is, we would say, on logical terms or operators—although some of the terms the medievals included here would not be logical operators for us) of William of Sherwood and Peter of Spain;[55] and second, a number of largely anonymous collections of sophismata.[56] The keynote of this literature is that we are here first witness to the influence, or perhaps better, intrusion, of "limit decisions" in the sense found in Aristotle's *Physics* and of other things that appear in the later physical literature such as that of Walter Burley. We find, for example, an analysis of the terms 'incipit' and 'desinit' related to the distinction between permanent and successive things and a good sprinkling of the vocabulary of first and last instants.[57]

But we also find something that will become one of the hallmarks of *incipit/desinit* treatises: the translation, as it were, of "limit decisions" expressed physically by reference to first and last instants into *related* expositions of the terms 'incipit' and 'desinit'. Thus, to speak merely of 'it begins' or 'incipit', we are told that when something begins to be it can either begin by (1) the positing (*positio*) of the present and a removal (*remotio*) of the past, or by (2) a removal of the present and a positing of the future. To translate this back into the corresponding "physical way" of putting it, in the first case we have to consider the existence of a first instant of being, an intrinsic limit, to the something in question (which fits the way normal permanent things are held to begin to be). In the second case—removal of the present and positing of the future—we have to consider the existence of a last instant of not being (which fits the beginning limit held to be proper for successive things).[58]

In Peter of Spain in particular we are witness to even further awareness of the connection between the "logic" of 'incipit' and 'desinit' and the "physics" involved in limit decisions. We see, for instance, an explicit awareness of the relevance of the continuity of time.[59] But, more importantly, Peter gives a constellation of rules for all relevant combinations of *incipit/desinit*, being and not-being, and permanent and successive entities. This enables him to set up the proper spectrum of limit decisions, but then he brings what he has done "back to logic" by using these results to point out why and how each of the terms 'incipit' and 'desinit' have different significations.[60]

Although this all looks terribly encouraging, nevertheless, when we look to the resolution of the actual sophisms involving the terms 'incipit' and 'desinit' in Peter and the rest of this "segment two" literature, the "physical strand" that has been established is not applied. Logical rules and conceptions are utilized instead.[61] And again, the difficulties treated and solved in the sophisms stand in either discrete or continuous time.

Thus, the general conclusion to be drawn from this second, thirteenth-century, segment of *incipit/desinit* literature is, I believe (and I think Norman Kretzmann agrees in this), that the essentially physical material dealing with limit decisions occurs as an adjunct and not as something inextricably connected with the logic of 'incipit' and 'desinit' in these tracts. We have, so to say, the mere *juxtaposition* of the logical and the physical or, in other terms, of the metalinguistic and the physical. There is also a missing piece in that part of the historical story told by this thirteenth-century literature: we do not know why it was that the Aristotelian problem about limit decisions became associated with the sort of logical analysis of the terms 'incipit' and 'desinit' that was already present for other reasons. (But perhaps it would be wrong to look for anything more in this "association" than a simple tendency toward a syncretism that put resembling things and conceptions together.)

Another missing piece in the story comes to view, unfortunately, as soon as we approach the third segment of our *incipit/desinit* literature, since we then have before us a literature that expresses the genuine integration of the logical and the physical, not merely their juxtaposition. How this integration came about, we still do not know. But it did occur, taking the form of a radical metalinguistic treatment of the problem of limit decisions.

This is seen in a work belonging to what might be considered a "first strain" in this third segment of our literature: the *Tractatus de incipit et desinit* ascribed to Thomas Bradwardine, written, it would seem, some time in the 1320s.[62] It is instructive to see just how the "metalinguistic jump" is made in this work. One of the two explicit *suppositiones* with which it begins is clearly stated in the physical, object language: "There is no last instant in the existence of a permanent thing, but there is a first instant in its existence" (that is, a permanent thing has no *last* intrinsic limit, but it does have a *first* intrinsic limit).[63] However, Bradwardine's other explicit *suppositio* gives the standard *positio-remotio* analysis of the two senses given to the terms 'incipit' and 'desinit' and explicitly connects this with propositions by claiming that *positio* amounts to an affirmative proposition and *remotio* to a negative proposition.[64] Given this, plus a single preliminary distinction which speaks, not of permanent versus successive *things*, but of *dictiones* or *termini* that are signs of, or stand for, permanent or successive things,[65] the stage is quite prepared for the metalinguistic approach. To see something of the "play" to be presented on this stage, we can look at Bradwardine's first conclusion. It is, again, stated in the object language: "Whatever among permanent things begins to exist is now and was not previously"[66] (that is, there is a first instant of being for such things). But then his first "corollary" immediately translates this into his metalanguage:

> Every proposition composed out of terms (standing for) permanent things in which the verb 'it begins' occurs is to be expounded by the *positio* of the present and the *remotio* of the past. For example, if one says 'Socrates begins to be', this proposition is to be expounded into [the two propositions] 'Socrates in this instant is' and 'Socrates was not before that instant', one of which two expounding propositions is affirmative and called *positio* of the present, the other negative and called *remotio* of the past.[67]

And this metalinguistic treatment continues through Bradwardine's *Tractatus*. For example, he employs such means in the investigation of sophism-like conclusions dealing with the space traversed and the places occupied at the inception of a given local motion.[68] Or, somewhat more generally, in the treatment of difficulties presumably implied by saying that something beginning to be entails that it *will* be, he examines the situation in terms of the truth of future contingent propositions.[69]

If in reflecting upon the kind of "metalinguism" we see in Bradwardine there is still a puzzle about how things proceeded from what we find in the thirteenth-century juxtaposition of the logical and the physical to the integration we see in his work, it is nevertheless true that this work was composed at a time when the metalinguistic analysis of all manner of other problems was extremely prevalent. Our citation of Ockham's analysis of the existence of indivisibles is an excellent case in point. Bradwardine marks, therefore, a very good fit with his time.

The second strain in our third segment of *incipit/desinit* literature brings out yet another kind of fit. We might say that this strain can be initially characterized by the massive reintroduction (although there here lurks another "missing piece" in the story) of sophisms, something that was in general an outstanding "disputational element" in fourteenth-century university activities.[70] But unlike the *incipit/desinit* sophisms of the thirteenth century, these *incipit/desinit* sophisms are now directly connected to limit decision problems. Any number of works populate this new strain of *incipit/desinit* literature, but among the most important are, in chronological order, the *Sophismata* of Richard Kilvington,[71] the fourth chapter of William Heytesbury's *Regule solvendi sophismata,*[72] and, tolerably later in time, the chapter on 'incipit' and 'desinit' in Paul of Venice's *Logica magna.*[73] I shall, however, start with Heytesbury and confine most of my remarks to his work, largely because he illustrates what was involved in a clearer and more impressive way.

Apart from the fact that the *incipit/desinit* chapter in Heytesbury's *Regule* is much more complex than corresponding fourteenth-century work either before or after him, one of its characteristics is that, although he begins the chapter in the usual "textbook" fashion by giving the standard two-fold exposition of the terms 'incipit' and 'desinit',[74] he is clearly not "textbookish" in what follows. That is, he does not go on to set down exhaustively and in proper fashion all of the relevant rules for the traditional cases of *permanentia* versus *successiva*. That something "different" is as a matter of fact going to follow is even presaged by the first words he utters after the standard exposition of 'incipit' and 'desinit': "However, in whatever way one or the other [of these terms] is understood . . ."[75]; the usual distinctions and rules, he seems to be telling us, are not going to be very important.

In fact, the rules that Heytesbury does give are not at all very commodious for the treatment of "normal" cases of permanent and successive things. As they are phrased, they contain too much "extra baggage" for easy application to such cases. They are, as we shall see, specifically keyed to the particular sophisms whose resolution will form the substance of Heytesbury's whole chapter.

However, acknowledging the fact that what we have before us fits very well with the popularity of *disputationes de sophismatibus* in general, what advantage did sophisms have in treating limit decision problems? Put abstractly, at least part of the answer to this question is that, when one might have had one's head tolerably clear about what decision should be made with respect to the limiting of this or that kind of thing, the formulation of an appropriate sophism might serve to reveal that things weren't so clear after all and that, consequently, the particular limit decision in question should be investigated further. (And this is true for the role of sophisms in treating all manner of other problems in the fourteenth century.) For instance, let us say that (a) you were white *after* any *past* instant; does it not follow as a general rule that (b) you were white immediately *before* the present instant (it not being relevant whether you are white or not at the present instant)? Does not (a) always imply (b)? This might seem true. But one can imagine a *casus* that makes a sophism out of this presumed general rule. Take the past hour and divide it into proportional parts with the smaller proportional parts in the direction of the present instant; furthermore, assume that you were white in any even-numbered proportional part of this past hour, but black in any odd-numbered one. (Thus, you were black in the first half-hour of the past hour, white during the next quarter-hour, black in the next eighth, white in the next sixteenth, and so on.) Now, in the past hour thus divided, since there is no last proportional part that immediately precedes the present instant, one cannot claim that you were white immediately before the present instant, even though it *is* true that at some point *after* any instant of the past hour you were white. But this is to deny outright the presumably general rule. The lesson is that the sophism has revealed that it need not be observed in all cases.[76]

Another instance of a sophism "clarifying" matters about limits by revealing that things were really not so clear or simple as might have been imagined can be taken from Heytesbury himself (although Heytesbury does not introduce the sophism in the way I shall describe; he just introduces it, no explanation given). Let us suppose that something successively possesses or "runs through" all of the values of a given finite continuum (of whiteness or of size, for example) *except* the final value or point terminating that continuum. One can then very well claim that the values had by that thing are *extrinsically* limited by the least value it does not come to have. Instantiating, if I grow in size from one foot up to six feet in such a way that I am successively all of the sizes from one to six *except six itself*, then six is the least size I will not have had; my sizes are extrinsically limited by six. But can anything *more* be said about the sizes that I *will* have had? Apparently not; there is surely no greatest size that I will have had. But such a negative answer to what more might be said need not be so if one constructs a sophism comparing my growth with that of someone else over the same time span. Let us set aside my magnitude and speak instead, with Heytesbury, of the imagined cases of Socrates and Plato. Assume that Socrates is now one foot tall, Plato two feet tall; and let each of them grow uniformly throughout the next hour, Socrates twice as fast as Plato, stipulating further that three feet is the smallest size that neither of them will have, since both cease to exist at the end of the hour at which moment both would have been three feet tall had they then existed. As of the present instant, as of now, what can we say about Socrates' and Plato's sizes? Naturally that Socrates *is* not now of such a size as Plato is or will be. But what about, as of now, the truth of the proposition 'Socrates will be of such a size as Plato will be' and the proposition 'Socrates begins or will begin to be of such a size as Plato will be'?[77] I will postpone an answer since the investigation of this particular sophism forms the major burden of Heytesbury's chapter on 'incipit' and 'desinit'. At this point what we should note is that the sophism is meant to bring out features about a limit decision that would not otherwise present themselves.

Let us examine, not the details, but rather the structure of how Heytesbury goes about resolving this sophism comparing the hypothetical growth of Socrates and Plato. His method is, to be sure, metalinguistic, but his approach takes a subtler form than that which we observed in Bradwardine. He begins with the following: "Whatever something will begin or will cease to be, it will begin or will cease to be such in some *instant*."[78] With this, he has directly connected beginning and ceasing with some instant. But since he will be operating metalinguistically, this "some instant" amounts to a *proposition* that was, is, or will be *true* at some instant. This becomes clear if we look at his first principal—admittedly rather complex—rule:

> If we have to do with a negative proposition about the present joined to an affirmative proposition about the past or the future for the truth of which affirmative proposition there is required some instant at which it will be true, then a beginning with respect to either the present or the future follows; on the other hand, if that same past or future affirmative proposition does not require such an instant for its truth, but an interval of time, then it is not necessary that a beginning of this sort follow.[79]

An example given by Heytesbury will make what is covered by this rule slightly clearer. If the *true* present negative proposition in question is 'Socrates is not now white' and the future affirmative proposition is 'Socrates will be white', then there *must* be some instant for which the proposition 'Socrates will be white' can be verified. This is so because, if 'Socrates will be white' is now true, then, as a matter of fact, Socrates will be white at some instant (although Heytesbury doesn't trouble to tell us the reason why there must be an instant at which this in fact will be true, which is, of course, because Socrates' being white is a permanent thing *durans per tempus* at any instant of which he naturally will be white). But if some instant is required for the truth of 'Socrates will be white', then, by Heytesbury's rule, it follows that Socrates will begin to be white.[80] Heytesbury doesn't trouble to give another example applying his rule to the case of a successive thing[81]—he is not so "textbookish" as to do that—but proceeds directly to his sophism of the growth of Socrates and Plato.

How does the rule apply there? Again, if we are given the negative proposition as true now—namely, the proposition 'Socrates is not now of such a size as Plato will be'—then according to the two alternatives stipulated by the rule we must *either* specify the *instant* required for the truth of the future affirmative proposition 'Socrates will be of such a size as Plato will be' *or* the *time interval* required for this latter proposition to be true. Now, given the *present* sizes of Socrates and Plato and the way they are stipulated by the sophism to grow, it is clear that there is no *instant* for which 'Socrates will be of such a size as Plato will be' can be verified (since that would entail that Socrates and Plato will at some instant be equal in size). However, if we see that for Heytesbury the proposition 'Socrates will be of such a size as Plato will be' means that Socrates will have all of the sizes that Plato will have and will have no size greater than those had by Plato, then it is clear that the future affirmative proposition 'Socrates will be of such a size as Plato will be' will be true *if* we are given the time interval from now up to, but not including, the end of the next hour (since neither Socrates nor Plato exist at the end of the next hour). The truth of this future affirmative will then obtain because it is during that (open-ended) time interval that Socrates will have all of the sizes Plato will have and none greater. On the other hand, it doesn't follow that Socrates will *begin* to be of such a size as Plato will be, because that would involve (according to Heytesbury's rule) that the future affirmative proposition in question be true for some instant.[82] Q.E.D. – the sophism is solved.

The significant thing to note, however, is that Heytesbury's sophism and the metalinguistic treatment of a limit decision that it contains did enable him to say something more about the sizes of Socrates and Plato beyond the fact that these sizes are limited extrinsically by a least size (viz., 3) had by neither of them. We would phrase this "something more" by saying that "Socrates will have all of the sizes Plato will have and none greater," while Heytesbury, quite thoroughly metalinguistic, accomplishes the same thing by saying that the proposition 'Socrates will be of such a size as Plato will be' will be true *per aliquod tempus*. Indeed, as we have seen, it is because that *aliquod tempus* is the interval during which Socrates will possess all of those sizes that allows Heytesbury to express the same "fact" metalinguistically.

We should not be hasty to conclude that Heytesbury was the only one to propose this particular sophism for resolution or that all agreed with him concerning his conclusions about it. As a matter of fact, apparently before him, Richard Kilvington treated an all-but-identical proposition. ('Socrates will be as white as Plato will be white') and concluded that it would require that there be a most intense degree of whiteness in which Socrates will be white or in which Plato will be white in order for it to be true.[83] Similarly, long after Heytesbury, Paul of Venice agrees that his Socrates-Plato "sophism proposition" is true, but only when stated in a different form (in, roughly, the same words, but with these words having different positions within the proposition). The qualification is necessary, Paul felt, because this will make the proposition about Socrates' and Plato's future sizes jibe with the doctrine of supposition and, furthermore, make it more consistent with the dictum asserted by Heytesbury himself claiming that any beginning occurs at some instant. To render the whole yet more complete, Paul even troubles to set forth specific rules revealing just which propositions require an instant for their verification and which do not. Heytesbury's metalinguism was being filled out.[84]

Before concluding this account of *incipit-desinit* literature and bringing it back to confront what we have seen about Ockham and the existence of indivisibles, it will be worthwhile to set down a few final comments about this third, genuinely metalinguistic, segment of this literature. As I have already noted, this segment has been characterized as the "logical phase" of the investigation of limit decision problems.[85] But we should be careful about such a label. The emphasis should be on the *integration* of the logical and the physical. It was that integrating which occurred, as I have suggested, as one moved from thirteenth-century treatments of 'incipit' and 'desinit' to fourteenth-century ones. This means that we should be quite clear that, when we look at the work of Bradwardine, Kilvington, or Heytesbury, although there is a good deal of logic in these works, their authors are not *doing* logic. They are doing physics or natural philosophy but with decidedly logical, metalinguistic, tools. In point of fact, the works of Heytesbury and his associates are no less natural philosophy or physics than any other application of metalinguistic analysis and logic in medieval philosophy or theology—something easily and plentifully observable in the likes of Ockham, Holcot, Buridan, Gregory of Rimini, and others—at Paris as well as at Oxford.[86] In all of these cases the *content* was natural philosophy or theology; it was the *method* that was more or less "logic dominated"—and method need not, and in many fourteenth-century instances did not, affect content.

Still, if one singles out the kind of thing that Heytesbury does in his *Regule*, it is true that there is much more of the same at Oxford, especially among his Mertonian colleagues, than at Paris. Why so? In attempting to answer this almost unanswerable question, one is tempted to see a reflection of the difference between the essentially "extensional" logic developed in England in the fourteenth century and the earlier "intensional" logic more characteristic of Paris and the Continent. But considerably more sources need to be analyzed to say much more about the hypothesis of that difference as a partial cause of the English phenomenon exhibited by Heytesbury and his associates.

Yet another partial cause might be elicited if we return for a moment to the fact that a concern for problems involving indivisibles was very much part of Aristotelian physics, especially in those areas and problems that dealt with the investigation of the continuity of motion and time and the "limit decisions" relevant to these continua. Indeed, the kind of concern with indivisibles and instants that we find in scholars like Heytesbury is what might "naturally happen" if one goes more deeply into all of the twists and turns of Aristotle's *Physics* and then attempts to develop in detail some of the most salient problems and conceptions it contains. Noting this, if one then turns to the frequency with which Aristotle's *Physics* was commented upon at Oxford versus Paris in the later thirteenth and earlier fourteenth centuries, one comes away with the fact that commentaries at Oxford outnumbered those at Paris by a factor something like two to one, an imbalance that is not true concerning commentaries on almost all other works of Aristotle.[87] The suggestion is, then, that greater attention paid to Aristotle's *Physics* may have contributed to making fourteenth-century Oxford natural philosophy what it was, Heytesbury and the whole so-called calculatory tradition around him included.

On the other hand, if one sets this difference between Oxford and Paris aside, it is certainly true that the utilization of sophisms, the application of logic, and metalinguistic analysis constitute something that is generally characteristic of fourteenth-century philosophy and, in many respects, of fourteenth-century theology as well. These things represent a good part, I would maintain, of what made the fourteenth century "analytic." It is presently difficult to say just why such a way of approaching and resolving problems increased so markedly in this century. Surely, the very central position occupied by logic in medieval university curricula was a contributing factor. Yet if we focus our attention more strictly upon the phenomenon of metalinguistic analysis, then it seems extremely plausible that another cause of the rise of *that* kind of "being analytic" is to be found in the rapidly growing belief in the absolute contingency of the natural world and in the concomitant concerns with the certitude of knowledge and with the grounding of this certainty, not in contingent *things*, but in *propositions* as the only possible bearers of the requisite universality and necessity characteristic of demonstrative knowledge. To return to some of my initial comments, it is of course this belief in the contingency of the natural world that was bound up with the empiricism Moody has noted as a notable feature of fourteenth-century philosophy. But as I have tried to show by example, when fourteenth-century scholars got down to the business of doing natural philosophy or "science," many of them left this contingency, its accompanying empiricism, and, in the bargain, nature far behind. It was not terribly relevant to what they were trying to do. Logic and logical techniques, on the other hand, decidedly were. It was from such that so much of their *method* arose.

I have talked today about only a few examples of that method, but I believe that they are fully representative of a great deal in fourteenth-century thought. In point of fact, I also believe that if one is concerned most adequately to reveal what was characteristic of fourteenth-century learning, of how it was analytic and critical, more often than not it is not content that is indicative, but method: tools of analysis, techniques of reasoning, and criteria of evidence. What is more, method is far more acceptable as "common tender" by scholars of different philosophical or theological persuasions than is content. In fact, this ability to utilize techniques and methods of analysis developed in philosophical contexts in dealing with problems in theology was one of the phenomena that I appealed to in criticizing Moody's assertion of the withdrawal of philosophy from theology in the fourteenth century. It was, I would guess, probably the most important of such phenomena. Lest one think that this interchange between fourteenth-century philosophy and theology was a limited and infrequent thing, one can point to the utilization in theological contexts of something as specific as the conceptions involved in limit decisions and the language of first and last instants and 'incipit' and 'desinit'.[88]

As might be expected, if we forget instants and indivisibles, metalinguistic analysis taken broadly was even more prevalent in philosophy and theology. The "objects" or "things" treated in these two realms were naturally regarded as distinct, radically distinct. But the language in which both had to be treated, or the structure—one might even say the "logic"—of that language, was, equally naturally, the same. Why not, then, see what yield the metalinguistic treatment of problems in both of these disciplines might have? The dissenting view to such a suggestion was from time to time that this would be to seek refuge in mere *verba grammaticalia* (especially if Ockham's metalinguistic analysis was at stake) and then one ought to *nauseare super dictis eorum* and simply say: *Contra verbosos noli contendere verbis.*[89] One should deal with *things*, with what really is, not just words. But such an approach seems to fail to appreciate what was being done in metalinguistic analysis. Things and objective events *were* being dealt with, and to use logical conceptions and a metalinguistic approach in dealing with them no more means that one is doing logic or grammar and *not* dealing with reality than to utilize mathematics in natural philosophy is simply to do mathematics and no natural philosophy. Ockham himself has a related reply to those who do not wish to speak of words, but only of things: "Although you may wish to speak only of things, that is only possible by means of words or concepts or other signs, and therefore it is according to what those signs—whatever they may be—signify and connote or do not connote" that one ought to proceed.[90]

Of course, one might object that, even if one grants the necessity or at least value of doing a good deal of natural philosophy metalinguistically, still the kind of *things* and *events* whose metalinguistic treatment I have spoken of today are certainly not representative of what goes on in nature. But that is just the point. That is to say, if there was no metalinguistic analysis at all and all of these arguments about indivisibles and limit decisions were stated in a physical, object language, there would clearly still be no "match" with nature. But *that* is because these fourteenth-century natural philosophers were, as I mentioned at the outset, proceeding *secundum imaginationem.*[91] Such a procedure was itself one of the things that made the fourteenth century analytic and, as a consequence, much of its natural philosophy *praeter cursum naturae.* And metalinguistic analysis and sophisms were, I have wanted to say today, another.

Finally, lest you think that such problematic entities as points and instants were the "culprits" in pulling natural philosophy away from nature, let me assure you that if we put them as much out of the picture as possible and look instead to what fourteenth-century natural philosophers did with more "normal" problems such as what motion is, how we should "measure" it by applying the doctrine of the intension, remission, and latitude of forms or by appealing to rules dealing with the velocities of bodies undergoing rotation,[92] the same features of proceeding *secundum imaginationem*, of metalinguistic analysis, and of the invocation of sophisms are plentifully present.

Then, too, we had a natural philosophy that often had less to do with nature than we might like.

Notes

1. This article first appeared in the *Philosophical Review* 67 (1958): 145–63, and was reprinted in Moody's *Studies in Medieval Philosophy, Science, and Logic: Collected Articles 1933–1969* (Berkeley/Los Angeles/London, 1975), pp. 287–304. References below will give the relevant page numbers for both publications, that of the *Collected Articles* in parentheses.

2. Any number of the somewhat older standard histories of medieval philosophy could be cited in this regard, but see, in particular, Etienne Gilson's *The Unity of Philosophical Experience* (New York, 1937), chap. 4 and the historians referred to by Moody in his article.

3. Moody, p. 161 (301).

4. Moody, p. 161 (302).

5. Moody, p. 159 (300).

6. Moody, p. 160 (301).

7. Moody, p. 159 (300).

8. It seems far better to emphasize the role and influence of a *particularist ontology* (only individual, permanent things exist) rather than an *empiricist epistemology* in the development of fourteenth-century natural philosophy.

9. Thus, in commenting on William Heytesbury's *secundum imaginationem* example of a body undergoing a uniform motion of rotation while at the same time being rarefied throughout and suffering corruption at its circumference, Gaetano da Thiene gives the equally imaginative "natural confirmation" of a wheel of ice rotating in an oven (see William Heytesbury, *Regule solvendi sophismata* [Venice, 1494], fol. 38r). Note should also be made of the fact that, although empiricist epistemology was of little effect in such *secundum imaginationem* procedures, the underlying particularist ontology frequently did "come through."

10. Moody, p. 159 (300).

11. J. Murdoch, "From Social into Intellectual Factors: An Aspect of the Unitary Character of Late Medieval Learning," in J. Murdoch and E. Sylla, eds., *The Cultural Context of Medieval Learning* (Dordrecht/Boston, 1975), pp. 280–89.

12. See J. Murdoch and E. Sylla, "The Science of Motion," in David Lindberg, ed., *Science in the Middle Ages* (in press); J. Murdoch, "*Mathesis in philosophiam scholasticam introducta*: The Rise and Development of the Application of Mathematics in Fourteenth-Century Philosophy and Theology," in *Arts libéraux et philosophie au moyen âge*, Actes du Quatrième Congrès International de Philosophie Médiévale (Montreal/Paris, 1969), pp. 225–33, 238–46; J. Murdoch, "*Subtilitates Anglicanae* in Fourteenth-Century Paris: John of Mirecourt and Peter Ceffons," in Madeleine Cosman et al., eds., *Machaut's World: Science and Art in the Fourteenth Century* (in press).

13. See J. Murdoch and E. Sylla, "The Science of Motion," (above, n. 12); E. Sylla, "Medieval Quantifications of Qualities: The 'Merton School,'" *Archive for History of Exact Sciences* 8 (1971): 9–39, and "Medieval Concepts of the Latitude of Forms: The Oxford Calculators," *Archives d'histoire doctrinale et littéraire du moyen âge* 40 (1973):223–83.

14. *Physics* 3. 1. 200b15–21.

15. See, for example, William of Ockham, *De sacramento altaris*, ed. T. Bruce Birch (Burlington, Iowa, 1930), p. 72: "Nusquam invenitur quod Aristoteles ex intentione pertractavit illam questionem an punctus sit res indivisibilis distincta realiter ab omni re divisibili." Although Birch utilized several manuscripts as well as the fifteenth- and sixteenth-century editions of the *De sacramento altaris*, the resulting text is in many places far from reliable. Therefore, in most cases below, I have corrected Birch's text by employing one or more fourteenth-century manuscripts.

16. *Physics* 6. 1–2. At times, Aristotle's refutation of any indivisibilist composition of continua was reputed to imply that he admitted the existence of indivisibles. See, for example, this argument as presented in the *De sacramento altaris* (ed. Birch, pp. 48, 80, and MS Basel F. II. 24, 23v, 25v) and Ockham's reply to it: "Item, ibidem (scil. *Phys.* 6) dicit Philosophus quod linea est divisibilis et punctum indivisibile et per hoc probat quod linea non componitur ex punctis ne aliquod continuum ex indivisibilibus, quod esset vanum nisi essent talia indivisibilia preter continua. . . . Ad aliud quando dicitur quod Philosophus probat quod nullum quantum componitur ex indivisibilibus, dicendum est quod verum est, et illa, cum sit negativa, non infert aliquam talem affirmativam: 'aliquod indivisibile est'. Et quando dicitur quod vanum fuisset ita diffuse probare quod continuum non componitur ex indivisibilibus nisi essent aliqua talia indivisibilia, dicendum est quod non est vanum probare unam conclusionem per diversa media, quamvis possit sufficienter probari per unum. Unde sufficiens medium fuit probare nullum indivisibile esse, sed tamen alia non superfluunt, et specialiter in isto casu."

17. The *De sacramento altaris* also provided a theological context for Ockham's discussion of *quantitas*.

18. See text quoted in n. 23 below.

19. Ockham brings forth similar arguments against the separate existence of instants (*De sacr. alt.*, ed. Birch, pp. 50–62). Thus, strictly speaking, it should be said that the only separately existing things for Ockham are spatially extended bodies and temporally extended intervals of time, although we shall ignore the latter in what follows.

20. I have in mind the establishment of the concepts of point, line, and plane in the works of the likes of Moritz Pasch, *Vorlesungen über neuere Geometrie* (Leipzig, 1882; 2d ed., Berlin, 1926) and G. Veronese, *Fondamenti di geometria* (Padua, 1891; translated into German as *Grundzüge der Geometrie* Leipzig, 1894). Comparison also might be made with Whitehead's "method of extensive abstraction"; see his *An Enquiry into the Principles of Natural Knowledge* (Cambridge, 1919), pt. 3, and *The Concept of Nature* (Cambridge, 1926), chap. 4.

21. *De sacramento altaris*, ed. Birch, pp. 8–28.

22. *De sacramento altaris*, ed. Birch, pp. 30–36.

23. *De sacramento altaris*, ed. Birch, pp. 36–38; MSS Basel F.II.24, 23r; Rome, Angelica 1017, 66r: "Et si queratur quid est punctus, aut est res divisibilis aut indivisibilis, dicendum est quod, si sic dicendo 'punctus est aliquid' vel 'punctus est res' vel huiusmodi li 'punctus' supponat pro aliquo ita quod habeat precise vim nominis et non includat equivalenter unum complexum ex nomine et verbo vel aliquid consimile quod secundum proprietatem vocis potest reddere suppositum verbo, debet concedi quod punctus est aliquid et quod punctus est res; et hoc quia debet concedi quod punctus est linea et punctus est quantitas, quia tunc hoc nomen 'punctus' equivalet toti isti: 'linea tante vel tante longitudinis' sive 'linea non ulterius protensa vel extensa' vel alicui toti composito ex adiectivo et substantivo vel alicui toti composito ex nomine et verbo mediante coniunctione vel adverbio vel hoc pronomine 'qui', secundum quod placet dare diversas diffinitiones exprimentes quid nominis illius nominis 'punctus'. Et ideo sicut hoc predicatum 'res divisibilis' predicatur de tali substantivo et per consequens de composito ex adiectivo et substantivo, ita predicatur de puncto." On the distinction between real and nominal definitions and "connoting" in Ockham, see Ernest Moody, *The Logic of William of Ockham* (London, 1935), pp. 55–57, 106–11.

24. *De sacramento altaris*, ed. Birch, p. 42; MSS Basel F.II.24, 23v; Rome, Angelica 1017, 66v: "Et sicut dicitur de istis propositionibus, ita dicendum est de consimilibus; et non tantum est hoc verum de hoc nomine 'punctus', sed etiam de omnibus nominibus verbalibus et omnibus nominibus formatis ab adverbiis, coniunctionibus, pronominibus, prepositionibus, et universaliter ab omnibus sincategoreumatibus, et universaliter ab omnibus que non sunt precise habentia virtutem nominis ita quod sine omni figura et etiam proprietate sermonis non possunt esse extrema propositionis distincta a copula."

25. *De sacramento altaris*, ed. Birch, p. 40; MSS Basel F.II.24, 23r; Rome, Angelica 1017, 66v: "Si autem hoc nomen 'punctus' equivaleat in significando alicui composito ex nomine et verbo vel coniunctione vel adverbio et hoc pronomine 'qui' vel ex obliquo et verbo composito quod secundum proprietatem sermonis non potest reddere suppositum verbo loquendo grammatice, et per consequens omnis oratio in qua ponitur non est secundum proprietatem sermonis, sed est figurativa locutio et potest reduci ad figuram que vocatur a grammaticis "ypalage," de qua dicunt quod ypalage est conversio casuum vel constructionis vel quandocumque totius sententie."

26. *De sacramento altaris*, ed. Birch, pp. 42–44; MSS Basel F.II.24, 23v; Rome, Angelica 1017, 66v: " . . . que inveniuntur in dictis sanctorum et philosophorum et in scriptura sacra sunt figurative per aliquam figuram grammaticalem excusande. Nec est inconveniens concedere quod philosophi et sancti sic figurative loquebantur, cum multa talia in scriptura sacra reperiantur, non tantum accipiendo dicta scripture sacre in sensu spirituali, sed etiam in sensu litterali. Immo etiam frequenter vulgaris et communis modus loquendo talibus figurativis locutionibus utitur, sicut manifeste per dicta grammaticorum de talibus determinantium potest probari. . . . Et sicut translatio secundum grammaticos fit triplici de causa—quia aliquando causa metri sicut in poetis, aliquando causa ornatus sicut in rethorica locutione, aliquando causa brevitatis sive utilitatis sicut in philosophia, et omnibus istis modis fit translatio talis in theologia—ita impositio talium nominum, sive sint abstracta sive concreta, fit triplici de causa, scilicet, metri, ornatus, et utilitatis sive brevitatis."

27. *De sacramento altaris*, ed. Birch, pp. 64, 70, 74; MSS Basel F. II. 24, 24v, 25r; Rome, Angelica 1017, 68r–v: "Ad aliud dico quod Philosophus non intendit quod punctus cadit in diffinitione linee, tamquam aliquid de essentia linee vel tamquam importans aliquid de essentia linee et distinctum a linea; sed intendit quod in diffinitione exprimente quid nominis ipsius 'linee' ponitur hoc nomen 'punctus'. . . . Nec est tamen intelligendum quod punctus sit aliqua privatio distincta totaliter a linea sicut homines communiter imaginantur, quia impossibile est imaginari, scilicet quod punctus sit aliquid vel privativum vel positivum secundum se totum distinctus vel non idem cum linea. Immo secundum proprietatem sermonis nec est concedendum quod est positivum nec quod est positivum. . . . Sed . . . ista opinio nec magis ponit quod punctus est privatio quam positivum, quamvis in diffinitione exprimente quid nominis ipsius debeat poni unum nomen negativum vel conceptus negativus. . . . Et ideo Philosophus per illam propositionem: 'partes linee copulantur ad unum terminum communem' (*Categ.*, 5a1–3) intendit illam propositionem: 'inter partes linee nihil est medium et ille faciunt per se unum'."

28. *De sacramento altaris*, ed. Birch, p. 80; MSS Basel F. II. 24, 25v (directly follows the last text quoted in n. 16): "Nam probare quod nihil est indivisibile in istis inferioribus non potest fieri nisi per rationes subtiles quas mathematici et alii minus subtiles et exercitati in metaphysica

et logica non possunt comprehendere. Sed probare continuum non componi ex indivisibilibus per aliqua media, etiam si essent talia indivisibilia, potest fieri per rationes magis apparentes mathematicis et aliis quibuscumque, sicut alias ostendetur; et ideo rationes non sunt superflue." Ockham was quite historically accurate in claiming that arguments congenial to those versed in mathematics were utilized in investigating the possible composition of continua out of indivisibles. On this topic, see J. Murdoch, "Superposition, Congruence and Continuity in the Middle Ages," *Mélanges Alexandre Koyré*, vol. 1, *L'aventure de la science* (Paris, 1964), pp. 416–41; J. Murdoch and E. Synan, "Two Questions on the Continuum: Walter Chatton (?), O.F.M. and Adam Wodeham, O.F.M.," *Franciscan Studies* 26 (1966): 212–88. Ockham's presumed reference to his own forthcoming treatment (*sicut alias ostendetur*) is most likely to his *Quodlibeta* 1, Q. 9, 1491; reprinted., Louvain, 1962): Utrum linea componatur ex punctis.

29. See his *Super quatuor libros sententiarum* (1495; reprint ed., London, 1962), 2, Q. 9: "Utrum motus sit vera res extra animam differens realiter a mobili et a termino" (ad sig. P, Q); 2, Q. 12: "Utrum tempus habeat esse reale extra animam a motu" (ad. sig. CC–MM). Cf. *The Tractatus de successivis attributed to William Ockham*, ed. P. Boehner (St. Bonaventure, N.Y., 1944).

30. Thomas Bradwardine, *Tractatus de continuo* (MS Torun, Gymnas. Bibl. R.4°. 2, p. 192): "Superficiem, lineam sive punctum omnino non esse. Unde manifeste: Continuum non continuari nec finitari per talia, sed seipso."

31. Many of the relevant texts are quoted in V. Zoubov, "Jean Buridan et les concepts du point au quatorzième siècle," *Mediaeval and Renaissance Studies* 5 (1961):43–95.

32. Paul of Venice, *Logica magna* (ed. Venice, 1499), pars I, 64r: " . . . dicunt quidam quod nullus terminus connotans indivisibilitatem debet ingredi expositiones vel probationes." The context of this remark is the investigation of 'incipit' and 'desinit' which we shall go into in some detail below.

33. For Albert of Saxony, see his *Sophismata* (ed. Paris, 1495, unfol.; MS BN 16134, 43v): " . . . precisius loqui possumus imaginando instantia indivisibilia in tempore, licet talia in rei veritate non sint; nihilominus expedit ea imaginari . . . ita in proposito non plus neque minus dico quod expedit ea imaginari ad explicandum certas et precisas mensuras motuum et mutationum quas sine imaginatione instantium indivisibilium ita precise exprimere non possumus; nec ex hoc sequitur aliquod inconveniens, quoniam sermones de talibus indivisibilibus per alias longas orationes debite exponuntur, propter quas etiam orationes prolixas evitandas expedit tales terminos ponere quos aliqui (ed. antiquos!) crediderunt supponere pro rebus veris indivisibilibus, licet tales res indivisibiles non sint nisi secundum imaginationem." For Oresme, see his *Questiones super libros physicorum* (MS Sevilla, Colomb. 7–6–30, 67v): "Quod non est negandum

indivisibilia esse, large et equivoce capiendo esse et ymaginando aliter quam mathematicus ymaginatur, quia talia sunt significabilia . . ." For Heytesbury, see the text quoted by Curtis Wilson, *William Heytesbury: Medieval Logic and the Rise of Mathematical Physics* (Madison, 1956), p. 179, n. 55.

34. The context was, again, the opening chapters of Book 6 of the *Physics*.

35. See J. Murdoch and E. Synan, "Two Questions on the Continuum . . ." (above, n. 28).

36. See J. Murdoch, "The Equality of Infinites in the Middle Ages," *Actes du XIe Congrès International d'Histoire des Sciences* (Warsaw/Cracow, 1968), 3:171–74, and "*Mathesis* . . ." (above, n. 12), pp. 221–24.

37. Again, the appeal was always to *Physics* 6. 1–2.

38. Henry of Harclay, *Questio de infinito et continua* (*Inc*: "Utrum mundus poterit durare in eternum a parte post"), MS Tortosa 188, 88r: "Certum est quod Deus modo intuetur omne punctum quod possit signari in continuo."

39. Harclay, ibid.: "Accipio igitur primum punctum in linea incoativum linee; Deus videt illum punctum et quodlibet aliud punctum ab isto in hoc linea; usque ad illum punctum immediatiorem quem Deus videt intercipit alia linea aut non. Si non, Deus videt hunc punctum esse alteri immediatum. Si sic, igitur cum in linea possint signari puncta, illa puncta media non erant visa a Deo. Probatio huius consequentie: nam per positum linea cadit inter hunc punctum primum et quodlibet aliud ab hoc puncto quod Deus videt, et ideo, per te, modo inventum punctum medium Deus non videbat."

40. One should note that this particular use of the doctrine of supposition in clarifying that involved in continua and continuity was not only present in the reply (which will be detailed in n. 42) to Harclay's argument, but also in the works of other fourteenth-century natural philosophers; see J. Murdoch, "*Scientia mediantibus vocibus*: Metalinguistic Analysis in Late Medieval Natural Philosophy," in *Sprache und Erkenntnis im Mittelalter*, Acts of the Sixth International Congress of Medieval Philosophy" (Bonn, 29 August–3 September 1977, in press).

41. For an exposition of this doctrine see, for example, Ernest A. Moody, *Truth and Consequence in Mediaeval Logic* (Amsterdam, 1953).

42. I have given a resumé of William of Alnwick's reply to Harclay's argument (which he cites, naming Harclay as its author): Alnwick, *Determination 2* (MS Vat. pal. lat. 1805, 14r–v): "Dico autem breviter quod ista est vera: 'inter primum punctum linee et omnem alium punctum eiusdem linee cognitum a Deo est linea media'. Quelibet enim singularis est vera et eius contradictoria est falsa. Et hoc ideo est, quia 'linea media' in predicato sequens mediate signum universale stat confuse tantum. Hec tamen est falsa: 'est linea media inter primum punctum et omnem alium punctum eiusdem linee visum a Deo', quia nulla est linea media inter primum punctum et omnem alium punctum visum a Deo. Non enim contingit dare aliquam talem lineam mediam, sic enim mediaret inter primum

punctum et seipsam; nec illa linea esset visa a Deo. Et ideo, cum infertur: si sic, igitur cum in linea possent puncta signari, et cetera, ibi 'linea' stat particulariter et ideo arguitur a superiori ad inferius affirmative et sic facit fallaciam consequentis. Similiter arguitur a termino stante confuse tantum ad eundem terminum stantem determinate sive particulariter, et commutatur quale quid in hoc aliquid, et fit fallacia figure dictionis." In summarizing Alnwick's reply, I have spoken of "mean points" in place of the "mean line" in which such points can be designated, but the structure of the argument is precisely the same.

43. This is just what Alnwick claimed Harclay *was* in effect doing. See the last two sentences of the text quoted in the preceding note.

44. *Physics* 6. 5, in particular 235b30–236a27.

45. *Physics* 6. 5, 236a7–15.

46. In particular *Physics* 8. 8. 263b9–26.

47. Roger Bacon, *Opus tertium*, ed. J. S. Brewer (London, 1859), pp. 145–48.

48. Herman and Charlotte Shapiro, "*De primo et ultimo instanti* des Walter Burley," *Archiv für Geschichte der Philosophie* 47 (1965): 157–73.

49. Something that existed for but an instant naturally had that instant as an intrinsic beginning and ending limit. On all of these distinctions, see the treatise of Burley cited in the preceding note.

50. Curtis Wilson, *William Heytesbury* (above, n. 33), pp. 32, 38.

51. The most recent and most complete investigation of this literature is Norman Kretzmann, "Incipit/Desinit," in *Motion and Time, Space and Matter*, ed. P. K. Machamer and R. G. Turnbull (Columbus, Ohio, 1976), pp. 101–36.

52. For reference to the relevant De Rijk editions as well as the analysis of the texts in question, see N. Kretzmann, pp. 105–7.

53. The relevant texts are in N. Kretzmann, pp. 106–7.

54. Since "discrete time," by definition, is made up of instants immediately next to or in contact with one another, there would be no reason why all permanent and successive things should not be intrinsically limited by the first and last instants of their existence. Hence there would be no corresponding *incipit-desinit* puzzle.

55. J. R. O'Donnell, "The *Syncategoremata* of William of Sherwood," *Mediaeval Studies* 3 (1941): 75–78; translated by N. Kretzmann (Minneapolis, 1968), pp. 106–16. Peter of Spain,. *Tractatus syncategorematum*, trans. J. P. Mullally (Milwaukee, 1964); those parts of the *Tractatus* relevant to *incipit-desinit* have been translated by N. Kretzmann in "Incipit/Desinit" (above, n. 51), pp. 122–28. Since an edition of the Latin text of Peter's *Tractatus* was not available to me, I have relied on Kretzmann's translation. Finally, mention should be made of the fact that, although the *Tractatus syncategorematum* is ascribed to Peter, its contents seem to belong to a stage in the history of medieval logic tolerably later than what seems to be the date of Peter's undoubtedly genuine *Summulae logicales*.

56. Sophisms dealing with the terms 'incipit' and 'desinit' are found in

the following collections of sophismata: Vat. lat. 7678, 1r–72v; Paris, BN 16135, 3r–103v; Worcester Cath. Q. 13, 24v–53v.

57. William of Sherwood, *Syncategoremata* (above, n. 54), text, p. 76; trans., pp. 108–9. Peter of Spain, trans. Kretzmann (above, n. 54), passim.

58. These *incipit/desinit* "translations" of first and last instant distinctions have been accordingly added in Figs. 1 and 2.

59. Peter of Spain, *Tractatus syncategorematum* (trans. Kretzmann [n. 54], p. 123): ". . . just as there is no interval between a time and its limit, so there is none between (some thing's) being and its not being."

60. Peter of Spain, *Tractatus syncategorematum* (ibid.): "Because the verb 'begins' indicates the outset of a thing's being, it has different signification with permanent and successive things."

61. See the references in n. 54 to William of Sherwood and Peter of Spain.

62. The work is extant in MSS Vat. lat. 3066, 50v–52r; Vat. lat. 2154, 24r–29v.

63. MS Vat. lat. 3066, 50v; Vat. lat. 2154, 24r: "Quod non est dare ultimum instans rei permanentis in esse et quod est dare primum instans rei permanentis in esse.

64. Ibid.: "Quod positio de presenti vocatur una propositio affirmativa de presenti, et remotio de presenti vocatur una propositio negativa de presenti; et positio de preterito vocatur una propositio affirmativa de preterito; et remotio de preterito vocatur una propositio negativa de preterito. Item positio de futuro vocatur una propositio affirmativa de futuro, et negatio (! *sed lege* remotio) de futuro vocatur una propositio negativa de futuro." Note that Bradwardine is very explicit about the fact that *propositions* are involved and is not satisfied with simply speaking of *positio* and *remotio*, or even *affirmatio* and *negatio*.

65. Ibid.: "Distinctio premittendam est hec: quod alica nomina vel alice dictiones sunt signa rerum permanentium et alia sunt signa rerum successivarum. Dictiones sive termini rerum permanentium dicuntur, non quia non significant res successivas, sed quia significant aliquas res, quamvis iste non moveantur. Et huiusmodi dictiones sunt 'homo', 'animal', 'albedo', 'album', 'quantitas', 'quantum', et sic de aliis. Dictiones sive termini rerum successivarum dicuntur, non quia non significant res permanentes, sed quia non significant res permanentes nec alicas alias nisi ille res moveantur. Et talia vocabula sunt ista: 'motus', 'tempus', 'movere', 'acquirere', 'pertransire'."

66. Ibid.: "Prima conclusio est ista: quicquid incipit esse in rebus permanentibus, hoc nunc est et prius non fuit."

67. MSS Vat. lat. 3066, 50v: Vat. lat. 2154, 24v: "Ex ista conclusione sequitur generaliter quod omnis propositio affirmativa composita ex terminis rerum permanentium in qua ponitur hoc verbum 'incipit' debet exponi per positionem de presenti et remotionem de preterito. Verba gratia, sic dicendo: 'Sortes [Socrates] incipit esse', ista propositio debet exponi: 'Sortes in hoc instanti est' et 'Sortes non fuit ante illud instans', quarum

duarum propositionum exponentium una est affirmativa et vocatur positio de presenti, alia est negativa et vocatur remotio de preterito."

68. MSS Vat. lat. 3066, 51r–v; Vat. lat. 2154, 25v–27v: "Alia conclusio est . . . quod illa consequentia est bona: 'Sortes incipit moveri localiter, igitur immediate post hoc aliquod spacium erit pertransitum'. . . . Alia conclusio est hec: quod illa consequentia est bona: 'Sortes incipit moveri, igitur Sortes immediate post hoc erit in duobus locis . . . et nullum erit tempus antequam Sortes erit in duobus locis'. . . . Alia conclusio est quod ista consequentia est bona: 'Sortes incipit moveri localiter, igitur Sortes non movebitur antequam sit in alio loco quam nunc est'. . . . Alia conclusio est quod ista consequentia est bona: 'Sortes incipit moveri localiter, igitur immediate post hoc pertransibit aliquod spacium quod non immediate post hoc instans pertransibit'."

69. Bradwardine begins a lengthy discussion of this matter with the following (MSS Vat. lat. 3066, 50v; Vat. lat. 2154, 25r): "Habeo igitur probatum quod ista consequentia sit bona: 'Sortes nunc est, igitur Sortes erit', et per consequens erit bona consequentia: 'Sortes incipit esse, igitur erit'. Contra istam propositionem arguo sic: si ista propositio esset vera, sequitur quod de futuris contingentibus esset determinata veritas et quod futura contingentia possent determinate sciri; sed hoc est contra Aristotelem primo *Peryermenias*."

70. See Martin Grabmann, *Die Sophismataliteratur des 12. und 13. Jahrhunderts mit Textausgabe eines Sophisma des Boetius von Dacien*, Beiträge zur Geschichte der Philosophie und Theologie des Mittelalters, 36, 1 (Münster, 1940); J. Murdoch, "A Central Method of Analysis in Fourteenth-Century Science," *XIVth International Congress of the History of Science, Proceedings No. 2* (Tokyo, 1975), pp. 68–71; J. Murdoch, "From Social into Intellectual Factors . . ." (above, n. 11), pp. 303-7.

71. Kilvington's *Sophismata* exist only in manuscript form, but are currently being edited by Norman and Barbara Kretzmann.

72. William Heytesbury, *Regule solvendi sophismata*, cap. 4 (Venice, 1494), fols. 23v–27r.

73. Paul of Venice, *Logica magna*, (Venice, 1499), prima pars, fols. 63r–70v.

74. See Curtis Wilson, *William Heytesbury* (above, n. 33), pp. 41–42.

75. *Regule solvendi sophismata*, (Venice, 1494), 23v: "Qualitercumque autem intelligitur unum vel aliud. . . ."

76. The example is taken from Paul of Venice, *Logica magna* (cap. de isto termino 'immediate') (Venice, 1499), 61v: "Capio horam elapsam dividendo illam in partes proportionales proportionalitate dupla, minores versus hoc instans presens, et quod in qualibet parte proportionali pari fueris albus et in qualibet impari fueris niger, . . . et in hoc instanti rubeus. Isto posito patet veritas istius: 'post quodlibet instans preteritum tu fuisti albus' et quod hec sit falsa: 'immediate ante instans quod est presens tu fuisti albus' probo."

77. William Heytesbury, *Regule solvendi sophismata*, 23v: "Posito quod

Sortes sit tantum pedalis quantitatis, Plato vero bipedalis, et quod uterque illorum uniformiter augmentetur per eandem horam quousque neutrum illorum erit, et quod tripedalis quantitas sit minima quantitas quam non uterque illorum habebit; sequitur quod Sortes erit tantus quantus erit Plato et quod ipse non est tantus quantus erit Plato, quia ipse non est bipedalis, et tamen nec incipit nec incipiet esse tantus, et cetera." See Curtis Wilson's discussion of this sophism in *William Heytesbury* (above, n. 33), pp. 47–50.

78. *Regule solvendi sophismata*, 23v (directly following text in n. 75): "Qualecumque incipiet aliquid esse vel desinet, ipsum in aliquo instanti incipiet vel desinet esse tale." Directly following this, Heytesbury connects any change from not being such and such to being such and such (or vice versa) with *beginning* or *ceasing* to be such and such and, hence, on grounds of what he has just said, with beginning or ceasing to be such at an instant: "Et qualecumque erit aliquid quale ipsum nunc non est, ipsum incipit vel incipiet esse tale; et qualecumque fuerit aliquid cuiusmodi ipsum aliquando non erit, ipsum vel desinit vel desinebat esse tale."

79. Ibid., 24r–v: "Circa quod tamquam regula est tenendum vel notandum quod ab affirmativa de preterito vel futuro cui negativa annectitur de presenti, quam ad hoc quod vera fuerit requiritur pro instanti aliquo vera fore de presenti aut futuro, sequitur inceptio; eam quoque que instans taliter non requirit, sed tempus, non oportet inceptionem huiusmodi ullam sequi." Although Heytesbury's rule is applicable to cases in which the affirmative proposition is in the past tense, in what follows we need deal only with the case of an affirmative future proposition.

80. Ibid., 24v (directly following the rule quoted in the preceding note): "Verbi gratia, signetur illa affirmativa de futuro: 'Sortes erit albus', cui copuletur illa negativa de presenti: 'Sortes non est albus'; et notum est quod ex illa copulativa sequitur quod Sortes incipit vel incipiet esse albus, et causa est quia illa affirmativa, si sit vera, pro aliquo instanti verificatur; sequitur enim 'Sortes erit albus, ergo in aliquo instanti Sortes erit albus': et ideo sequitur 'si Sortes non est albus et Sortes erit albus, igitur ipse incipit vel incipiet esse albus'."

81. Although Heytesbury does not consider a simple example of a successive thing, it seems that his rule would cover such a case. Thus, let the relevant present negative proposition be 'Sortes non currit' and the future affirmative to which it is joined 'Sortes curret'. But in this instance there can be no instant on behalf of which the future affirmative can be verified, the reason being the (thoroughly Aristotelian) fact that no motion, let alone running, can occur in an instant (and hence no proposition like 'Sortes currit' can be true for an instant). But, by Heytesbury's rule, the fact that verification of an instant cannot obtain in this case means that *inception* must be denied for Socrates' running (i.e., Sortes non incipit nec incipiet currere). Note that, although Heytesbury does not say so himself, in the case of the *admitted* inception for the *res permanens* of Socrates' being white, the kind of inception is that of having a first in-

stant of being white (which corresponds with the standard scholastic doctrine of a *primum instans esse* for all *res permanentes*). Accordingly, in the example we have formulated of Socrates' running, the kind of inception denied is that of a first instant to this running. This does not mean that Heytesbury would deny inception for Socrates' running in terms of a last instant of his *not* running (which would yield the standard scholastic *extrinsic* beginning limit for *res successive*). Heytesbury was aware of the different (intrinsic vs. extrinsic) ways of taking *incipit* and *desinit*, since he begins his whole chapter on these terms by stipulating just such a distinction (see n. 74); but he does not appeal to that distinction as relevant to the substance of his chapter (which consists in the resolution of the various sophisms he had constructed).

82. *Regule solvendi sophismata*, 24v: "Verbi gratia, ex illa copulativa: 'Sortes erit tantus sicut erit Plato et Sortes non est tantus sicut erit Plato' non sequitur quod Sortes incipit vel incipiet esse tantus sicut erit Plato; et causa est quia ad hoc quod Sortes erit tantus sicut erit Plato non requiritur quod in aliquo instanti erit ipse tantus sicut erit Plato." Of course, as I have tried to indicate in explaining Heytesbury's procedure in solving this sophism, we must always keep in mind the *casus* he had specified for the sophism (see n. 77), since that *casus* gives information about the growth of Socrates and Plato that is absolutely necessary to the proper resolution of the sophism.

83. Richard Kilvington, *Sophisma 6* (after text established by Norman and Barbara Kretzmann, unpublished): "Socrates incipiet esse ita albus sicut Plato erit albus. . . . Ad sophisma dicendum est quod est falsum . . . Et ad probationem dicitur quod antecedens est falsum—videlicet, quod Socrates erit ita albus sicut Plato erit albus [thus, we have a proposition parallel to that of Heytesbury]. Et quando arguitur quod illud antecedens est verum sic—"Socrates erit albus, et Plato erit albus, et Socrates non erit albior quam Plato erit albus"—dicitur quod non sequitur, et maxime cum verbo de futuro. Cum verbo tamen de praesenti bene sequeretur; verbi gratia, bene sequitur 'Socrates est albus, et Plato est albus, et Socrates non est albior quam Plato est albus, nec econtra; igitur Socrates est ita albus sicut Plato est albus'. Et causa quare tales consequentiae bene valent cum verbis de praesenti et non cum verbis de futuro est ista, quia arguendo cum verbis de praesenti per antecedens supponitur aliquem esse maximum gradum albedinis per quem in praesenti Socrates est albus et consimiliter quod aliquis est maximus gradus per quem Plato est albus. Sed arguendo cum verbo de futuro, ut prius argutum est, non supponitur in aliquo antecedente quod aliquis erit maximus vel intensissimus albedinis per quem Socrates erit albus vel per quem Plato erit albus, quod tamen requireretur ad hoc quod consequentia valeret." It is true that Kilvington's sophism is itself different from that of Heytesbury, but the crucial antecedent involved in the resolution of Kilvington's sophism is—as indicated above—parallel to Heytesbury's central future affirmative proposition. It is also true that Kilvington does not specify an increase of whiteness for

Socrates and Plato that is parallel to that stipulated by Heytesbury for their increase in size, but instead specifies a *casus* that has Socrates and Plato of equal whiteness at the outset and posits their equal increase of whiteness throughout time ("Posito quod Socrates et Plato sint equaliter albi, et quod vivant per aequale tempus praecise, et intendantur albedines in Socrate et Plato aequaliter per totum tempus quo vivent Socrates et Plato"). Nevertheless, Kilvington is admittedly dealing with a *casus* that entails that Socrates will have all of the degrees of whiteness Plato will have and no greater and vice versa ("quantumcumque gradum albedinis habebit Socrates, tantum gradum et ita intensum habebit Plato, et econtra"), which is parallel to Heytesbury's *casus* of Socrates' having all of the sizes Plato will have and none greater (the lack of "vice versa" being of no effect relative to the point at issue). But, unlike Heytesbury, Kilvington denies that we can therefore validly infer that "Socrates will be as white as Plato will be white" and the reason is that, due to the presence of a future tense verb, there will be no most intense degree of whiteness that will be had by either Socrates or Plato ("nam non sequitur 'quantumcumque gradum . . . [text as above] . . . et econtra; igitur Socrates erit ita albus sicut Plato erit albus'. Et causa est quia nullus erit intensissimus gradus albedinis per quem Socrates erit albus vel per quem Plato erit albus").

84. Paul of Venice, *Logica magna* (Venice, 1499), 66r–v: Paul begins with the same connections Heytesbury made (n. 78) between change, beginning and ceasing, and instants: "Adduco regulas communes materie inceptionis et desinitionis correspondentes, primo supponendo quod omne quod incipit vel desinit esse aliquale, ipsum in aliquo instanti incipit vel desinit esse tale. . . . Isto supposito sit hec prima regula: qualecumque erit aliquid quale ipsum iam non est, ipsum incipit vel incipiet esse tale" (and he goes on to give corresponding rules for past *inceptiones* and for all manner of *desinitiones*). Paul then raises Heytesbury's sophism as an objection to this *prima regula* (for Heytesbury's own resolution of the apparent inconsistency to which Paul is here referring, see Curtis Wilson, *William Heytesbury*, n. 33, p. 49): "Contra primam regulam arguitur sic: tu eris tantus sicut erit Plato et iam non es tantus sicut erit Plato, et tamen tu non incipis nec incipies esse tantus quantus erit Plato; igitur regula falsa. . . ." Paul follows with a *casus* that is the same as that of Heytesbury (n. 77): "Et pono quod tu sis pedalis quantitatis et Plato bipedalis et quod uterque vestrum uniformiter augmentetur per totam istam horam ita quod tripedalis quantitas sit minima quam neuter vestrum habebit, et quod ultimum instans istius hore sit primum non esse tam tui quam Platonis. . . ." After establishing how this *casus* can be brought to bear in establishing the objection in question and raising several other objections to his *prima regula*, Paul sets down a second series of rules that specify the relevant connections that obtain between various kinds of propositions that require verification at an instant and the resultant *inceptiones* or *desinitiones*; among them is one that gives one "half" of the rule Heytesbury

applied (above, n. 79) in resolving the "Socrates-Plato growth" sophism: "Ad hec respondendo premitto quasdam regulas . . . quarum prima est ista: ex copulativa duarum demonstrativarum unius de presenti negative et alterius de futuro affirmative requirentis instans pro sui verificatione, sequitur inceptio de presenti vel de futuro. . . ." These rules in hand, Paul next turns to resolving the inconsistency he had proffered as existing between his initial *prima regula* and the "growth sophism," at the same time restating the sophism in what he takes to be its proper form (i.e., one that is not inconsistent with his *prima regula*): "Et tunc ad probationem nego illam consequentiam: 'tu habebis tantam quantitatem quantam habebit Plato et non maiorem et econtra, igitur tu eris tantus sicut erit Plato,' quia antecedens non requirit instans pro sui verificatione, sed consequens bene requirit instans. Ex illo enim antecedente sequitur precise quod (a) 'quantuscumque tu eris tantus erit Plato' vel (b) 'quantus tu eris tantus erit Plato,' ex quo postea non sequitur quod (c) 'tu eris tantus sicut erit Plato,' eo quod ly 'eris' in antecedente stat confuse tantum et in consequente determinate. . . ." Thus, in Paul's eyes, the proper form of Heytesbury's sophism is either (a) or (b), not (c). It is (c) that is inconsistent with his (and Heytesbury's: n. 78) *prima regula*, not (a) or (b). Finally, somewhat later, Paul completes the whole matter by giving several rules that reveal just which kind of propositions require verification at an instant: "Et ut solutio istius primi et secundi melius intelligatur, pono tres regulas quibus apparebit que sunt propositiones pro instanti verificabiles et que non. Prima regula est ista: quelibet propositio de presenti cuiuscumque verbi respectu cuiuscumque appositi vel de preterito aut de futuro, primo termino probabili carente apposito, est pro instanti verificabilis [examples by Paul are 'tu es vel curris', 'tu est tantus sicut tu fuisti vel sicut erit Plato']. . . . Secunda regula est ista: quelibet propositio de preterito vel futuro verbo substantivo primo termino probabili respectu cuiuscumque appositi est pro instanti verificabilis nisi determinetur per terminun significantem fluxum [examples: 'tu eris albus vel fuisti niger'; 'tu eris tantus sicut erit Plato']. . . . Tertia regula est ista: propositio de verbo adiectivo apposito preteriti vel futuri temporis non exponibili, officiabili vel habente causas veritatis non est pro instanti verificabilis nisi forte gratia materie, videlicet quando actus verbi respectu appositi potest pro instanti procedere [examples: 'tu tanges Sortem et Platonem'; 'tu pertransibis A spatium']."

85. See n. 50.

86. See J. Murdoch, "*Scientia mediantibus vocibus* . . ." (above, n. 40) and J. Murdoch, "The Development of a Critical Temper: New Approaches and Modes of Analysis in Fourteenth-Century Philosophy, Science, and Theology," in *Medieval and Renaissance Studies* 7, ed. Siegfried Wenzel (Chapel Hill, 1978):51–79.

87. I have derived the statistics from tabulating the relevant material in Charles Lohr, "Medieval Latin Aristotle Commentaries," *Traditio* 23 (1967): 313–413; 24 (1968): 149–245; 26 (1970): 135–216; 27 (1971): 251–351; 28 (1972): 281–396; 29 (1973): 93–197; and 30 (1974): 119–44.

To cite but one resulting correlation, there seem to have been thirty-one *Physics* commentaries done at Oxford in the thirteenth century and the first thirty years of the fourteenth, while only fifteen appear to have been realized at Paris during the same period.

88. See J. Murdoch, "From Social into Intellectual Factors . . ." (above, n. 11), pp. 289–97; J. Murdoch, "*Subtilitates Anglicanae* . . ." (above, n. 12).

89. The complaint is that of the Augustinian Michael of Massa in the second book of his *Commentaria sententiarum* (ca. 1325–26), cited by Damasus Trapp, "Notes on Some Manuscripts of the Augustinian Michael de Massa († 1337)," *Augustinianum* 5 (1965): 109: "Sicut dixi hic est error quorundam modernorum qui secundum rei veritatem conantur diffundere inter vera dicta physicae multa semina falsitatum et, in omnibus tamquam verbosi, habent recurrere ad "verba" grammaticalia sophistice utendo eis. Nec forte melior modus esset nisi nauseare super dictis eorum et dicere "Contra verbosos noli contendere verbis" quia secundum veritatem errores ipsorum non sunt cum magna diligentia pertractandi et ideo expediamus nos de illo errore quem asserunt circa realitatem motus. Dicunt enim quod motus non est distinctus a mobili."

90. Ockham, *Comm. Sent.*, I, dist. 2, quest. 1 (ed. S. Brown and G. Gál), p. 47: "Si dicas: nolo loqui de vocibus sed tantum de rebus, dico quod quamvis velis loqui tantum de rebus, tamen hoc non est possibile nisi mediantibus vocibus vel conceptibus vel aliis signis."

91. See J. Murdoch, "From Social into Intellectual Factors . . ." (above, n. 11), pp. 281, 297.

92. See the references in n. 13. What I have here termed "normal" is somewhat unfairly determined by a tacit appeal to more modern notions of what science amounts to.

Comment

BY

Norman Kretzmann

John Murdoch's papers are typically so rich as to give the impression of being infinitely divisible into interesting topics, and this one is no exception. I couldn't comment on all the things that have caught my attention without producing a paper as least as long as his own; and if the few I choose to discuss in the short space allotted to me are mainly things about which we disagree, that's only because we're most likely to make progress by concentrating on those rather than on the many more things I have learned from him or about which he and I agree. I'll begin with some specific observations and conclude with an assessment of his general thesis.

Ockham's discussion of the existence of indivisibles is chosen by Professor Murdoch to illustrate two features characteristic of fourteenth-century philosophy as he views it: the careful attention to questions concerning indivisibles, and the choice of linguistic analysis as the method for dealing with such questions. Although Professor Murdoch remarks in passing that Ockham's discussion is "impressive" in "its philosophical competence" (p. 177), the discussion as presented in his paper is unlikely to seem so. If his presentation is accurate, as it seems to be, then his admiration of Ockham's treatment of indivisibles strikes me as unwarranted. Near the beginning of his presentation Professor Murdoch reports Ockham as taking divisibility in three dimensions to be at least a necessary condition of existence as a real thing and says "Thus, in the final analysis, only bodies exist as things, divisible in all dimensions . . ."(p. 178). Surfaces, lines, and points all violate that necessary condition in different ways. But Professor Murdoch sums up the first part of his presentation of Ockham's position by saying that we have been provided with "a 'metalinguistic translation' of the fact that only bodies and time intervals exist as things" (p. 179).

Temporal instants obviously violate the criterion of three-dimensional divisibility in the same way points do (or at least in an analogous way); but, aside from all the other difficulties introduced by considering temporal intervals to be real things, how are they supposed to survive the application of that criterion of real existence?

The focus of Professor Murdoch's interest in Ockham in this paper is not on metaphysical difficulties, however, but on what he describes as Ockham's technique of "metalinguistic translation," his application of linguistic analysis to the problem of the existence of indivisibles. Ockham is reported, quite accurately, as maintaining that "the term 'point' signifies the same thing as the phrase 'a line of such and such a length' " (p. 179; *De sacramento altaris,* p. 38). A proposition containing the term 'point' may nevertheless be accepted "once we realize that . . . the term 'point' is being used in place of its nominal definition, in place of a phrase equivalent to it" (p. 179). The sense in which this Ockhamist translation of 'point' is metalinguistic is only the sense in which any nominal definition is so; nor can it be considered more than a stage in a series of translations that would, presumably, replace 'line' with 'a surface of such and such an area' and 'surface', in turn, with 'a body of such and such a volume'. Still, we can test the technique by attending to just the translation Professor Murdoch singles out. On that basis we are evidently entitled to accept the proposition 'Between every two points there is another point' "once we realize that" it signifies the same as the proposition 'Between every two lines of such and such a length there is another line of such and such a length'—but that, of course, is absurd, and the absurdity of the result is in no way mitigated by characterizing the technique as metalinguistic. We don't have to *infer* all the shocking implications; Ockham presents us with enough of them in his own voice. Soon after introducing his astonishing nominal definition of 'point' he goes so far as to say that "Just as we grant the proposition 'A line is divisible,' so, in virtue of signification, we grant these: 'A point is a line', 'A point is divisible' " (*De sacramento altaris,* p. 38). And, of course, he would also grant the proposition 'A point is indivisible'. An application of linguistic analysis that yields such results inspires no confidence in its power to clarify *any* problems regarding the nature and existence of the indivisibles, especially because the first result of the analysis is the obliteration of the very characteristic that makes their nature and existence problematic. And so I can't share Professor

Murdoch's appraisal that "this metalinguistic analysis takes adequate account of the other distinctions and conceptions that are traditionally connected with points. It explains, in other words, just what is involved in the most important propositions in natural philosophy in which the term 'point' appears" (p. 180f.). I do, however, wholeheartedly agree with the contention he means to be illustrating—namely, that the consideration of problems associated with indivisibles by means of linguistic analysis is very important in, even characteristic of, fourteenth-century natural philosophy. It's just that Ockham, or at any rate Ockham presented uncritically, doesn't serve his purpose nearly so well as others might have done.

Because of my own work on the subject, I'm particularly interested in the progress Professor Murdoch has made in filling out and explaining the development of the analysis of beginning and ceasing. I have some misgivings about the "segments" and "strains" in terms of which he organizes the historical development of that sort of analysis, but they are thought-provoking working hypotheses, and at this stage of our understanding of the literature of *incipit/desinit* no one is in a position to offer more than that.

When it comes to Thomas Bradwardine on *incipit/desinit,* however, Professor Murdoch very likely knows more than anyone else does; but his zeal in uncovering evidence of a "metalinguistic jump" seems to have led him to credit Bradwardine with a move that is certainly not original generally and is misguided in the one respect in which it may be distinctively Bradwardine's. Professor Murdoch suggests that it is one of Bradwardine's accomplishments in linguistic analysis that he "explicitly connects" the "standard *positio-remotio* analysis of the two senses given to the terms 'incipit' and 'desinit' . . . with propositions" (p. 190); "Bradwardine is very explicit about the fact that *propositions* are involved and is not satisfied with simply speaking of *positio* and *remotio*, or even *affirmatio* and *negatio*" (n. 64). For more than a century before Bradwardine the analysis of incipit- and desinit-propositions in terms of *positio* and *remotio* was indeed "standard," and since *positio* and *remotio* are affirmation and negation, and affirmation and negation are in any case inevitably connected with propositions, there is nothing whatever remarkable in Bradwardine's connecting that analysis with propositions. But *the way* in which Bradwardine makes the connection is worth noting, if only as an example of misguided reductionism. For, as Professor Murdoch quite correctly reports him, Bradwardine claims that "*positio* amounts to an affirmative proposition and *remotio* to a negative proposition" (p. 190); and such an identification is, if not distinctive, at least nonstandard in the literature of *incipit/desinit*. Perhaps the identification is merely terminological and thus harmless in this restricted context; but since an affirmative proposition is susceptible of negation as well as of affirmation and a negative proposition may be affirmed as well as negated, it would create a muddle if it were applied generally. Because I don't see Bradwardine's approach as novel in any *relevant* respect or as *distinctively* metalinguistic, I'm inclined to be hesitant about adopting the associated distinction of "strains" within Professor Murdoch's "third segment."

Professor Murdoch offers two examples of analysis drawn from the literature centering around sophismata, the first from Paul of Venice and the second from William Heytesbury. I think he shares my conviction that it is in this sophisma literature that the power and originality of fourteenth-century natural philosophy and logic are most evident, but it is easy to lose sight of the virtues of this literature (as the renaissance humanists did) in the face of the apparently—but *only* apparently—frivolous and certainly bizarre details. The power and the logical point of the example from Paul of Venice (p. 192) may be appreciated better if it is generalized a little further. It is certainly not *prima facie* implausible to consider the following conditional proposition as a promising candidate for the status of a thesis in a logic of tenses: 'If for *every* instant t before now x was A after t, then x was A *immediately* before now'. The weird details of Paul's example are very likely to obscure the fact that in it he is presenting a decisive counter-instance to that apparently obvious general truth. Part of the disguised power of the sophismata lies in the flexibility of the examples that at first glance seem absurdly overly detailed. For instance, approximately three-quarters of a century before Paul of Venice, Richard Kilvington used an example with the same basic structure as this one of Paul's in Sophisma 16 of his *Sophismata* in order to challenge a much more fundamental logical principle—the law of noncontradiction.

I want to conclude by commenting on Professor Murdoch's general thesis, which deserves more careful scrutiny than I can give it here. I agree with his assessment of Moody's thesis regarding fourteenth-century philosophy; and so I am ready to agree with his broadest claim—namely, that the philosophy of the fourteenth century is more accurately described as analytical than either as speculative or as empirical. Furthermore, I think he is certainly right to suggest that the ubiquitous employment of one or another form of linguistic analysis as a method is one of the strongest reasons for calling this philosophy analytical. Professor Murdoch frequently cites the dominance of logic as an important force shaping the character of fourteenth-century philosophy. He's right in doing so, but he may be misunderstood by twentieth-century readers who tend to think of logic as *formal* logic. In the Middle Ages, of course, semantic theory and techniques of linguistic analysis were also part of logic, and much the most interesting and important part of it. So I take his claims that fourteenth-century philosophy is strongly characterized by linguistic analysis and dominated by logic to be two ways of saying very nearly the same thing, a thing he is certainly justified in saying. He makes those claims, of course, primarily about natural philosophy rather than about philosophy generally, but as I learn more about fourteenth-century philosophy I become less certain about the distinguishing characteristics of fourteenth-century natural philosophy. A simple and apparently sensible criterion is to accept as medieval *natural* philosophy all and only such medieval philosophy as deals with concepts—such as speed, qualitative change, or limits—that subsequently became part of the subject matter of mathematics or natural science. Adopting that criterion provisionally—I think it must be very close to the one Professor Murdoch has adopted—I want to consider a few of the more specific claims he makes about fourteenth-century natural philosophy.

He ends his paper by pulling together his main themes in these words: "fourteenth-century natural philosophers were . . . proceeding *secundum imaginationem.* Such a procedure was itself one of the things that made the fourteenth century analytic and, as a consequence, much of its natural philosophy *praeter cursum naturae.* And metalinguistic analysis and sophisms were . . . another" (p. 199). Having already agreed with him about linguistic analysis, I want to sort out the other factors mentioned here. First of all, I certainly agree that fourteenth-century natural philosophers do proceed *secundum imaginationem;* but I don't see why such a procedure, which is surely just as important in nineteenth-century speculative metaphysics or twentieth-century theoretical physics, is "one of the things that made the fourteenth century analytic." Secondly, I think that the way in which proceeding *secundum imaginationem* does characterize fourteenth-century natural philosophy is manifested in the peculiar and pervasive use of sophismata, *all* of which are *secundum imaginationem*; so I think that for purposes of characterizing fourteenth-century natural philosophy the use of sophismata and proceeding *secundum imaginationem* should be considered together, and that considered *together* they *are* distinctive of late medieval natural philosophy. But, whether considered together or separately, they do not help to make that philosophy *analytical*.

Finally, as Professor Murdoch observes, the sophismata are used not only, or even primarily, to *resolve* problems in natural philosophy, but also, and perhaps primarily, to *pose* such problems. One of the things that I think is distinctive, and perplexing, about the natural philosophy of the late Middle Ages is that its practitioners do not merely—like *any* natural philosophers or, indeed, natural scientists—perform thought experiments or extrapolate from observed cases *secundum imaginationem,* they get their *cases* from imagination rather than from nature. And it is precisely in that respect that much of their natural philosophy is *praeter cursum naturae*. They get their cases from imagination not because they could not observe cases of the sorts that might have suited their analytic procedures, but, apparently, because it never occurred to them to look. Why not? I can't believe that they thought of themselves as natural philosophers but failed to realize that nature ought to be observed in connection with natural philosophy or that they were crippled with embarrassment at their total lack of reliable instrumentation and objective, conventional standards of measurement. I think that it didn't occur to them to think of themselves as philosophers of nature. The great majority of the men who devised and disputed over the so-called "physical" sophismata were in their own eyes *logicians*, and to the eyes of someone trained in twentieth-century analytical philosophy most of their work looks less like natural philosophy than like conceptual analysis that happens to focus on certain concepts because they tend to illustrate or generate logical, grammatical, semantic, or metaphysical problems in which those men happened to be interested. The fact that many (but by no means all) of those concepts later appeared as part of the subject of physics or mathematics is of course no evidence in itself that those sophismatists were proto-physicists or proto-mathematicians.

Twentieth-century analytical philosophers interested in vagueness have painstakingly examined the concept of a poem or of a bottle without thereby becoming involved in the work of literary criticism or the Bureau of Standards.

I want to be careful not to push this nonnaturalism too hard. There seems to be a continuum in the work of the "physical" sophismatists, with Richard Kilvington near the end that trails off into medieval logic of a sort that would not tempt anyone to think of it as natural philosophy, and with Richard Swineshead and Nicole Oresme, perhaps, near the other end, which leads into natural science and mathematics. And I suppose that it is in the flow of mingling ideas along that continuum that the recognizable beginnings of modern natural science are to be found. It is a rich, complex, fascinating field of inquiry, as Professor Murdoch has helped so much to show. Perhaps we only deepen its formidable difficulties if we designate all of it natural philosophy in virtue of the concepts it focuses on, just as we would do if we called all of it logic in virtue of its methodology.

Note: Since 1976 Professor Murdoch and others have published further discussions of the topics considered in his paper and my comment. See, e.g., the section on natural philosophy in *The Cambridge History of Later Medieval Philosophy*, ed. N. Kretzmann, A. Kenny, J. Pinborg (Cambridge: Cambridge University Press, 1982), and *Infinity and Continuity in Ancient and Medieval Thought*, ed. N. Kretzmann (Ithaca, NY: Cornell University Press, 1982), especially the chapters by John Murdoch and Eleonore Stump.

Approaches to Nature in the Middle Ages includes six major papers which explore the ways in which medieval philosophers, scientists, writers and artists of the Middle Ages dealt with the subject of nature. The authors consider such topics as methods of study used in the Middle Ages, the symbolic roles assigned to nature, and medieval conclusions about nature and its place in human life.

The collection includes "Nature in *Beowulf* and *Roland*," by Bernard F. Huppé; "Some Implications of Nature's Femininity in Medieval Poetry," by Winthrop Wetherbee; "*In Principio*: The Creation in the Middle Ages," by Dorothy Glass; "The Origin of the Fleur-de-lis and the *Lilium Candidum* in Art," by Robert A. Koch; "Aristotle's Concept of Nature: Avicenna and Aquinas," by James A. Weisheipl; and "The Analytic Character of Late Medieval Learning: Natural Philosophy Without Nature," by John E. Murdoch. A critical commentary by a respondent follows each essay.

Lawrence D. Roberts is Associate Professor of Philosophy at the State University of New York at Binghamton and has been a Visiting Senior Member at Linacre College, Oxford. He is the author of several articles on Duns Scotus and St. Augustine.

mrts

medieval & renaissance texts & studies
is the publishing program of the
Center for Medieval & Early Renaissance Studies
at the State University of New York at Binghamton.

mrts emphasizes books that are needed —
texts, translations, and major research tools.

mrts aims to publish the highest quality scholarship
in attractive and durable format at modest cost.